Earl Nichols
Dec. 25, 1979

Spiritual
Roots
of Human
Relations

Spiritual Roots of Human Relations

By Stephen R. Covey

Published by
DESERET BOOK COMPANY
SALT LAKE CITY, UTAH
1978

Library of Congress Catalog
Card No. 72-119477
ISBN Number 87747-315-3

Lithographed by

DESERET PRESS

in the United States of America

To Sandra, a true helpmate.

ACKNOWLEDGMENTS

To acknowledge by name all those who have contributed to the development of the thoughts expressed in this book is a virtual impossibility. Many I know and many I do not know.

I do know that my family is central, and I am deeply grateful for the love and believing support of my father, my mother, my brother and sisters, my wife, and my six children. Experiences in my homes have developed an underlying attitude toward life reflected explicitly and implicitly throughout this book and have provided many of its illustrations. The awareness and memory and unspoken challenge of my heritage, particularly my grandfather, Stephen L Richards, have been a constant inspiration to keep my expressions responsible.

The examples and stimulation received from many individuals and the insights gained from relationships with them were major influences in shaping the ideas expressed here. I feel indebted to many former teachers and students, including BYU Education Week patrons, to missionaries (to whom the missionary material was initially directed) and Saints of the Irish Mission, to members of the former BYU 12th Ward, and to many friends and colleagues on the BYU faculty and staff. I also thankfully acknowledge the learning and inspirational influence of several Church leaders whom I was privileged to associate with in connection with my responsibilities; I particularly thank President N. Eldon Tanner, Elder Spencer W. Kimball, Elder Mark E. Petersen, Elder Bernard Brockbank, President Ernest L. Wilkinson, the late Henry D. Moyle, and my own mission president, A. Hamer Reiser. The teachings, example, and touch of our recent prophet, President McKay, have been pervasive and powerful in their influence on this work.

Inasmuch as most of the thinking in this book came directly out of having responsibility to do what was necesary, consistent with true principles, to fulfill those responsi-

vi

bilities, I am especially grateful for the training and service opportunities in The Church of Jesus Christ of Latter-day Saints and for the teaching and administrative responsibilities at Brigham Young University. I also appreciate the training in analytical thinking given at the Harvard Business School.

Thanks is expressed to *The Instructor, The Church News, The Relief Society Magazine,* the MIA general board, and BYU Extension Publications for permission to use some of the material prepared originally for their use.

I have dedicated this book to my dear wife, Sandra, because of her constant support during its preparation, her intuitive human insight and understanding, her candid constructive criticisms and suggestions in light of this natural wisdom, and her magnificent second-mile spirit.

Finally, I give heartfelt thanks to Alva Parry for encouragement years ago to prepare such a manuscript, to William James Mortimer for recent encouragement and professional assistance, to Eleanor Knowles for expert editorial work and counsel, to Lela Dalton for splendid secretarial help, to President Owen J. Cook and many others in Laie, Hawaii, for an ideal environment in which to write.

Contents

Introduction: An Overview

"For every thousand hacking at the leaves of evil there is one striking at the root." (Henry David Thoreau.)

This book is an attempt to strike at the root.

The roots of the problems we face in the world, in our national life, and in our family and personal lives are spiritual. The symptom manifestations (leaves) of these problems are social, economic, and political. But the roots are moral and spiritual. And they lie first within each individual and then within the family.

Since the problems are rooted spiritually, the solutions are also. To not accept and act on this fact is comparable to giving aspirins for headaches and covering sores with bandages. We must work on the causes, the roots.

This book is essentially a compilation of articles written and speeches given over the last few years focusing on the spiritual roots of human relations. The section headings represent what I believe these roots to be.

1. VISION.

> An eternal perspective toward life, its problems and challenges, should influence all decisions and actions.

2. COMMITMENT.

> Once we understand "the big picture" (who we are, why we're here, and so forth), the next logical step is to decide or to commit ourselves to act accordingly.

3. UNDERSTANDING AND EXAMPLE.
   The quality of our own lives and the depth of our understanding of others are the fundamental roots in succeeding with people.
4. COMMUNICATION.
   Communicating (human and divine) is the most important single activity of man.
5. SELF DISCIPLINE.
   To do and act consistent with commitment and vision is the root source of integrity and effectiveness as parent, teacher, leader, or missionary.

Each chapter is self contained and can be understood without reading the earlier chapters. Basic themes and principles recur throughout several of the chapters, which I hope will serve to reinforce and deepen understanding of the basic spiritual roots of life, many of which are common and fundamental to most areas and problems in life.

I

VISION:

An Eternal Perspective

1

Our Purpose Here:
Obedience

By obedience to the principles and the ordinances of the eternal gospel of Jesus Christ, man will gradually become a "partaker of the divine nature" and will feel comfort and confidence in the presence of his Eternal Father and his Elder Brother, the Lord Jesus Christ. This is the purpose of life.

It all may be summarized in another way—*growth toward Godhood.* When the Lord revealed that it was his work and his glory "to bring to pass the immortality and eternal life of man," he essentially outlined the two great parts or programs or objectives of all that he has attempted to do among men since the beginning.

The first grand part or objective is immortality, which was achieved through the miracle of the resurrection. With the seeds of mortality or death and immortality or life flowing in his veins, Christ willingly laid down his own life and took it up again. Through his resurrection, *all* mankind will be resurrected into immortality.

The second grand design of the Lord is eternal life, which has to do with the *quality* of the resurrection. While immortality is a free gift to all mankind, eternal life is a personal *achievement* by each individual, made possible through the atonement of the Lord Jesus Christ.

The gospel may be studied from different points of view, and each makes its own valuable and unique contribution. The traditional viewpoints are what we might term "definitional" and "legalistic." The definitional viewpoint involves essentially coming to a clear understanding of what various gospel terms mean—such as faith, repentance, baptism, immortality, eternal life, salvation, etc. The legalistic way of thinking views God as the judge and jury, man as the defendant, the principles of the gospel as the laws of celestial society, judgment as the verdict, punishment as jail or hell, and so forth.

There is an additional, extremely fascinating, and immensely useful study framework that we might term a *behavioral* viewpoint. Let us analyze eternal life from this viewpoint.

In life man is immersed in various kinds of values: physical, social, material, family, spiritual. Life can be seen as a series of alternative choices within these value systems. Many times man finds himself in conflicting situations where he must choose to accept one value, and, by so doing, he knowingly or unknowingly rejects another.

This choosing process is the growth process. If a man loves God more than pleasures, he will grow to become like God. If he loves his worldly pleasures more than God, he will choose and grow in another direction.

From this perspective, what, then, is eternal life? Eternal life is essentially that quality of character and personal integrity achieved through Christlike service and lifetime obedience to the principles of the gospel which enables an individual to be so changed—gradually and almost imperceptibly, in his very nature—that his "confidence waxes strong in the presence of God." If he had not so grown from within, he would feel like a stranger and foreigner and would shun the presence of this perfect and holy Being, and would feel more comfortable with those who have lived a lower order or a lower law, such as found in a terrestrial or a telestial level.

What is judgment? It is the divine process of God revealing man to himself. We are only as good as we *are*. "Ye cannot say, when ye are brought to that awful crisis, that I will repent, that I will return to my God. Nay, ye cannot say this; for that same spirit which doth possess your bodies at the time that ye go out of this life, that same spirit will have power to possess your body in that eternal world." (Alma 34:34.)

There is no mystery about this business. It is very simple. The laws of the gospel are the laws of human growth toward godhood. The Sermon on the Mount contains the perfect laws of social, mental, and spiritual health.

When Christ said that it was life eternal to know God, he again taught the behavioral principle that *true knowledge is a state of being*. (Study 2 Peter 1:3-11 and John 7:16-17.)

This behavioral approach to the study of the gospel reveals the transparent error and inconsistency of manmade doctrines regarding salvation and eternal life. Deathbed confession or mere ordinance work do not change man's nature. This is the reason Satan's plan would have failed, for there could never be a returning to the presence of the Eternal Father without a testing in the face of opposites and temptation and the continual choosing of the highest good over lesser goods and over evil.

Any other approach to salvation ignores this process of growth and turns it all into some kind of an arbitrary and awesome mystery that, to many, is the hallmark of spirituality.

From this behavioral viewpoint every principle of the gospel can be prayerfully studied again, and new light and understanding and motivation will result. The blessings of God come in the form of divine growth, and the cursing of God in the form of a lack of divine growth, or a growth in the opposite direction.

Repentance is change of mind resulting in confessing and forsaking and in good works—divine growth. The after-life cursing or hell amounts to that kind of anguish which follows a clear recollection of misdeeds and acknowledgment that the judgment is just and self-chosen, with a quickened realization of the enormous loss and the widened gap between God's nature and the man's nature. "Of all the words of tongue and pen, the saddest are these: 'It might have been.'"

To summarize the purposes of life from a behavioral standpoint, I would suggest that every principle of the gospel is so calculated that through obedience to it there is an *immediate* growth or blessing. Through continued faithfulness, sin gradually loses its pull and attractiveness, and man loses all desire for anything but continued service to mankind and obedience to higher and higher laws of the gospel. The Savior taught that man must be "born again." Man is born of the water in baptism and is born of the Spirit as he obeys the injunction given at his confirmation ("receive the Holy Ghost") to so live as to receive the continued purifying and sanctifying and perfecting influence of the Holy Ghost.

Man as a begotten spirit child of God has the laws of the gospel implicit within his very nature. The revelations of the Lord through prophets make those implicit internal laws and his preexistent memory (shrouded by the veil of mortality) explicit or open to mortal understanding and response.

Through obedience and selfless service, man becomes a celestialized personality and thus fulfills his promise and purpose. This is a divine miracle.

2

Six Days of Creation:

Process of Growth and Development

The Lord took six days to create the world. Each day was important—each in its own time.

A child learns to turn over, to sit up, to crawl, then to walk and run. Each step is important. No step can be skipped.

In school we study mathematics before we study algebra. We can then go on to geometry and calculus. We simply can't do calculus until we understand algebra.

So it is with spiritual growth and development within the Church. Repentance precedes making a covenant in the waters of baptism. We meet the requirements of the Aaronic Priesthood before assuming the obligation of the Melchizedek Priesthood.

This is true with all phases of life, with the development of all skills, whether it be piano playing or communication. It is true with individuals and it is true with groups and families.

In all of life there are stages, or processes, of growth and development. We know and accept this fact of process in the area of physical things, but understanding it in emotional area, in human relations, and even in the spiritual area, is less common and more difficult. And even though we may have this understanding, to accept it and to work on that basis is even less common and more difficult. Things in the physical area are seen, and constant evidence is supplied; but things in the other areas are largely unseen, and evidence is not as direct or as plain. Therefore, we sometimes look for a shortcut, preferring to skip some of these vital steps in order to save the time and effort and still reap the reward desired.

For the purposes of understanding and clarity, let us use the idea of the six days of creation to represent this process of growth and development. Then let's reason together.

Consider your answer to this question: What happens when a person attempts to shortcut this process in his development? For instance, if you are only an average tennis player at, say, day three, but decide to play today at day six in order to make a better impression, what will result?

What would happen if you were to lead your friends to believe you could play the piano at day six, while your actual present skill was at day two?

In sports if you who are at day three level skill in golf or tennis were to compete against someone at day five, would positive thinking alone beat him?

The answers are obvious. It is simply impossible to violate, ignore, or shortcut this development process. It is contrary to nature, and any attempt to seek such a shortcut will result in confusion and frustration. If I am at day two, in any field, and desire to move to day five, I must first take the step toward day three. A thousand-mile journey begins with the first step, one step at a time— "line upon line, precept upon precept," here a little and there a little. This is the law of the harvest (you reap as you sow), the law of justice, a natural law of God.

No bypassing, no shortcutting, no pretending or appearing, no making impressions will compensate. "There is a law, irrevocably decreed in heaven. . . ." This involves accepting the fact that I am at day two and the refusal to pretend to be anywhere else. If you don't let a teacher know at what level you are—by asking a question, or revealing your ignorance—you will not learn or grow. You cannot pretend for long, for you will eventually be found out. This admission of our ignorance is often the first step in our education.

Let me illustrate. While serving a mission in England, we held regular street meetings as a proselyting method to meet people. One elder would never participate. He had a different excuse every day—a cold, sore throat, other duties, etc. His father was a prominent and successful civic, Church, and business leader. Everyone expected his young missionary son to also be successful. The missionary enjoyed the inheritance of being well thought of, receiving admiration for qualities others assumed he had. He did not want to reveal himself—and the fact that he too had to start at the beginning, at day one. He did not know the scriptures and could not preach with clarity and persuasion, and so he would not participate. Until the time he was willing to pay the price of revealing the level he was at, he could not grow or move from the tortuous task of pretense.

Now, instead of skill or knowledge growth, let us consider the internal growth (emotional and spiritual) of an individual. Let us say, for instance, that a particular mother is at day five intellectually but at day two emotionally. Everything is okay when the sun is shining or when things go well. But what happens when fatigue and/or the pressure of screaming kids, diapers, dishes, and telephones join together? Or struggling with uncooperative teen-agers and a husband who is always gone?

This emotionally immature mother may find herself absolutely enslaved to the emotions of anger, impatience, and criticalness. She may find herself incapable of acting upon what she knows in her mind is right, because of the built-in, ingrained habit of losing her temper. All this adds to her guilty feeling. And yet in public, when things are going well, one may never detect this internal deficiency, this emotional immaturity. She has a good mind and seems to be patient and in control.

I recall an occasion when two daughters came to me tearfully complaining about their father's harshness and lack of understanding. They were afraid to open up with either of their parents, for fear of the consequences. And yet they needed almost desperately the kind of love, understanding, and guidance that can really only come from parents. I talked with the father, and he agreed with the complaints and was intellectually aware of what was happening. But while he admitted he had a temper problem, he refused to take responsibility for it and to honestly accept the fact that he was, in a sense, emotionally at day two. It was more pride than he could swallow to take the first step toward day three.

This is obvious with tennis or piano playing, where it is impossible to pretend. But it is not so obvious in emotional and spiritual areas. We can "pose" and put on a friend. We can pretend. And "for a while" we can get by with it—at least in public or on "one-night stands." We might even deceive ourselves. Yet I believe that most of us know the truth of what we really are inside, as do some of those we live with and work around.

To relate effectively with our wife, husband, or children requires emotional strength, because we must learn to listen. Listening involves patience, openness, and the desire to understand. And when we are really open, we run the risk that we may be changed—we may be influenced. And if we are so sure that we are right, we don't want to change. We find it easier to be closed and to tell and dictate. It is easier to operate from our day two emotional level and to give day six advice.

Let me illustrate from my own experience how I once attempted to teach the value of sharing to my daughter.

One day I returned home to my little girl's third-year birthday party only to find her in the corner of the front room defiantly grasping all of her presents, unwilling to let the other children play with them. The first thing I sensed was the presence of several parents witnessing this selfish display. I was embarrassed, and doubly so because I was serving as a bishop at the time and was also a college teacher in the field of human relations. And I knew, or at least felt, the expectation of these parents.

The atmosphere in the room was really charged up— the children crowding around my little daughter with their hands out, asking to play with the presents they had just given, and my daughter adamantly refusing. I said to myself, certainly I should teach my daughter to share. The value of sharing is one of the most basic things we believe in. So I proceeded through the following process.

My first method was to simply make a request: "Honey, would you please share with your friends the toys they've given you?"

A flat "No."

My second method was to use a little reasoning. "Honey, if you learn to share your toys with them when they are at your home, then when you go to their homes they will share their toys with you."

Again, "No!"

I was becoming a little more embarrassed, for it was evident I was having no influence. The third method was bribery. Very softly: "Honey, if you will share, I've got a special surprise for you. I'll give you a piece of gum."

"I don't want a piece of gum!" she exploded.

Now I was becoming exasperated. My fourth method —fear, threat: "Unless you share, you will be in real trouble!"

"I don't care. These are my things. I don't have to share!"

Last method—force. I merely took some of the toys and gave them to the other kids. "Here, kids, play with them."

Perhaps my daughter needed the experience of possessing the things before she could give them. (In fact, unless I possess something, can I ever really give it?) Because, at that moment, I valued the opinion those parents had of me more than the growth and development of my child and our relationship together, I simply made an initial judgment that I was right: she should share, and she was wrong in not doing so. Based on that judgment, I proceeded to manipulate her until I ultimately forced her. Perhaps she was at day two and I at that moment superimposed a day five expectation—simply because on my own scale I was at day two emotionally.

I was unable or unwilling to give patience or understanding, so I expected her to give things.

If I had been more mature, I may have allowed her to make a free choice as to whether she wanted to share or not to share. Perhaps after the reasoning method, I could then have attempted to turn the attention of the children to an interesting game, thus taking all that emotional pressure off my child. I've learned that once my children gain a sense of real possession, then they share very naturally, freely, and spontaneously.

My experience has been that there are times to verbally teach and times *not* to teach. When your relationships are strained and the air charged with emotion, an attempt to verbally teach is often perceived as a form of judgment and rejection. But to take the child alone, quietly, when the relationship is good and to discuss the teaching or the value seems to have real merit. But again, this requires patience and internal control—in short, emotional maturity.

Indeed, a sense of possession should precede a genuine giving, just as algebra precedes calculus. Must not we as parents be patient enough to allow our children the sense of possession? We must also be wise enough to teach them the value of giving and to provide the example ourselves. Perhaps many who give mechanically or refuse to give and share in their marriages and families have never experienced what it means to possess, which would include a feeling of one's own worth and identity (possessing one's self).

This story is an example that focuses on the principle of sharing or giving and how the teaching approach distorted the very principle itself. What about other principles

—such as work, responsibility, appreciation, honesty, virtue? Isn't it possible that they too might be distorted in the mind and life of the child or student when the parent or teacher does not exemplify or embody his or her own teachings?

When Borrowing Strength Builds Weakness

In addition to parents, many employers, leaders, teachers, or others in positions of authority may be competent, knowledgeable, and skillful (at day six) but are emotionally and spiritually immature (at day two). They too may attempt to compensate for this deficiency, or gap, by borrowing their entire strength from their position or from their authority.

How do these immature people react to pressure? How does the boss react when subordinates don't do things his way? The teacher when the students challenge her viewpoint?

How would such an immature father treat his teen-age daughter when she interrupts his convenience with her problems? How does he discipline the younger children when they get in the way? How does he handle a difference with his wife on an emotionally potent matter?

Such an emotionally immature, although intelligent, father will tend to borrow strength to make up for his character imbalance. Because he lacks the internal control and the wisdom to handle each situation as it comes up and on its own merit, he may react almost blindly by relying upon his sheer physical size, perhaps with the younger children, or on his intellectual prowess with his teen-age daughter or his wife. He may end up losing his temper and borrow strength from his angry volume, his position, even his priesthood.

Eventually this father discovers, and inwardly knows, that when he borrows strength, he builds weakness. He builds weakness in three places: First, he builds it in himself. Borrowing strength from position or authority alone reinforces his own dependence upon external factors to get things done in the future.

11

Second, he builds weakness in the other person involved, because the younger child, the teen-ager, or wife learns to act or react in terms of fear or position alone, and this leaves little room for their own reasoning, freedom, and growth in internal discipline.

Third, he builds weakness in the relationship. It becomes strained. Fear replaces the spirit of cooperation. And then each person involved becomes a little more arbitrary, a little more sharp and quick with the other person, a little more defensive.

If to win an argument he uses his intellectual abilities to reason the children and his wife into a corner, he will poison the atmosphere. No one likes to breathe poisonous air. Even though he wins the argument, he loses. Everyone loses. His very strength becomes his weakness.

If this father has the habit of borrowing strength from his size or position, from threatening, bullying, and spanking almost at will, what happens when the children grow up and he can no longer do these things? Unless he repents and uses other more effective methods of influence and discipline, he may then find himself without influence.

His children may then feel belittled and crushed with little sense of worth or identity or individuality. Others may become rebellious and strike back in their own way. Sometimes their way is to strike back against the very things that the father seemingly loves and treasures the most: the Church and the gospel plan. And sometimes then it's almost too late for such a father to change his methods of influence and to use the higher forms: consistent example, high goals and standards, persuasion, kindness, patience and discipline based on well-understood principles and rules, not on the mood of the moment.

When trust or credibility is low, even the best of intentions and the finest of influence methods will be viewed with suspicion and mistrust.

"No power or influence can or ought to be maintained by virtue of the priesthood, only by persuasion, by long-suffering, by gentleness and meekness, and by love unfeigned." (D&C 121:41.)

In fact, whenever we build our security or borrow strength from our possessions or our credentials (the letters following our name), or from our appearance or our memberships in certain social cliques, or from status symbols or past achievements, or from someone else's faith and testimony, what happens to us when these things change or are no longer there? Obviously we remain with our developed weaknesses, for these things are all external to man himself.

From what sources, then, can we borrow strength without building weakness? Only from sources that build the internal capacity to deal with whatever the situation calls for. For instance, a surgeon borrows strength from his developed skill and knowledge; a mile runner from his disciplined body, strong legs, powerful lungs; a missionary from his developed capacity to love and teach and testify.

In other words, we ask the question: What is it that the situation demands? What strength, what skill, what knowledge, what attitude? Obviously the possessions, the appearances, or the credentials of the surgeon, the athlete, or the missionary are only symbols of what is needed and are therefore worthless and deceiving without the substance.

But when we borrow strength from divine sources and from eternal principles, the very nature of the borrowing demands our living better, and we thus build strength inside.

"Labour not for the meat which perisheth, but for that meat which endureth unto everlasting life. . . ." (John 6:27.)

Summary

Based on the above analysis, I see six significant implications:

First, we have learned that the growth process is a natural one that follows God's laws; precept upon precept, you reap as you sow; math, algebra, calculus; crawling before walking. ". . . all things must be done in order." (Mosiah 4:27.)

Second, we are also aware that we all are at different "days" (levels of growth) in the physical, social, emotional,

13

intellectual, and spiritual realms. I am at a different level than you. Perhaps things I need to work on and overcome you have already conquered, and vice versa. Your day four may be my day two, or vice versa. (The time, the circumstance, and the others involved are other variables that influence the manifestation, at least, of the level we're at. It is a complex matter, and we must not oversimplify or generalize from one or two selected instances.)

Third, we must be aware of the dangers of comparing.

"Tom, there is simply no reason for you to bring home a report card like this. If only you'd apply yourself like your brother, you could get good grades too!" This may be true, but if our children's (or our own) sense of worth and personal security comes from being compared with others, how insecure and anxious they will be—feeling superior one minute and inferior the next. Opinions, customs, fashions are fickle, always changing. There is no anchorage or security in changing things. Internal security simply does not come externally. Borrowing strength from any source that does not build and internally strengthen the borrower will internally weaken him.

Such comparing and borrowing breeds complacency and vanity on the one hand, and discouragement and self-dislike on the other. It encourages people to seek shortcuts, to be ruled by opinion, to live by appearances, and to borrow more strength from external sources.

While we must learn from good examples and keep always in mind the bigger goal, we must compare ourself only with ourself. We can't focus or base our happiness on another's progress; we can focus only on our own. We should compare our child against his own potential and then exercise faith in that potential and his effort. We should ask, How is he doing with what he's got? instead of comparing one child against another and meting out love or punishment on the basis of that comparison.

Fourth, there is no shortcut. If I am at day two (to use the analogy of the six days of creation) and desire to move to day six, I must go through days three, four, and five. If I pretend to be at day six in order to impress others, eventually I will be found out. Trying to be all things to all people results in the loss of everybody's respect, including one's own.

If the order, harmony, and mutual understanding (communication) in my home are at day two and my neighbor's are at day six, I must move through each of the intervening steps. If I try to push too hard or to go too fast in order to shortcut the process, I may further strain the relationships and drop back to day one.

If my family, or my son, or the priest's quorum, or the Sunday School class is at day three, it is futile and hurtful to compare and criticize them because they aren't at day five or six. There simply is no shortcut.

"Be not deceived; God is not mocked: for whatsoever a man soweth, that shall he also reap." (Galatians 6:7.)

Fifth, we all need to begin to improve, starting from where we are (not from where we should be, or where someone else is, or even from where others may think we are).

By doing one more pushup each day, I could do 30 in a month. Likewise, in any area of improvement, I could also exercise a little more of what it takes, such as a little more patience, a little more understanding, a little more moral courage, slowly increasing my capacity through daily effort and discipline.

I believe that days one and two for most of us involve getting more control over the body—such as getting to bed early, arising early, exercising regularly, eating in moderation, staying at our work when necessary even though tired, etc. Too many are trying to conquer other higher weaknesses (days four, five, and six), such as procrastination, impatience, or pride, while still a slave to their appetites. If we can't control the body and its appetites, how can we ever control our tongue (a part of the body) or overcome the emotions of anger, envy, jealousy, or hatred. Can I truly love and gossip also? Algebra precedes calculus.

Many pray for the blessings of days five and six (love, spirituality, wisdom, specific guidance in decision-making), and are unwilling to obey the laws of days one, two, three, and four (mastering appetites and passions). One may give lip service to the principle of consecration and yet not participate in quorum projects or magnify his home teaching calling.

Until we gain, to some degree, a control over the lower laws, we can never hope to take the next steps. President David O. McKay continually stressed the importance of mastering our appetites and passions. He stated: "There can be no fullness of life where there is slavery, and the man who is subject to his appetite is the most abject slave. He who can rule his passions is greater than a king."

We will not be able to effectively teach our children about the evils of smoking, drinking, and drugs if we ourselves have a flesh problem—no control over appetite or our tongue, no ability to be moderate, to exercise, to get up early. Where is our power if we don't live the principles? We can't testify effectively of prayer unless we pray fervently and regularly. We need to gain control of ourselves before we can exercise control over others or before we can give up control of ourselves to the Lord.

Priesthood ordinance work, Church activity and service embody perfect opportunities for the exercise of both *belief* power and *will* power. Such a combination will build character or *reserve* power to meet the stresses and tests of life.

Sixth, an accurate understanding of our weaknesses and the power to overcome them comes from the Lord (and from active involvement in his programs).

Many of us simply don't know where to start. We don't always know what things come before other things. Someone else's pattern and process may differ from ours. What is someone else's "day five" may be our "day two." At one time we may be in "day four" and at "day one" another time—even on the same matter! At times we will need to do some work at each day or level simultaneously.

We must not over simplify a complex, variable subject merely to not feel confused. We may really be confused. Moreover, we may find ourselves bogged down in a circular habit pattern of making resolutions, then breaking them, remaking them, then breaking them again.

Where then is the light through our confusion? What is the answer? It lies with the Lord—for he understands all this and infinitely more. He understands exactly where we are and what we need to do. He knows these divine processes and promises to help and guide us if we come to him and obey his voice (our conscience).

"And if men come unto me I will show unto them their weakness. I give unto men weakness that they may be humble; and my grace is sufficient for all men that humble themselves before me; for if they humble themselves before me, and have faith in me, then will I make weak things become strong unto them." (Ether 12:27.)

3

The Three Temptations:
Understanding and Overcoming

It has always been interesting to note the time in the Savior's life and ministry when he was led into the wilderness "of the Spirit to be tempted of the devil." Chapter 1 of Matthew records the genealogy of Christ, his conception, birth, and the special message to Joseph from the angel. Chapter 2 tells of the visit of the wise men, the flight into Egypt, and the slaying of the children by Herod. Chapter 3 introduces John the Baptist and records the baptism of Christ in the Jordan. Chapter 4 records the temptations of the Savior. Immediately afterward he began preaching and teaching. Chapters 5, 6, and 7 contain the greatest sermon ever given to man— the Sermon on the Mount. It is noteworthy that the temptations *followed* baptism and *preceded* his great teaching and ministry. Think about it.

I believe the sequence is significant and has its parallel in many lives. Conquering and overcoming temptation often seems to be a prelude to becoming or self development and to understanding others and their temptations, problems, and feelings. Paul informs us that Christ was touched with the feeling of our infirmities, for he was in all points tempted "like as we are."

"For we have not an high priest which cannot be touched with the feeling of our infirmities; but was in all points tempted like as we are, yet without sin." (Hebrews 4:15.)

Perhaps a deep personal understanding of these temptations is necessary before we can understand and effectively influence others.

Many are sorely tried and tempted before their baptism, thinking such temptations will cease once they have been baptized. From my observation, this is not the case. The temptations often increase, although they may change in character. The greater the growth, the more subtle the temptation. Yet we are told that we are never tempted beyond our capacity to endure and overcome, so no one can say he was forced or seduced by a temptation. He chose to give in. Moreover, there is always a way to escape the temptation, if there is a belief and will to do so. God is faithful and will provide the way. "There hath no temptation taken you but such as is common to man: but God is faithful, who will not suffer you to be tempted above that ye are able; but will with the temptation also make a way to escape, that ye may be able to bear it." (1 Corinthians 10:13.)

Let us now consider each of these temptations that came to the Savior and that come to all of us.

The first temptation. Consider very carefully these words:

"Then was Jesus led up of the Spirit into the wilderness to be tempted of the devil.

"And when he had fasted forty days and forty nights, he was afterward an hungred.

"And when the tempter came to him, he said, If thou be the Son of God, command that these stones be made bread.

"But he answered and said, It is written, Man shall not live by bread alone, but by every word that proceedeth out of the mouth of God." (Matthew 4:1-4.)

What is the nature of this temptation and of the Savior's response to it? Put briefly, could it not be stated *"Flesh versus the spirit"?* Is it the temptation of *appetite,* of bodily longings, of that which is physiologically based?

Flesh versus the spirit . . . After forty days and forty nights of fasting, the Savior must have been very weakened and incredibly hungry. Satan knew this and appealed to the Savior's appetite by pointing to little limestones resembling somewhat a Jewish loaf of bread, saying, "If thou be the Son of God, command that these stones be made bread." But the Savior would not subject himself to the tauntings and directions of Satan. His spirit ruled his flesh, and his spirit was subject to every word that proceedeth out of the mouth of God, his Father.

Each of us faces temptations of appetite or of bodily longings. There are many. Let's consider two of them: First, *food*. Many people today are literally slaves to their stomach! Their stomach controls their mind and their spirit rather than being in subjection to their mind and spirit. To eat to an excess or to gorge oneself is gluttony, which is a perversion of a God-given appetite. To knowingly take things into the body that are harmful or addicting or that simply put on weight is foolishness. It betokens again the control of the stomach or the taste buds or whatever you might call the flesh.

Considered in this light, it becomes obvious that gluttony or ingesting harmful substances doesn't hurt just the body—it also hurts the spirit. It becomes a spiritual matter; and to the Lord all things are spiritual, and all of his laws and commandments are spiritual.

"Wherefore, verily I say unto you that all things unto me are spiritual, and not at any time have I given unto you a law which was temporal; neither any man, nor the children of men; neither Adam, your father, whom I created.

"Behold, I gave unto him that he should be an agent unto himself; and I gave unto him commandment, but no temporal commandment gave I unto him, for my commandments are spiritual; they are not natural nor temporal, neither carnal nor sensual." (D&C 29:34-35.)

How great is the wisdom in the Word of Wisdom, found in Section 89 of the Doctrine and Covenants! Particularly is this so in our affluent society, with an overabundance of things to eat and to satisfy the cravings of the body.

Many researchers and nutrition experts and doctors believe that many more people in America die of overeating than of hunger. "I saw few die of hunger—of eating, a hundred thousand." (Benjamin Franklin.)

I can bear personal testimony of the effect on the spirit of overeating, for I have learned for myself that when I over-indulge, I lose sensitivity to the needs of others. I become angry with myself and sense the tendency to take that anger out on others at the earliest provocation. Sir Walter Scott puts my learning succinctly: "He who indulges his sense in any excesses, renders himself obnoxious to his own reason; and to gratify the brute in him, displeases the man, and sets his two natures at variance."

Now let us look at another temptation of the appetite or bodily longing: *sleep*.

Think about your own situation. How many times do you set the alarm or your mind to get up early, knowing all of the things you have to do in the morning, anxious to get the day organized right, to have a calm and orderly and enjoyable breakfast with the family, to have an unhurried and peaceful scripture reading and a sweet family prayer before sending everyone off? What happens during the night so that when the alarm does go off, your good resolves seem to dissolve? Mind versus mattress! Often the mattress wins. You find yourself getting up just a little too late, then beginning a frantic, desperate rush to get dressed, to get organized, to get fed and be off. In the spirit of rush you grow impatient and begin yelling at one another. Nerves get frayed, tempers short; and by the time you get everyone to family prayer, there often just isn't any "prayer spirit" left. And all because of giving in to the temptations of the flesh to sleep in. A chain of unhappy events and sorry consequences often follows not keeping the first resolution of the day. That day may begin and end in defeat.

The extra sleep is hardly ever worth it. In fact, considering the above, such sleep is terribly tiring and exhausting.

But what a difference if you organize and arrange your affairs at night in order to get to bed at a reasonable time. (I find that often the last hour or two before retiring is the most inefficient and is often spent just fussing around.) Then when the alarm (mechanical or mental) goes off you get up, have a private prayer, and then get at the task of preparation for the day. Such an early-morning victory gives a sense of conquering, of overcoming, of mastering, and this sense is good and clean and propels one on to conquer further difficulties. Success begets success, and a day with an early victory over self is on its way to many more.

Now let us examine the *second temptation.* Ask yourself as you read it, What is its nature?

"Then the devil taketh him up into the holy city, and setteth him on a pinnacle of the temple,

"And saith unto him, If thou be the Son of God, cast thyself down: for it is written, He shall give his angels charge concerning thee: and in their hands they shall bear thee up, lest at any time thou dash thy foot against a stone.

"Jesus said unto him, It is written again, Thou shalt not tempt the Lord thy God." (Matthew 4:5-7.)

The Jews expected their Messiah to come in great power and glory and to dramatically right the wrongs perpetuated on their nation. If only Satan could get the true Messiah to fulfill their wants, their expectations, how he could frustrate and thwart the purposes of God?

And again the taunting "*if* thou be the Son of God," the desire to prove himself, to demonstrate his superior power, to call angels from heaven to bear him up. What an appeal to vanity and to pride!

What is the nature of this temptation? I suggest it might be put in these terms: *appearances vs. reality.* In other words, pretending to be vs. being. The Lord knew who he was. He had a divine definition of himself. It was given to him by his Father—in fact, just before his temptations. At the time of his baptism the Father confirmed to his beloved Son how pleased he was with him.

"And Jesus, when he was baptized, went up straightway out of the water: and, lo, the heavens were opened unto him, and he saw the Spirit of God descending like a dove, and lighting upon him:

"And lo a voice from heaven, saying, This is my beloved Son, in whom I am well pleased." (Matthew 3:16-17.)

If our definition or concept of ourself comes from what others think of us, we will find ourselves gearing our lives to their wants and their expectations; and the more we live in terms of what others expect of us, the more insecure we will become. Expectations change. Opinion is fickle. One person or one group may expect certain things while another individual or group expects other things. Which should you please? The teen-age son may desire to please both his parents and the peer group to which he seeks belonging, but they demand different things; they hold different standards. If he is true to one, he is untrue to the other; but if he learns to pretend or to put on appearances, he might be able to get by, so he thinks. However, in the long run he discovers that by trying to become "all things to all people," he eventually is discovered for what he is, and he loses the respect of others as well as of himself. The only sure anchor to personal security is in God and in God's definition of man.

Consider anger or hatred or envy or jealousy or most any other negative emotion or passion, and you will discover that their roots lie in the desire to be accepted and approved and esteemed of those who are "alienated from the things of God." Thus the temptation to pretend or to appear to be.

The tendency to cram in school or to take a shortcut is a form of appearing or pretending to be a good student. The reality or truth of the matter is that there is no shortcut. The student needs to obey the law of the harvest, but in order to please everyone (teachers, parents, friends) he searches for a shortcut to "beat the system."

Once a student visited me in my office asking how he was doing in the class. After developing some rapport, I confronted him directly: "You didn't really come in to find out how you were doing in the class. You came in to find out how I thought you were doing. You really know how you are doing in the class far better than I do, don't you?"

He acknowledged meekly that he did, and so I asked him, "Just how are you doing?"

He admitted that he was trying to get by. He had a host of reasons and excuses for not studying as he ought and for taking the shortcut, and he came in to see if this was working (if he had "psyched" me out, as it's put).

Satan tempted Christ to appear in all his power and glory to prove himself and to thwart the divine plan. Christ did not come to prove himself, for he already knew who he was. Instead, he came to teach others that they needed to change, to repent, and that they could not rely upon their Messiah to change outside things for them. They didn't want this. They didn't like it, but they needed it.

If people go on long enough playing roles or pretending, giving in to their vanity and to their pride, they will gradually deceive themselves. They will find themselves frequently buffeted and threatened by various circumstances and people and will then fight to maintain their false front.

But if they come to accept the reality or truth about themselves and then will follow line on line and precept upon precept, the laws and principles of the gospel of Jesus Christ, living always the law of the harvest, they will gradually develop (receive) a divine definition or concept of themselves.

The effort to "keep up with the Joneses" puts one on a treadmill that only seems to go faster and faster, almost like chasing a shadow. But it will never satisfy. To build one's security on good looks or fashionable clothing or possessions or status symbols or anything vain and prideful will prove to be a snare and the undoing of that person. Edwin Hubbell Chapin said: "Fashion is the science of appearances, and it inspires one with the desire to seem rather than to be."

Perhaps we could call the second temptation one of passion or emotions, as contrasted to the first temptation, the appeal to the appetites.

If we lose our temper, we are controlled by the emotion of anger. What a tyrant to be ruled by! Nothing good could ever come by it.

Even the Savior, before he cast the money changers out of the temple, braided his whip; he was in full control of himself in the exercise of his righteous indignation.

We need to concern ourselves only with the truth about ourselves from the Lord's point of view. We should be interested in others' opinions and perceptions so that we might learn to be more effective with them, but we would refuse to accept their opinion as a fact and then act or react accordingly.

"Thou shalt not tempt the Lord thy God!"

The third temptation. Consider what the thrust of the third temptation is:

> "Again, the devil taketh him up into an exceeding high mountain, and sheweth him all the kingdoms of the world, and the glory of them;
> "And saith unto him, All these things will I give thee, if thou wilt fall down and worship me.
> "Then saith Jesus unto him, Get thee hence, Satan: for it is written, Thou shalt worship the Lord thy God, and him only shalt thou serve." (Matthew 4:8-10.)

Here Satan is dealing with the desires or motives of man. Here he appeals to our love of power and wealth, to our desire for position and domain.

Let us term this temptation *"aspiration vs. consecration."* By aspiration I mean the seeking for one's own glory, the "what's in it for me" attitude. By consecration I mean seeking for God's glory, the attitude of "how can I best serve?" A consecrated person has given or dedicated all that he has or ever will have to the Lord's purposes. He then looks on his time, talents, and possessions as a stewardship—one to which he is to give an honest accounting from time to time. Nothing is his own, in this sense. Everything is the Lord's, even his own children. He is an agent—the Lord is his principal—and he seeks only to serve God's purposes.

The aspiring individual is deeply concerned with his own things. He even regards his children as possessions and often attempts to wrest from them the kind of behavior that will win him more popularity and esteem in the eyes of others. This kind of possessive love is destructive. Instead of being an agent or a steward, he sees himself as a principal and becomes a law unto himself. He then interprets everything in life in terms of what it will do for him, and everybody, in a sense, becomes a competitor. His relationships, even close, intimate ones, tend to be competitive rather than cooperative. He uses various methods of manipulation to achieve his ends, such as threat, fear, bribery, pressure, for he is unable to learn the lesson that the only real power and honor that has enduring quality comes from obeying the principles of righteousness.

"Behold, there are many called, but few are chosen. And why are they not chosen? Because their hearts are set so much upon the things of this world, and aspire to the honors of men, that they do not learn this one lesson—That the rights of the priesthood are inseparably connected with the powers of heaven, and that the powers of heaven cannot be controlled nor handled only upon the principles of righteousness." (D&C 121:34-36.)

The Lord was a perfect model of the consecrated life. He refused Satan's appeal to love of power and wealth and reaffirmed his commitment to follow the will of the Father. In the Sermon on the Mount he clearly taught that it is impossible to serve two masters—that is, to seek both your own glory and the Lord's glory. It is like trying to walk east and west at the same time. We can see this, perhaps, in all of us. Until an individual acquires the spirit of service and consecration, he might say he loves the Church, but inwardly he might despise the demands the Church makes on his own life and conveniences. He often moves and tries to escape from these demands, only to find the home teachers and the bishopric visiting him again.

"No man can serve two masters: for either he will hate the one, and love the other; or else he will hold to the one, and despise the other. Ye cannot serve God and mammon." (Matthew 6:24.)

The apostle James put the matter squarely: "A double minded man is unstable in all his ways." (James 1:8.)

Double-mindedness is having two conflicting motives or interests. It inevitably sets a man at war within himself, and under storm conditions this internal civil war breaks out into war with others.

"From whence come wars and fighting among you? come they not hence, even of your lusts that war in your members?

"Ye lust, and have not: ye kill, and desire to have, and cannot obtain: ye fight and war, yet ye have not, because ye ask not.

"Ye ask, and receive not, because ye ask amiss, that ye may consume it upon your lusts." (James 4:1-3.)

The opposite of double-mindedness is self unity or integrity. When a man controls himself and knows himself and is unified in all his feelings and desires to the Lord's cause, this is integrity. This is sincerity. ". . . with full purpose of heart, acting no hypocrisy and no deception before God, but with real intent. . . ." (2 Nephi 31:13.) This is a man who lives what he teaches. This is the Son of God, who said, "I am the truth." He didn't just say this is the truth. He said, "I am the truth." He is our exemplar and our model, and he tells us to become like him, to be perfect even as he and our Father in heaven are perfect. (See 3 Nephi 12:48.) To achieve this is a very real possibility and arises through the consecration of ourself to his divine purpose—that is, to selfless gospel service of others.

President McKay taught regarding these three temptations: "Nearly every temptation that comes to you and me comes in one of those forms. Classify them, and you will find that under one of those three, nearly every given temptation that makes you and me 'spotted,' ever so little as it may be, comes to us as: (1) *a temptation of the appetite;* (2) *a yielding to the pride and fashion and vanity of those alienated from the things of God;* or (3) *a gratifying of the passion or a desire for the riches of the world or power among men."* (*Instructor,* September 1962, p. 290.)

How instructive to understand that these three temptations of the Savior are also the same temptations that come to us! This very understanding yields power to resist, to conquer, and to overcome. For instance, if we find ourselves in a situation in every-day affairs where, by compromising slightly our integrity, we would seem to gain in position or power or influence or esteem, we can then introspect and sense that this is a temptation. Once we see it clearly as a temptation, we can then marshal our will to resist it. When we know that our tendency to gluttonize is not just a little foible of our nature but a real giving in to a fundamental temptation, it encourages us to conquer and be the master of ourself.

Relationship of the Three Temptations to Each Other

The practical implications for our personal lives of understanding the relationships between the three temptations are tremendous.

I may be over-simplifying, but I have come to believe that until we conquer to a considerable extent the first temptation, we will be unable to conquer the second one; that is, unless we acquire control of our appetites, our flesh, our body, we will not be able to control our passions and our emotions and place them in subjection to our spirit. Similarly, unless we conquer the second temptation to a considerable extent, we will not be able to successfully consecrate ourself. We will, instead, find ourself a victim of our passions and thereby would naturally yield to the temptation of seeking or aspiring our own glory in the form of wealth and dominion, prestige and power.

Yet, in another sense, all of us face all three temptations simultaneously and we must work (resist and overcome) at all three levels.

It is possible to conquer, at least to a large extent, the first temptation without conquering the second or the third; similarly, it is possible to conquer the first and the second temptations to a considerable extent without consecrating ourselves to the Lord's cause and to his value system. We have known of great athletes who have amazing discipline over their bodies, who have trained and developed their bodies so as to be able to do almost Herculean feats of skill and speed, and yet in other areas of their lives they lack discipline. As students, they lack the disciplined power to mentally concentrate and achieve in their studies. Others are highly volatile and temperamental.

We have also seen people who have, to a considerable extent, acquired a great mental and emotional discipline. They have learned to concentrate and discipline their minds and school their feelings so as to create and accomplish fantastically. I have met many such individuals and feel enormous respect for their self-discipline, intellectual prowess, and emotional control. Yet, by their own admission, they are not consecrated to the Lord's purposes and the doing of his will, but instead have consecrated themselves to their own causes (their own glory), or to laying up for themselves treasures on earth, "where moth and rust doth corrupt, and where thieves break through and steal." (Matthew 6:19.) Their aspiring self-control focuses upon temporal rather than eternal pursuits and values.

Yet I have never known a man who was thoroughly consecrated to the Lord's purposes who had not also control of his own passions and appetites. Have you?

I have taken the opportunity in the last several months to read and reread many of the sermons and messages and articles of President McKay. Again and again I am impressed with what seems to me to be a dominant theme he continually emphasized: We need to rise above the physical, the animal existence through the conquering of our appetites and our passions and to live a spiritual existence. President McKay defined spirituality, in part, as "a consciousness of victory over self."

I will never forget one of the missionaries in the Irish Mission. When he first came out, and for several weeks, he followed a slovenly, irresponsible, undisciplined, and selfish pattern. He seemed to lack control of anything about him. He was not only a slave to his appetites, but also to his tongue and temper. Sleep itself became a form of escape from accepting the responsibilities of missionary work. If his companion slept in, he would sleep in. He was unable to concentrate in his study, to memorize scriptures, to master the teaching discussions. He resented tracting, using the excuse that he hated to intrude himself into other people's lives. He gorged himself at every chance and grew "fat and sloppy."

With all of this you would naturally expect him to have relationship problems with any companion who refused to take the course of least resistance. Such was the case. His hair-trigger temper flashed again and again, snapping and biting and wounding. When I counseled with him regarding these problems, he often became softened and open and teachable, and he would express an eagerness and determination to conquer these tendencies and to be a good missionary. Yet again and again, under various stresses, he found himself unable or at least unwilling to keep his resolves.

One day, after weeks of counseling, he asked me to transfer him to a new area and assign him to a new companion. The relationship he had with his present companion was so poor he was afraid of what he might do in a fit of anger. Up to that point I had listened attentively to him and tried to counsel him to learn to be kind and to obey and to give himself to the work. Then I began to realize that I was asking him to conquer the third temptation before he had conquered the first, and that perhaps this is somewhat similar to expecting a child to walk before it could crawl, or for a student to conjugate verbs before he can even distinguish between verbs and nouns.

I decided to change the approach of my counsel and to focus heavily on the first temptation, the first level, by encouraging him to master his flesh.

I knew he wasn't getting up regularly at 5:55 in the morning when the missionaries were expected to, so I asked him if he would do this every morning for one full month. His response was most interesting. He said, "I came to talk to you about my companion and my problems with him, and here you tell me to get up at 5:55."

I replied, "Let's get to work at conquering the flesh first and then later you'll deal with these emotions and your relationships. Will you get up at 5:55 for one full month?"

He answered, "I am not really sure I can."

I told him not to make a promise unless he knew he would keep it, and that if he wasn't sure he could keep it for a full month, could he keep it for a week? He said he was sure he could do that, and he made a commitment.

What a beaming face after a week! He was thrilled with his achievement. However small it may appear to others, to him it was a major overcoming. I congratulated him on his integrity, and we then determined on the next step, which was to continue getting up at that time but also to put in two and a half hours of solid individual and companion study in the morning. He didn't think he could do this, for his mind was so undisciplined it would constantly jump from one thing to another. He was distracted by most any and every interruption. So I directed, "All right, then merely commit yourself to sit there and to try, but do not get up."

Several days later I was able to commend him again; then we moved to the next step, that of getting out and beginning tracting each morning at 9:30. He honored the commitments and he grew in a sense of integrity and honor; and gradually, little by little, line upon line, he acquired control over his flesh. His consciousness of victory over himself became such a thrilling thing to him that he started to get up at 5:30 in the morning so that he might have a little more time to study. He began to exercise his developing self-power over his tongue, which was also part of his body. Even though he often felt anger and jealousy, he held his tongue. He didn't say the nasty thing as he had done before.

Gradually he found an increase in his power to study and to concentrate in his prayers, to express the feelings of his heart. He sought God's blessings upon his emotions that he would acquire the power to control them, to subject them to God's spirit. He had no more companion or relationship problems.

To make a long story short, he became one of the most powerful and influential teaching missionaries in the entire field. He became highly esteemed and respected because of his selflessness and his tendency to go the second mile in serving others. When he was put into a top leadership position in the mission, his example and spirituality were so well-known and esteemed that the zone over which he presided immediately leaped forward in application and dedication and shortly thereafter in accomplishment.

What an absolutely inspiring thing it was to witness this transformation, this second birth! I am convinced the same principle holds in many of our lives. If we could merely be strong in certain of the hard moments, then when other temptations come, we would be amazed at the reserve strength we would have for all the rest of our difficult moments.

I believe that most of us are struggling with some of these problems and that if we would begin by conquering some of the basic appetites first, we would be amazed at the power that would come to us to accurately discern and then to conquer higher level temptations.

Most men and women, for one reason or another, have a tendency to overeat and thus are rather heavy. It makes many of them feel self-conscious and ugly, and it depresses their whole spirit. What an emotional and spiritual transformation would begin to take place if they could get back to normal weight through a strict program of self-mastery. They would not only look better, but they would also feel better and would thereby treat others better. They would grow in a "consciousness of victory over self." And with this increased power they would have the capacity to do many other things they have only longed to do before.

In the mission field we had a motto that somewhat expresses or capitalizes on this entire concept: "Until you can say 'I am my master,' you cannot say 'I am thy servant.'" In other words, a missionary or anyone of us might profess to be a servant of the Lord. We might feel very sincere in that particular moment, but under the right pressure or stress we might find ourself controlled by a particular passion or appetite. We lose our temper. We become jealous or envious or lustful or slothful. Then we feel guilty. We make promises and break them; make resolutions and break them. We gradually lose faith in our own capacity to make any professions or promises, or we do so only mechanically. Despite our profession to be the Lord's servant, we become the servant or the slave of whatever masters us.

This reminds me of the plea of Richard Rich to Thomas More in the movie *A Man for All Seasons.* Richard Rich admired More's honesty and integrity and wanted to be employed by him. He asked, "Employ me."

More answered, "No."

Again Rich pleaded, "Employ me," and again the answer was no.

Then Rich made this pitiful yet endearing promise: "Sir Thomas, employ me. I would be faithful to you."

Sir Thomas, knowing what really mastered Richard Rich, answered, "Richard, you can't even so much as answer for yourself tonight," meaning "You might profess to me faithfulness now, but all it will take is a different circumstance, the right bribe or pressure, and you will find yourself so controlled by your pride, your spleen, your vain ambition, that you could not be faithful to me."

Sir Thomas More's prognosis came to pass that very night, for Richard Rich betrayed him!

The real key to growth is to learn to make promises and to keep them. In the ordinances of the gospel, the

Lord has provided magnificent opportunities for promises or covenants. He himself enters into the covenants and promises to give us his spirit and power if we are true to our covenant. I believe that, daily prayer is the most appropriate time to renew, in a very private way, our promises or covenants.

We must never make a promise or a covenant we do not intend to keep. If we can't make the larger ones, then we should begin by making the smaller ones. But we must begin somewhere to conquer temptations and unworthy habits.

I think most of us need to start with acquiring control over our body. We know in our minds what we need to do. Our problem is not a lack of knowledge—it is habit. The body is sacred. It is the house in which the spirit lives. Paul, the apostle, called it a temple.

"Know ye not that ye are the temple of God, and that the Spirit of God dwelleth in you?

"If any man defile the temple of God, him shall God destroy; for the temple of God is holy, which temple ye are." (1 Corinthians 3:16-17.)

I tend to believe that through the power of the Savior's atonement and resurrection we will participate in resurrecting ourselves, but until the spirit has control over the flesh, the spirit body may be unable to go to the grave and pick up the flesh and unite with it.

We are told that those who will come with the Savior in his second coming, and those who will rise in the air to meet him, are those who have "overcome"—meaning, as I understand it, they have overcome the flesh and the world. With God's help they become their own master and then fully submit themselves to the mastery of the Lord. The Savior himself, when he delivers up the kingdom and presents it unto the Father spotless, will say: "I have overcome and have trodden the wine press alone, even the wine press of the fierceness of the wrath of Almighty God." (Doctrine and Covenants 76:107.)

Through study of the scriptures and the teachings of

our modern prophets, it appears that our first and most basic stewardship is our body. To acquire a body was one of the main purposes of our coming to earth, and we are then to use this body as a divine instrument to perfect and train the spirit until the spirit has the full control and mastery of it under the direction of the Holy Spirit. If I do not honor the stewardship over my own flesh, how could I possibly honor my stewardship as a husband or wife, or father or mother?

I will never forget hearing one of our Church leaders report to a congregation counsel he gave to a brother who had lived in deep sin for a long period of time, to the effect that he should be very careful to take no chances or risks of an accident, since his body was so important in the overcoming of his sins and in making a full and complete repentance. The idea was presented that it would be infinitely more difficult to repent of sins of the body, in the spirit world, without a body.

Perhaps a sense of the buffetings of Satan is to be in the spirit world without a body, yet possessing the same disposition and character weakness there as in mortality, to have all of the appetites and desires and passions but without the instrument of expression. The controls would not lie in the spirit, but in the body, which is in the grave. What a hell this would be!

We need to conquer the first temptation first and continue working to conquer all unworthy passions, feelings, and emotions until we can realistically and deeply mean it when we consecrate ourself to the Church and to God's divine purposes.

Some Practical Exercises

Each individual must strive to know himself, that is, to know some of his tendencies and propensities and weaknesses, as well as his strengths and capacities. On this understanding and with some spiritual motivation he can build a practical program of self-mastery for himself. He will find, as he begins to control himself, his appetites, and his passions, that his knowledge of himself will also increase. The following steps may help in a program of self-mastery: First, whenever you set your alarm to get up, *get up*, regardless of how you might feel at the time. Second, have a program of daily exercise that is geared to your own general health and capacity. Third, practice moderation in diet and fasting. (It is easier for some to fast than to eat moderately.) "The worst education which teaches self-denial is better than the best which teaches everything else and not that." (Sterling.)

In regard to the second level, or the second temptation, I have found that the exercise of patience and understanding is a cardinal principle, one that helps fashion and develop other gospel virtues, including sincerity of life. If we will exercise patience when we are tempted to become critical or angered, we will find that many other things will fall into place.

At the third level, or dealing with the third temptation, I stress two exercises: first the habit of daily scripture study and meditation leading to some private commitments in prayer to live by the principles of righteousness that day; and second, anonymous service of others and/or "going the second mile," which involves magnifying a church or priesthood calling. Such service flows out of the spirit of consecration and also feeds and reinforces that spirit so that we do the "right things for the right reasons."

The essential element in overcoming all three temptations and in "practicing" the exercises outlined is self denial. "The secret of all success is to know how to deny yourself. Prove that you can control yourself, and you are an educated man; and without this all other education is good for nothing." (Roswell Dwight Hitchcock.)

"One secret act of self-denial, one sacrifice of inclination to duty is worth all the mere good thoughts, warm feelings, passionate prayers, in which idle men indulge themselves." (John Henry Newman.)

After the Savior conquered the three temptations, according to the scriptures, "then the devil leaveth him, and, behold, angels came and ministered unto him." (Matthew 4:11.)

When you and I learn to conquer the evil one and his temptations, whether open and blatant or insidious and subtle, then I believe that God's sweet spirit will also come to us and minister to us. Our character will absorb the power and fury of the temptation, and from this increased strength will emerge the power to resist future temptations and to work more righteousness.

4

Life's Central Challenge:
Building Relationships

1.   *The Nature of Relationships*

All relationships are interwoven with each other. To graphically illustrate:

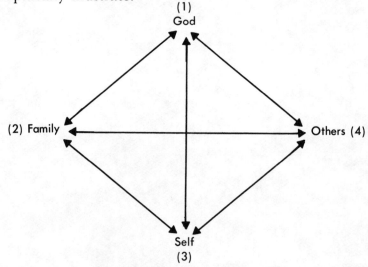

From the illustration, observe that our relationship with ourself (3) both affects and is influenced by our relationship with God (1), our family (2), and others (4). There is an interdependency here. Conversely, our relationship with God (1) is based on our relationship with ourself (3), our family (2), and others (4). To sense the interdependency, ponder these scriptures: ". . . and whosoever will lose his life for my sake shall find it. . . ." (Matthew 16:25.) "And the second is like unto it: Thou shalt love thy neighbour as thyself." (Matthew 22:39.) ". . . when ye are in the service of your fellow beings ye are only in the service of your God." (Mosiah 2:17.)

It is also true that our ability to "get along" well with others (4) flows naturally from how well we are getting along with ourself (3), from our own internal peace and harmony, which is itself a function of our peace with God (1) and our family (2).

The family is singled out, first, because of its preeminence throughout all eternity among other relationships, and second, because it involves a different and often more intense set of forces, problems, expectations, and challenges than found in relating to others.

It's senseless to work on one relationship without working on them all.

Let's think through an example. To grow closer to my wife (or husband), to build a richer and deeper respect for her and communication with her, I first need to draw closer to the Lord. The same principles that govern communication between people also apply in communicating with the Lord. There must be a desire to understand and to be understood—so with prayer. Communication must be two way—so with prayer. A regard (reverence) for the other's worth and dignity must be felt—so with prayer.

Now, one step further: to draw closer to the Lord will probably involve making some changes within myself, in my attitudes and behavior. I may need to repent of breaking his laws, which has resulted in a quarrel with my own conscience. I may have taken out my self anger on my wife or my children in moments of seeing their weaknesses or in other times of stress.

It isn't easy to repent. My pride will stand in the way. I need to ask forgiveness. I'll need to pray more sincerely from the heart and worship with real intent in order to be consistently more kind and less critical, more understanding and less judgmental.

Accomplishing this repentance, I feel better inside—more internal peace, less internal quarreling. I like and respect myself more and find it easier to like others more, to give of myself more freely and spontaneously. I love the Lord more. I'm less defensive and guarded, more open and respectful of my wife's feelings. We become closer.

In other words, to improve any of our relationships involves a simultaneous improvement in them all. How superficial and futile to work on one without working on all other relationships.

Two Relationship Tests

There are two real tests of the strength and quality of any relationship. The first comes under conditions of stress and strain. When all is fine, when the sun is shining, no deep-root relationship structure is required. Appearances seem sufficient, but when the storm breaks, appearances are thrown to the wind, and in the winds that blow then some of us lash out with an ugliness held deep within. We may wound—and wound deeply—the tender sensitive feelings of our spouses or children or others and thereby teach them to be defensive and guarded against such hurts in the future.

An article once depicted the figure of a little girl, burying her face in her mother's apron and weeping as her mother lashed out her venom and hatred on some colored children going into a recently integrated school. A social observer to this scene commented, "That child is not weeping because of the mother's prejudice but out of fear that someday, somehow, some poisonous hatred would be turned on her."

The other test of the quality of relationship is found in the little things of every day, little courtesies, little acts of kindness, the give and take in little moments.

"Men best show their character in trifles, when they are not on their guard. . . . It is in insignificant matters, and in the simplest habits, that we often see the boundless egotism which pays no regard to the feeling of others, and denies nothing to itself." (Arthur Schopenhauer.)

I used to write to new converts in the mission field inquiring what it was that impressed and touched them so deeply about the gospel and the Church. It's significant that a good percentage were most impressed by two things: first, the love missionary companions showed to each other (one new convert wrote, "I felt I could trust the love they gave me by the respect they showed to each other"); and, second, the consistent and unconditional love the missionaries gave the contacts when they were struggling, and even rebelling, under the new demands of the gospel and the social persecution heaped upon them.

"By this shall all men know that ye are my disciples, if ye have love one to another." (John 3:35.)

If the elders had returned unkindness for unkindness, the contacts would have felt justified in dropping the teaching. But how does a good person reject kindness?

Too many human relations formulas are sunshine philosophies, which sound simple and logical and do work when environmental conditions are freed of the "storms of life." But unless they work on the roots, deep within the character structure of an individual, they only temporarily tranquilize and anesthetize. Then individuals and relations "buckle" when the real storms move in, whether in the form of money problems, personal role conflicts, social pressures, physical suffering or affliction, death of a loved one, or simply every-day time pressures, minor household crises, deadlines, conflicting schedules, disappointing behavior of others. When these winds blow and rains descend, those built on the sand, with shallow root structures, are buffeted and uprooted. (See Matthew 7:24-27.) The person may lose his temper, shout, condemn, criticize, or otherwise take out his hostilities on others. Or he may walk out, withdraw into a numbed indifference, calloused and noncaring, and seek his satisfactions elsewhere. He may even turn on himself—self-condemning, self-hating, paralyzed by indecisiveness, fear, guilt. Lashing out and escaping are the two most common reactions of immature people when responsibilities and storms short-circuit their emotional root structure.

Valuing the Individual

The key in keeping the 99 sheep is in the treatment of the one. Valuing the individual, particularly the unlovable, the obnoxious, the awkward, the "drop out," communicates powerfully and persuasively to *all* the rest (many of whom may be on their guard, all of whom are unlovable or awkward in some way) your sincere regard and loving concern for them as individuals. In some way *each* of us is inactive in the Church—whether it be our poor attendance at meetings or in our inattention to the laws of love, particularly toward those who are difficult to love (the ungrateful, the rude, the obnoxious, the pushy, the haughty, etc.). We all need love, understanding, and acceptance; but fearing we may not receive such warmth, we learn to play roles and defend ourselves against being hurt, to guard our communication, to pretend and stand behind facades, to elevate ourselves above others by judging them. Because of this unlovable behavior pattern, we do not "receive" the love we need, even though given.

Sarcastically cut one of your children and all will fear your sarcasm. Gossip with your friend about another and the first storm on your seeming friendship may uproot it. Make fun of another, sarcastically dig at a weakness, belittle someone's sincere effort, laugh at someone's weakness, and you'll sow the seeds of destruction in all of your relationships. It may take some real storms to forceably teach you this truth.

We simply cannot violate a true principle toward one without doing so toward all, anymore than we can pray sincerely to God and be insincere to his other children.

Just as an injury or infection in any organ or limb of the human body affects the well being and feeling of the entire person, so it is with relationships.

We must all hold two pulses simultaneously—God's and man's. We can never serve man's deepest needs without God. Neither do we serve God and his purposes without serving his children in his way. Am I really feeling the pulse of the Lord—praying to him, receiving his Spirit, understanding his ways and designs—if I am unloving, critical, and judging of his children?

This truth became so clear in the mission field. Those missionaries who claimed to be so close to the Lord but were not to their companions and contacts served neither the Lord nor his children. They began to use the gospel, like the praying Pharisee, as a tool for judgment and rejection and self justification. Some of their opinions were right, but their spirits were wrong. Their unloving use of the religion of love distorted their perspectives, destroyed their effectiveness, and increasingly isolated them.

Some claimed to be close to the people, but were not to the Lord. Mistaking wants for needs, they became popular social friends with their contacts or the Saints but never really lifted lives. There was no vision, no strength in committing the people to repent and obey, no giving the bread of life to hungry souls.

Unless we hold the pulse of both heaven and earth, of God and man, learning from both, appreciating and loving both (God first), we hold neither. There is no power, no influence, no life in truth without love. There is no vision, no lifting power, no conviction, no light in life without truth.

Our greatest role in relationships is to be a light, not a judge.

2. The Root Cause of Breakdowns in Relationships

Relationships problems begin within the individual.

When Adam and his posterity were cut off from the presence of God for transgression, man's insecurity began. Whenever I or you sin against the light we've been given, we become estranged from God and his spirit. Further, we become split within and lose our wholeness and unity, our integrity. We feel insecure.

We read and hear a great deal on how to overcome insecurity and inferiority and how to acquire confidence and peace within. But which of these well-intentioned philosophers, scientists, or commercial advice-givers works on the roots? Who, among them, literally believes in and teaches of the human soul, of God and his laws and plan of life, of the effect of sin on personality and relationships, of the role of Christ, the one appointed to be the Savior of the human soul, the only ultimate source of personal security?

A correct understanding of the nature of man as a dual being is absolutely vital in giving an accurate understanding and counsel on overcoming insecurity and developing genuine self confidence.

President McKay taught, in the April, 1965, *Instructor:*

"Man is a dual being; and his life, a plan of God. Man has a natural body and a spiritual body. Man's body is but the tabernacle in which his spirit dwells. Too many, far too many, are prone to regard the body as the man, and consequently to direct their efforts to the gratifying of the body's pleasures, its appetites, its desires, its passions. Too few recognize that the real man is an immortal spirit, which "intelligence or the light of truth" animated as an individual entity before the body was begotten and that this spiritual entity with all its distinguishing traits will continue after the body ceases to respond to its earthly environment."

Inherent within the soul of man is a longing to return to its Creator, the Father of us all, and also the propensity to believe and to obey the laws that blessed reward is predicated upon. Disobedience and rebellion create a deep split within man's nature, between his body, his mind, and his spirit. This might be termed self alienation and is the root or fundamental cause of relationship breakdowns and most human problems. What many call insecurity is alienation or separation from God, our Father, caused by transgression.

This includes the transgressions of others as well as ourselves. How we are treated by others as human beings has a powerful influence, though not controlling, on how we think, feel, and behave. From others and traditions, we may learn false values and false principles. Our culture and models may teach us to exploit and manipulate relationships, to defend and to hurt before being hurt, to suspect and doubt, to pretend and to take shortcuts, to throw off the straight jacket of "outmoded moral codes," to gratify our appetites and selfish desires at the expense of others, if necessary.

But over and above negative cultural determinants is the light of Christ, our conscience, which prompts us regarding God's moral laws. If it is listened to and followed, more light comes. Gradually an individual becomes increasingly freed from the effects of his environment. We all know of individuals who have risen above their environments. Christ, our great exemplar, overcame all things and declared, "I have overcome the world."

If, on the other hand, we ignore or disobey the light of Christ (our conscience) by following the ways of the world, our internal world gradually deteriorates. President McKay, in the March, 1963, *Era,* taught of the effect transgression has on the human soul.

"You may cheat your fellow men and apparently for a while succeed, but nature is never deceived. She credits and debits according to merit; for here in this old world the law of retribution is just as constant as the law of compensation.

"The same conditions exist in the moral world. You cannot violate a moral principle without suffering the consequences. The world may not know of the violation, but there are two beings who do know it. One is God, and one is he who perpetrates the deed. In that connection Charles Kingsley has aptly said: 'The more I know intimately the lives of other men, to say nothing of my own, the more obvious it is to me that the wicked do not flourish nor is the righteous punished. The ledger of the Almighty is strictly kept and every one of us has the balance of his operations paid over to him at the end of every minute of his existence. The absolute justice of the system of things is as clear to me as any scientific fact. The gravitation of sin to sorrow is as certain as that of the earth to the sun; and more so, for experimental truth of that fact is within the reach of all, nay, is before us all in our lives, daily, if we have the eyes to see it."

"If law is operative in the physical, intellectual, and moral world, it is also operative in the spiritual world. Jesus Christ, our Redeemer, has given us laws, fundamental and eternal, by obedience to which we might enjoy abundant life, might keep the spirit free, and gain complete mastery over all things physical."

Roots of Strife and Prejudice

A breakdown or split within the individual translates itself into every relationship and becomes clearly evident in times of storm. James explains that war and strife among people stem from the war within, from lust, jealousy, selfish ambition, hatred. (See James 3.)

If we possess no *internal* security and if we feel no *external* security in a fickle world—nothing fixed—what can we depend upon? Too often, I fear, we take either the route of living for appearances, which only feeds the fires of envy and coveting, or the route of *freezing* our views and opinions and conclusions. This freezes our internal world and, to a degree, provides a modicum of security, something fixed or anchored to depend upon. This is one form and one cause of prejudice. Prejudice means pre-judgment or judgment of people, events, causes before understanding them. Understanding requires openness, sincere listening, empathy. But these efforts carry a risk insecure people can barely afford, the risk of changing, of modifying judgments, of unfreezing within, creating again the problem of having nothing fixed to feel secure with. Yet, we all know that understanding is the basis of communication and harmonious cooperative relationships. Look carefully at your own human relation problems to discover how many of these problems grew from making judgments before really understanding.

To judge someone before understanding him is a form of human rejection and feeds upon itself. It intensifies personal insecurities, necessitating more judgment (prejudice) and less understanding. The processes continue.

3. The Root Solution in Building and in Healing Broken Relationships.

Accepting Christ and his atoning sacrifice is *the* root solution to self alienation or personal insecurity, to estranged relationships with others, in addition to reconciliation between God and man.

Atonement means "at-one-ment." The atonement and resurrection of Christ is the most transcendently important event in all human history and profoundly affects all human life and all relationships. Every principle of the gospel becomes efficacious only in and through the suffering and sacrifice of the Lord Jesus Christ.

You ask: You mean to say my relationship with myself, my relationship with my wife and children and others is founded on my accepting the atonement of the Savior? I mean exactly that. To my understanding, the fall and the atonement are intimately connected with the development or deterioration of human personality and human relationships.

To understand how the atonement profoundly influences relationships, consider how it is we receive the transcendent gift of Christ and his atonement. Though we are all *given* the gift, unless we *receive* the gift, we rejoice "not in that which is given unto him, neither rejoice in him who is the giver of the gift." (D&C 88:33.)

To receive the gift of the atonement, we must first place our faith in the Lord Jesus Christ instead of on the "arm of flesh" (our learning, possessions, position, ability, etc.); second, repent of our sins, as evidenced by confessing and forsaking them; third, enter into sacred covenants at the waters of baptism (renewed in the sacrament); fourth, receive the Holy Ghost (the baptism of spirit or fire), which burns out the dross and gives us a new birth, a new mind, and a changed and pure heart.

These endeavors are not easy or mechanical. Great and consistent physical, mental, and spiritual effort is required.

"Merely an appreciation of the social ethics of Jesus, however, is not sufficient. Men's hearts must be changed. . . . Force and compulsion will never establish the ideal society. This can come only by a transformation within the individual soul—a life brought into harmony with the divine will. We must be 'born again.' . . . Christ is the light to humanity. In that light man sees his way clearly. When it is rejected, the soul of man stumbles in darkness. No person, no group, no nation can achieve true success without following Him who said: 'I am the light of the world; He that followeth me shall not walk in darkness, but shall have the light of life' (John 8:12)." (President David O. McKay, *Deseret News Church Section*, October, 1961.)

For a person to go through this gospel process necessitates subduing and overcoming the appetites and desires of the physical body, thus bringing a unity and harmony between the physical body and the spiritual body.

"From the 40-day fast on the Mount of Temptation to the moment on the cross, when He cried in triumph, 'It is finished,' Christ's life was a divine example of subduing and overcoming." (President McKay, *Instructor*, April, 1965.)

Having mastered our body and mind and placed them in subjection to our spirit, we then place our spirit in subjection to and harmony with God's spirit. Through continued obedience to the laws and principles of the gospel, and consecration to his divine purposes, a deep unity and integrity gradually develop inside. Harmony and real personal security replace estrangement and insecurity. In the very process of nurturing our faith in him through obedience, study, prayer, faith, confessing, repenting, covenant making, and serving, we gradually inculcate his qualities into our characters until we become "partakers of the divine nature." (See 2 Peter 1:3-8.) Christ literally is the healer, the unifier, the Savior of the soul. He was the only one so appointed. There is no other way. (See John 10:1, 9.)

Marriage and Christ

Why is the atonement so important to your marriage? No relationship is so demanding as marriage. To properly fulfill the divine purpose of marriage, that of bringing spirits into the world and raising them in the nurture of the Lord, will require the utmost in self-discipline, self-sacrifice, courage, love, humility, and integrity (self unity). Again, Christ taught, "I am the way." He was the perfect example of these character traits and instructs us to follow in his footsteps. In addition, the very nature of the process of receiving the divine gift of the atonement develops these character traits.

It is significant that there is no permanent marriage outside the gospel of Jesus Christ. Why is an eternal marriage found only in the highest degree of the celestial kingdom? I believe it is because a truly successful marriage, which can sustain any storm, must be a three-way divine partnership. The Savior and his atonement are the foundation of this harmonious partnership, this beautiful marriage. He is the Savior of the family relationship as well as of the individual soul.

So it is with our relations with others. Again, he is "the way." We forgive because he forgave. We love him because he first loved us. He suffered for us incomprehensively and described such suffering in a modern revelation. (D&C 19:16-19.)

Don't his suffering and love draw you to him and our Father in heaven and to all his other children? Once drawn, and born of him, our security comes from within, not from without—not from what others think of us, nor from our social station or our material possessions, which provide no real security at all. Therefore, anchored to light and truth, we can accept the risks of understanding and loving freely, nondefensively, without prejudging or asking for something in return.

To improve your relationships, don't look to others to change and don't look to easy, step-by-step shortcut, sunshine formulas that do not strike at the roots. Look to yourself. Be honest with yourself first—the roots of your problems are spiritual. So also, therefore, are the root solutions. The key lies in your own heart. "Keep thy heart

with all diligence; for out of it are the issues of life."
(Proverbs 4:23.)

You are called to be a light, not a judge. Build your
own character and relationships on the light of this world.
Build your home and family around him.

"And now, my sons, remember, remember that it is upon the
rock of our Redeemer, who is Christ, the Son of God, that ye must
build your foundation; that when the devil shall descend forth his
mighty winds, yea, his shafts in the whirlwind, yea, when all his hail
and his mighty storm shall beat upon you, it shall have no power
over you to drag you down to the gulf of misery and endless wo,
because of the rock upon which ye are built, which is a sure foundation, a foundation whereon if men build they cannot fall." (Helaman
5:12.)

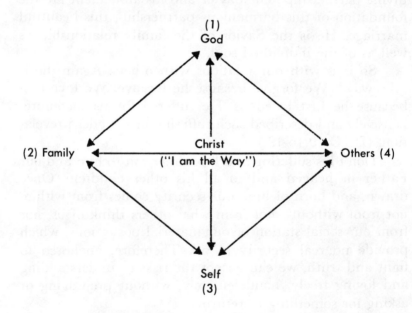

5

Conversion:

The Divine Miracle

The prophets Ezekiel and Jeremiah wrote of the divine miracle of conversion.

"And I will give them one heart, and I will put a new spirit within you; and I will take the stony heart out of their flesh, and will give them an heart of flesh:

"That they may walk in my statutes, and keep mine ordinances, and do them: and they shall be my people, and I will be their God." (Ezekiel 11:19-20.)

". . . I will put my law in their inward parts, and write it in their hearts; and will be their God, and they shall be my people." (Jeremiah 31:33.)

Not infrequently we hear faith-promoting stories of dramatic spiritual manifestations, of sudden, miraculous healings, of special inspiration and direction in times of need and decision. These are glorious, confirming blessings that are vital in the Lord's work today. Yet, it is my conviction that the divine purpose behind the gifts of the spirit and the greater manifestations of the Holy Ghost are largely fulfilled in the silent, peaceful, almost imperceptible workings upon the heart and mind of the person who is striving to know, to obey, and to love the Lord of life.

I fear that in our study of God and his dealings with us, we focus on the special, the sudden, the dramatic, and overlook his silent, natural, gradual workings within the breast of each individual who surrenders his will to a higher will.

We live in a shortcut world. Cities and human organizations are built apart from nature and are often governed by artificial, rather than natural, law. Can you imagine a farmer "cramming" in the fall to bring forth the harvest, as students have done, and still do, to pass examinations? Can you imagine a mile-runner "pretending" speed and endurance, or a concert pianist "putting on the appearance" of skill and proficiency? Obviously there is no shortcut, no "something for nothing," in farming or in developing a physical skill.

Yet when it comes to internal emotional and spiritual growth, we often apply the shortcut lessons of an artificial social world where we cram and pretend, get by on appearances or glib tongues, and literally think we do get something for nothing.

I have observed scores of missionaries come into the mission field, many with a "shortcut mentality" of wanting something for nothing or for very little. As the realities of mission life bore down, there often is a period of frustration, disappointment, and a desire for escape. The "shortcut artists" simply can not get by on good looks, fashionable clothing, clever talk, or past achievements. There is no way "to cram" someone into conversion, no pretending good discussions. There are no shortcuts anymore.

What a moment of truth! "No shortcuts"—"No one to blame but me"—"I've got to pay the price"—"Got to start right now, with me, a step at a time."

For every missionary, teaching and testifying with power and loving with deep sincerity, particularly when the storms break, emerge from deep well-springs of internal character growth, not from technique or a little knowledge combined with some persuasive and manipulative skills.

To an eager, youthful reformer, Tolstoi said. "Young man, you sweat too much blood for the world; sweat some for yourself first. . . . If you want to make the world better you have to be the best you can. . . . You cannot bring the Kingdom of God into the world until you bring it into your own heart first."

As the missionaries experience their "moment of truth," the divine miracle begins. Gradually, "line upon line, precept upon precept" through the days, weeks, and months of giving themselves over to faith and faithfulness, their souls unfold. Spiritual values replace physical and material values and transcend intellectual and social values. The doctrine of the priesthood distills upon their souls "as the dews from heaven," and the Holy Ghost becomes their companion. Through their devoted service the Lord writes his laws and his love into their lives, ". . . written not with ink, but with the Spirit of the living God; not in tables of stone, but in fleshy tables of the heart." (2 Corinthians 3:3.)

Shortly after beginning their labors, many missionaries feel they are leaving the Garden of Eden and going into a cold and dreary world. Their "life" is in their environment. But on departing from the mission field, with changed hearts, they feel they are leaving their "Garden of Eden" and going back into a cold and dreary world. Christ has become their life, and the Light of their lives.

Who would deny this miracle? No missionary who experiences it. Nor would his parents. But when does it take place?

The "second birth" and "new life," beginning with baptism, is a gradual, almost imperceptible process for most of us. The Savior said to Nicodemus:

"Marvel not that I said unto thee, Ye must be born again.

"The wind bloweth where it listeth, and thou hearest the sound thereof, but canst not tell whence it cometh, and whither it goeth; so is every one that is born of the Spirit." (John 3:7-8.)

I remember asking faithful, recently baptized converts if they knew when they had the Holy Ghost and when they did not. The answers, in almost every instance, were unequivocal. They knew they had come out of darkness into light. The contrast was simply too great to deny. And yet few testified to any special signs or unusual manifestations. They knew, for they had felt the pulsation of the Holy Ghost on hearing the missionaries testify and as they gave themselves over to a new, divine way of living.

These examples and experiences stem from the mission field, but the principle behind them is universal and applies to us all, in whatever circumstance we are in.

It is the principle of conversion. Conversion means change. Change implies repentance. Perhaps this perspective gives some understanding of the Lord's oft-given instruction to "say nothing but repentance unto this generation."

Testimony: Setting Out to Be True

In this process of conversion, which is the divine miracle, we acquire a testimony of the Lord Jesus Christ and his gospel. This kind of knowledge is as different from any other kind as a knowledge *of* sight differs from a knowledge *about* sight.

Try sometime to explain to a person who has never experienced sight what it means to see, or to a deaf person what it means to hear. We can communicate facts and ideas, but we cannot convey to a blind or deaf person a true knowledge or understanding of what it really means to see or hear.

And yet a blind person could make a lifelong study of the eye, the properties of light, the sight process, and become a great expert in the field. He might become so expert as to advise medical doctors who can see. But, in another sense, he would know nothing about sight. Such personal knowledge can come only from personal experience.

This is also true with divine knowledge, which is the kind of knowledge that comes from God to the spirit within man. It does not come from flesh and blood (see Matthew 16:17), nor from the reasoning and wisdom of man (see 1 Corinthians 2:9-14; 2 Nephi 9:28). Rather, it comes from God, as his spirit speaks to the spirit of man. A man could know a great deal about God and yet not know God. A man could understand God's dealings with his children through all dispensations and could impressively recite the principles and doctrines of the gospel and perhaps, from an intellectual standpoint, effectively teach a Sunday School class, yet have little or no personal soul-knowledge about God, the author of it all.

In Ireland we observed the conversion process of hundreds of people, amid struggles, doubts, fears, escapes, and fights. Over and over again we came to the conclusion that an individual would know the truth to the degree he was true to the truth. In other words, we found that a person would know that the gospel was restored if he became true to its unique teachings such as the Word of Wisdom, prayer, tithing, and study. We concluded that people did not really doubt the gospel; rather, they doubted themselves and their own desire and ability to live it.

What a startling discovery! The whole teaching approach changed! Instead of offering more logic, more scripture, more external evidence, in the spirit of love and testimony we asked each to look into his or her own heart, ". . . for out of it are the issues of life." (Proverbs 4:23.) The key to testimony was right there in the heart.

Some would try to escape from this fundamental responsibility, this reality, by seeking a shortcut or by mere intellectualization, thereby refusing to look within, to repent, to study prayerfully, to seek earnestly, or to pray sincerely from the heart. Others would fight and rebel as Amulek did prior to his conversion:

"Nevertheless, I did harden my heart, for I was called many times and I would not hear; therefore I knew concerning these things, yet I would not know; therefore I went on rebelling against God, in the wickedness of my heart. . . ." (Alma 10:6.)

The Father has promised to grant a witness of the divinity of his Son, through the Holy Ghost, to anyone who qualifies. The responsibility, then, is upon us to qualify.

It is not the Lord who must make up his mind to communicate. It is we who must change and prepare ourselves to receive the communication he has promised.

Once we clearly understand that "my thoughts are not your thoughts, neither are your ways my ways, saith the Lord" (Isaiah 55:8); that "the things of God knoweth no man, but the Spirit of God" (1 Corinthians 2:11); that "if any man will do his will, he shall know of the doctrine" (John 7:17); then we begin to look within for the key to this learning. We ask, "How sincere am I? Do I really want to know? Am I willing to pay the price to do whatever is necessary in study, prayer, repentance, and service, to qualify?"

Many then discover that it is not Christ—nor the prophets who testify of him—that they doubt. In their sincere introspection they cannot honestly lay the blame upon the Lord for their failure to receive a witness. What they really doubt is their own ability to make themselves worthy. They sense that the obstacle or weakness lies in them.

One investigator wrote, "I doubted whether I really could or even wanted to give up my smoking." Others also acknowledge, in this crisis of self-honesty, that the problem is within themselves—intellectual pride, perhaps, or sensuality, or materialistic desires, or hypocrisy. They see they have failed to gain a testimony of Christ's divinity "because their hearts are set so much upon the things of this world, and aspire to the honors of men, that they do not learn this one lesson—that the powers of heaven cannot be controlled nor handled only upon the principles of righteousness." (D&C 121:35-36.)

Many people do not like this principle because often it implies some agonizing admissions about oneself, and it promises hard effort to bring about personal change. There is no way to shortcut these admissions and this effort. It is not a matter of merely acquiring information while remaining one's old self. The person himself must change if he is to be able to receive a witness of the divinity of Christ and his restored Church.

This principle threatened the proud hopes of the Jews at the Savior's time, those who looked for a powerful political Messiah to take the responsibility of changing the world so they would not have to change.

They were looking for the spectacular. Their Messiah was to display great power and glory in overthrowing the Roman taskmasters and again enthroning Israel. Their Messiah did come—born naturally, in a manger, of a virgin. Instead of bringing a revolution among the nations, he taught of a revolution to take place within the breast of man.

We are too often like these early Jews, expecting others to change, looking for a miracle or manifestation outside ourselves, instead of within.

The Savior addressed these Jews directly and taught them this very principle.

"Now about the midst of the feast Jesus went up into the temple, and taught.

"And the Jews marvelled, saying, How knoweth this man letters, having never learned?

"Jesus answered them, and said, my doctrine is not mine, but his that sent me.

"If any man will do his will, he shall know of the doctrine, whether it be of God, or whether I speak of myself." (John 7:14-17.)

But this was too hard a doctrine for the learned Jews, for it demanded that they themselves change. They thought eternal life was in the scriptures, which they could study with their minds and then use to justify themselves and judge others. But they would not come to Christ, of whom the scriptures testified, and have life.

"Search the scriptures; for in them ye think ye have eternal life: and they are they which testify of me.

"And ye will not come to me, that ye might have life." (John 5:39-40.)

With all their pride and double-mindedness, the cost of humility and repentance and obedience to Christ was simply too great.

Divine knowledge is a function of humility and obedience to the laws of God. The laws of God are simply the natural, divine laws of eternal growth, obedience to which releases the divinity within and perhaps unlocks the contents of a veiled memory of covenants, convictions, and divine knowledge known before we came into this second estate.

There is no shortcut to this divine knowledge. The something-for-nothing philosophy—learning without obedience, intellectualizing without repentance, thinking without praying, accepting science without Christ—will fail utterly in bringing saving knowledge.

Peter beautifully outlines this process of acquiring divine knowledge, or a knowledge of God and his Son Jesus Christ (2 Peter 1:3-8), whom to know is eternal life (John 17:3). In becoming a "partaker of the divine nature," Peter outlines, first, the need for self-denial and self-mastery—"having escaped the corruption that is in the world through lust," and second, a diligent effort to develop the divine attributes of God, starting with faith and ending with charity. Net result:

"For if these things be in you, and abound, they *make* you that ye shall neither be barren nor unfruitful in the knowledge of our Lord Jesus Christ." (See 2 Peter 1:3-8. Italics added.)

Both levels of obedience are necessary, the second building on the first. Obeying lower laws builds internal discipline and strength of character and enables the individual to resist the higher temptations and to obey the higher laws of humility, love, and selfless service. To attempt to develop a divine character without leaving, through strict self-control, the worldly fountains is the height of self-deception. (See James 1:22-27.)

When a person can honestly say to himself, "I am my own master," so that his spirit masters his flesh, he is then fully in the position where he can say to the Lord, "Now I am thy servant." A servant looks to his master for direction, guidance, and correction.

So also a servant of the Lord looks to his Master. Therefore, he needs living contact with the spirit of the Lord. Generally, the medium of this contact is one's own conscience.

How does a person counsel with his conscience? Right now you may honestly ask yourself, "What should I do to get closer to the Savior?" Now listen. Meditate. Examine yourself. And again, listen. You will hear a voice speak to you: the still, small voice of conscience. You won't hear it in your ear. You will feel it within yourself—deep within yourself—in your heart and mind. It will tell you exactly what you must do to draw closer to the Lord. You will become aware of acts that call for repentance, someone to whom you should be kinder, someone whose forgiveness you must ask, some habit you must overcome, some virtue you must develop. What you hear or feel in your conscience is your personal formula for gaining a vital, living testimony of Jesus Christ.

The Lord may try to get through to us, while we harden our hearts against him, as Nephi indicated Laman and Lemuel had done: "Ye have heard his voice from time to time . . . but ye were past feeling, that ye could not feel his words." (1 Nephi 17:45.)

We then go through the motions of religious worship and service. Our prayers become one-way, mechanical, and ritualistic, offered out of duty, not desire. "They draw near to me with their lips but their hearts are far from me." Little wonder many of us lose faith in prayer: we have no response, no two-way communication with the Lord. We do not listen.

We should try "listening" in our prayers. When we ask for a particular blessing, let us quietly listen with our hearts to understand the law on which that blessing is predicated. (See D&C 130:20-21.) When we hear the answer in our hearts, let us carefully consider it and honestly examine ourselves to see if we are willing to obey that law. If so, let us answer back and commit or promise to the Lord that we will obey. If not, let us not ask for the blessing. If we are not willing to sincerely commit ourselves to qualify for a living testimony of Christ, we cannot expect to receive one.

"Be not deceived; God is not mocked: for whatsoever a man soweth, that shall he also reap." (Galatians 6:7.)

Few things will inspire self-honesty and humility more than a genuine, listening, two-way prayer. It brings us into living contact with the light and Spirit of Christ. In this attitude of perfect honesty, humility, reaching out, and dedication, we can literally have the Holy Ghost as our guide and companion; and he will bestow upon us a witness of the divinity of Jesus Christ.

However intelligent and knowledgeable we may be, unless we have a real and personal experience with the Spirit of God, we will know no more about Christ than the man blind from his birth knows about light and sight, however glib he may be in describing the anatomy of the eye or the properties of light.

This personal testimony is thus a living thing. It is neither borrowed from another nor from the remembrance of past spirituality.

It is rather a well of "living water" (John 4:10), arising from current and real experiences obtained through earnest prayer, study, repentance, convenant-making, obedience, and service—and all achieved through the empowering principle that it be done "with real intent."

"And when ye shall receive these things, I would exhort you that ye would ask God, the Eternal Father, in the name of Christ, if these things are not true; and if ye shall ask with a sincere heart, with real intent, having faith in Christ, he will manifest the truth of it unto you, by the power of the Holy Ghost.

"And by the power of the Holy Ghost ye may know the truth of all things." (Moroni 10:4-5.)

With the deepest conviction in my heart, I encourage a daily, earnest, prayerful study of the scriptures—which contain the feeling and thinking of the Lord—with the express purpose of finding him, to gain inspiration and enlightenment, to be humbled by the revelation of our own weaknesses, to be motivated to serve better, to sacrifice and obey, and to have the security, approval, and peace that come from within, rather than from without. ". . .

He that cometh to me shall never hunger." (John 6:35.)

The right to the companionship and blessings of the Holy Ghost has been given to all Latter-day Saints. To receive this divine gift, we must seek and pray and work and live for it. By doing so we will experience for ourselves, on a daily basis, direction, inspiration, comfort, strengthening, and testimony. Knowing how God works, we will come to know, to trust, and to testify of that still, small voice. The Savior said:

> "Behold, I stand at the door, and knock: if any man hear my voice, and open the door, I will come in to him, and will sup with him, and he with me." (Revelation 3:20.)

He did not say, "I stood"—he said, "I stand."

II

COMMITMENT:
Private Victory Precedes Public Victory

6

The Daily
Private Victory

Even his disciples fell asleep. The Lord went apart and knelt down in prayer. From the account given in the scriptures, both ancient and modern, the Lord indicates to us that his greatest trial and test began in the Garden of Gethsemane. In describing it, he used these words:

"Which suffering caused myself, even God, the greatest of all, to tremble because of pain, and to bleed at every pore, and to suffer both body and spirit—and would that I might not drink the bitter cup, and shrink—

"Nevertheless, glory be to the Father, and I partook and finished my preparations unto the children of men." (D&C 19:18-19.)

Gethsemane was the place that he renewed and deepened his internal commitment or covenant with his Father to go forth on the mission of his life, the very purpose for which he was sent to this world. And that mission was to suffer in some way incomprehensible to us as to take upon himself the full effects of our transgressions and our sins, which caused himself, "even God, the greatest of all, to tremble because of pain and to bleed at every pore, and to suffer both body and spirit." He committed himself in Gethsemane to give his life up on Calvary. No man took his life from him, remember. The Jews did not take the Savior's life. He even said, "No man taketh it from me, but I lay it down myself. . . ." (John 10:18.)

On Calvary he came to a point, unlike any other human being, even martyrs, where he had the power to call legions of heaven to save himself, but he willingly sacrificed his life and said, "Father, into thy hands I commend my spirit." (Luke 23:46.)

His Calvary was successful partly because his Gethsemane was successful. He won a private battle, which gave him additional power to win a public battle. He even returned to his private battle at Gethsemane two more times and fought it through until he had so mastered, I am sure, the fundamental issue of his life that he even cried out, "Oh, Father, if it be thy will, let this cup pass from me; but not as I will but as thou wilt." (See Matthew 26:42.) In other words, he fought the central issue that most masters people's lives; *my* will or *thy* will. He decided, he committed, he pledged, he promised, he covenanted with God, "Thy will be done." "All" he needed to do was to carry out this private decision in public.

Since Christ is "the way" for us, let us symbolically think of Gethsemane and Calvary as private and public battles respectively. All of us have our private battles— that is, the opportunities to live out our public battles in our minds and in our hearts *before* we ever come to them in fact. We can do this as the scriptures counsel—privately, in private prayer and communion. In this sense we can actually live out the trials and temptations and challenges of our day *before* they come. We can, in the unseen presence of God, deal with all of our unrighteous aspirations, our selfishness, perverse inclinations, touchiness, impatience, anger, impurities, procrastinating tendencies, or just our sheer irresponsibility and lack of discipline. We can fight these things through in the presence of God our Father, who seeth all things.

If we stay in that presence, seeking his Spirit, and make a deep covenant with him, we will have won the battle *before* it comes upon us in fact. Then when "the public battles" come—our public trials, the temptations, the pressures and stresses, the storms that descend upon our lives—

we will have the internal strength from the life and light of this world—the Savior of this world, the Redeemer of all men, to resist and to overcome. Our spiritual roots will have grown out of him naturally.

Winning such a private battle before going into the public battles is a form of spiritual creation. The scriptures tell us that the Lord created the world spiritually before it was created temporally or physically.

". . . And thus were their decisions at the time that they counseled among themselves to form the heavens and the earth.

"And the Gods came down and formed these the generations of the heavens and of the earth, when they were formed in the day that the Gods formed the earth and the heavens.

"According to all that which they had said concerning every plant of the field before it was in the earth, and every herb of the field before it grew. . . ." (Abraham 5:3-5.)

In a sense we all do this in many activities in our lives. For instance, in building a house, before we turn a shovel of earth we plan almost to the last detail the entire house in our mind, and this is reduced to a blueprint.

Therefore, I raise the question: Why should we not also create each day or each week or each year in our minds before we live them in fact? This is more than planning, for circumstances will change and plans will need to be altered accordingly. It also involves making commitments, private commitments, regarding those principles we will live our lives by, regardless of the circumstances. This process of thrashing the issues about in our minds, confronting directly mixed feelings and double motives and grappling with the forces within, is called the private battle. "The greatest battle of life," President McKay taught, "is fought out within the silent chambers of the soul."

Once we have resolved the inner conflict and have made up our minds, we have achieved a kind of spiritual creation or the private victory.

In speaking of this inner battle, President McKay went on to say, "There is a battle on with you, and with me, every day. The world's hope and destiny are centered in the Man of Galilee, our Lord and Savior, Jesus Christ. In your moment when you are fighting out the battle of the day, will you look introspectively and see whether you really believe that. . . ." (General priesthood session, October 2, 1964.)

I have learned these two basic lessons from my own experience and observation with this. We do not have a successful public victory—that is, an accomplished worthy task—unless we have a successful private victory. The opposite is also true. We seldom have deep, honest communication with God unless we also have a divine service to perform, where we feel the need to have God's Spirit to assist us, such as in the raising of our children and teaching them to anchor their lives to eternal values. We need to have this vital work to perform—before we will find ourself honestly communicating from our heart and pleading with a deep sincerity and hunger within ourself for the Spirit of God. Otherwise we can just go down a little checklist in a mechanical, almost ritualistic sort of way. If we have no deep commitment to a divine service, sharing the gospel, teaching our children, or magnifying a calling, we feel little need for a private victory.

The Savior says, "Seek ye first the kingdom of God, and *his* righteousness" (Matthew 6:33; italics added), not the righteousness of this world. The righteousness of this world only responds to that which is its own kind. When people treat you kindly, you are kind in return. But the power to respond with good in the face of evil comes from the righteousness of God, and Christ is his Son and the Way, and he led the way perfectly.

I would like, for an illustration, to paraphrase a few lines from the movie *A Man for All Seasons.* I think it is an excellent movie. I saw in it two great personalities who demonstrate this principle of private victories preceding public victories. Those of you who have seen the movie remember that Sir Thomas More was the man who opposed King Henry VIII in his desire to divorce his wife and marry Anne Boleyn. For various reasons it violated his conscience, and he would not take a particular oath of succession to the king. Because he was a man of such honesty and integrity, his influence, even in silence, assisted in disrupting things in the British Empire. As Cromwell, the king's minister, put it, his "silence thundered all up and down Europe," because people knew he was honest, and he would not subscribe to an oath contrary to his conscience.

He went through a process of gradually losing everything. He lost his station, his position, his wealth. He lost his physical comforts, for he was imprisoned in the Tower of London. Cromwell eventually took away his reading materials. His captors used every opportunity to tempt him and to induce him to "give in" and to sign the oath to the king. He wouldn't do it. He maintained silence.

While he was imprisoned in the Tower of London, their final strategy was to use his family to persuade him to give in. They brought to him his wife and daughter. His wife pleaded, "Oh, you've got to give in. I am afraid if they take your life, I'll hate you for it."

He needed the sustaining influence of his wife. Without it he wasn't sure he had the power and the courage to go forward. He pleaded with her, "You can't do this. You must understand. I dread to think what they might do to me but I dread even more what might happen inside to me if I do it."

And when she knew he meant it and that he was deeply committed to the truth within him, she embraced him and said, "You are the greatest man I have ever known or ever will know."

His daughter then came to him and pleaded, "Oh, Father, do you know what it is like at home without you? We can't even afford candles there. It is a miserable life. You've taught me all my life that God regards the heart, not the words of the lips. Father, take this oath with your lips, but think otherwise in your heart."

He answered her, "Daughter, what is an oath but words you speak to God!" And, cupping his hands, he continued, "My oath is my life. I hold it in my hands like water. If I ever open my hands, I can never expect to find my life again."

He then told his family to go out of the country because he knew he would never see them again. Eventually he was condemned to die, and right there at the guillotine he looked right at the anxious, hesitating executioner and said, "Do not begrudge your office. You only send me to God."

The Archbishop of Canterbury spoke up, "Oh, are you so sure of that, Sir Thomas?"

Sir Thomas answered, "God would not refuse one so blind."

In other words, his total commitment and faith resided in the unseen God. That was the oath he had made in the various private battles of his life.

The other fascinating character in the movie was Richard Rich. He gained many "kingdoms" and eventually also became chancellor of England. But at what a price! He sold his soul. He would lie and cheat, violate confidences and make and break oaths for the right bribe.

Once Cromwell, the king's minister, in an attempt to get certain evidence against More, put a bribe before Richard Rich that at first he resisted and then later gave in to. "That wasn't so bad was it," Cromwell observed.

Rich nodded affirmatively. He sensed his unworthiness and grew depressed, and Cromwell, observing this, stated: "It is a sad omen to see a person receive such a large favor and become depressed."

Rich answered, "Oh, I'm not depressed. It is just that I feel like I have lost my innocence."

Then Cromwell observed, "Oh, you just noticed? You lost it a long time ago."

Here are the two characters: Sir Thomas More, who became a "man for all seasons,"—in season or out of season, he was true to the source of his life, to God; and Richard Rich, who, like the chameleon which changes colors to blend into its environment, was buffeted constantly in his personal life. He would change with the seasons or with the force of another's personality or the pressure of the circumstance, and he was untrue to God, but true to *his* god, which was this fickle, changing, uncertain world, the source of his buffetings. That became the nature of his character.

More won and Rich lost their public battles in private. One was a totally buffeted life, and the other a life anchored and true and powerful, and very, very influential.

Someone inquired of a Hindu who had a great serenity and peace about him, no matter what pressures were put upon him, "How do you maintain that serenity and peace?" His answer: "I *never leave* my place of meditation." Every morning he meditated for thirty minutes. Then in his mind and heart he never left it—he maintained the spirit of that place all during his public life and pressures.

Joseph Smith had his Sacred Grove experience, and perhaps the greatest revelation or theophany ever given to man came there. The Father and the Son appeared. Yet even he, the Prophet of this dispensation, was chastened by the Lord for yielding at various times to the pressures, to "the persuasions of men." Once, after chastening him, the Lord said, "Behold, thou art Joseph, and thou wast chosen to do the work of the Lord. . . ." (D&C 3:9.) In a sense he is being told, "Never leave your Sacred Grove."

The Three Witnesses of the Book of Mormon—Martin Harris, Oliver Cowdery, and David Whitmer—had their marvelous, divine experience, but then they left it; they yielded to the persuasions of men under the pressures of this world, and they were buffeted. In the first several sections of the Doctrine and Covenants the Lord counsels these and other brethren again and again, essentially, to remember who they are, remember their calling, remember their divine experience.

I suggest that every day of our lives you and I can go to our place of prayerful study and meditation where we can "live out" the events that will transpire that day, master those issues that seem to dominate life in terms of true principles and God's way, and rededicate and commit ourselves to the source of light to which God has called us—to Jesus Christ, who is the father of our second birth and who is the author of the covenants we made in the waters of baptism, of the covenants we renew at the sacrament table.

God has ordained certain places and times for private victories: the private prayer, the sacrament, the temple, honest moments of meditation, fasting, scripture reading. We can prayerfully use our scriptures almost like our own Urim and Thummim, to translate our life, to help translate the will of God for us today. "Nevertheless thy vows shall be offered up in righteousness on all days and at all times." (D&C 59:11.)

But remember, we will not have deep, meaningful communion with God unless we honestly desire to serve and have some divine service—some great task ahead of us.

Try it, would you? Try it for 30 days. Don't judge it the first week. Judge it after a month. Try it every morning. Get up earlier. Discipline yourself—the very root of disciple means discipline. The root of discipline is disciple.

Whip those procrastinating, undisciplined tendencies, those inclinations toward weakness. Do it in private—and I am telling you you will sweat it out; it is not an easy thing —it is a most difficult thing—but take the time to do it, and watch the gradual serenity and power that will come into your life. More than anything I know it will help you to develop courage and integrity and to become a man or a woman "for all seasons."

Let me share a letter I received from a student whom I challenged, along with others, to prayerfully study the scriptures for 30 minutes a day for 30 days:

"Final examinations, graduation, and moving detained me from personally visiting with you and finalizing my part of our covenant wherein I promised to read in the scriptures for at least one-half an hour each day for a month with the express purpose of coming to know the Author through the experience. At the end of the thirty-day period I was to bear testimony to you of the effect of this daily spiritual nourishment on my life, and it is for this purpose that I have undertaken to write this letter.

"At the outset I must acknowledge that in addition to gaining from the reading itself, I also learned much about myself—about my character strengths and weaknesses in attempting to fulfill a personal commitment such as this. And I must confess to having missed four days during the month. The revealing thing to me was that these four days were in a row, that they were early in the month, and that having missed just one day, three others rather easily followed. To begin again on a fifth day was sheer effort, but once on the track again I was cautious to avoid another harmless-looking "just one day" that might lead to another serious void. Furthermore, I became more aware of my own rationalizations, my own double-mindedness, and those distractions and temptations to which I am vulnerable as I attempt to pursue a disciplined program of daily spiritual nourishment. Then in clarion terms came the most shocking realization of all—that the Prince of the earth was dismayed by my study and was literally seeking to avert my efforts. To not feed my soul daily was to daily pay homage to him and he had so long enjoyed that homage from me that he was determined to retain it!

In addition to these unexpected benefits and insights came those blessings which you unequivocably promised to those who would submit to a program of daily study. The content of the morning's reading I found was in my mind throughout the day. It began to become an important factor in my day-to-day relationships with my fellowman. The morning's reading gave me the Master's pattern for living, and his example began to influence and temper my daily decisions and actions. As I began to know the Son, I began to love him and better know his Father. And my prayers to the Father increased in scope and meaningfulness. And as this transformation continued I began to better understand the essence of your message to us that night in the fieldhouse. . . ."

This attitude, in my opinion, is the beginning of the greatest and most needed change that can take place in the world today, within our own heart and mind. It is then that we become a light to people, and not their judge.

I bear testimony that Christ lives. He is the Son of God. He is the Savior of the world, and there is a source of life within him that we can tap if we will take the time every morning to sink our spiritual roots deep, to have this successful private experience. Then we will have the power to be anchored, in time of temptation and stress, to eternal truths and eternal values in a world of change and turmoil.

7

Self-Fulfillment Through Self-Expression

The best a man can be, he must be. Achievement of the highest internal potential is self-fulfillment. As a child of God, spiritually begotten, man possesses his Father's nature, with all its potential. Man is, therefore, a God in embryo. The profound joy of which the scriptures speak (". . . and men are, that they might have joy" [2 Nephi 2:25]) is one of self-fulfillment and transcends all wordly joys or pleasures or happinesses, which offer only superficial and temporary satisfaction or comfort to man.

The world's culture in which we are enmeshed primarily embraces material and social goals and values, which are often inconsistent with the self-fulfilling goals and values. This is the real problem, in my judgment. The highest nature of man and the nature of the world's culture antagonize one another. To gain the one is to lose the other. A choice must be made, and each alternative requires sacrifices. Man's real enemy, then, is conformity—conformity to social pressures and group norms that do not contribute to self-fulfillment. Even though one might win acceptance and a sense of belonging through conformity, in another sense this is the highest cowardice. It is a betrayal of one's best nature. For in becoming all things to all people, one eventually becomes nothing to everybody—particularly to oneself. "Of all sad words of tongue or pen, the saddest are these: 'It might have been.' "

In this view, religion is not an external set of rules and regulations and laws, but rather principles and laws natural to, and internalized in, man's highest nature (divine self). Conformity to these *divine* laws requires the highest courage and amounts to being true to oneself. In one sense, the revelations of the Lord and the inspired admonitions of our prophets and leaders make *explicit* the laws that are *implicit* in our nature, adherence to which guarantees the highest self-fulfilled growth. In such growth we may achieve a condition of development that allows us to feel comfortable and natural in the celestial and exalted presence of God our Father. One wars with himself if he resists true religion. This is why one cannot sin with *all* his heart and soul. It will *split him apart,* for it is a conflict with his own divine nature. But, for the same reason, one *can* serve truth and live righteously with *all* his heart and soul.

A physically healthy person is active. If inactive over a long period of time, the body atrophies and becomes easy prey to accident and disease. Without adequate food or rest, serious deficiencies may develop. A different kind of sickness, somewhat intangible but nevertheless a real sickness, overtakes one who is intellectually, emotionally, or spiritually inactive or starving. One's mental faculties are to be cultivated and used in creative and productive effort, or they will also atrophy. One who does not move outside himself into the lives of others with love, empathy, and kindness eventually becomes increasingly isolated, lonely, unlovable, and emotionally sick. Spiritual health embodies *both* intellectual and emotional health. One must actively think and feel in order to effectively serve others and to worship God.

Let us call these mental, emotional, and spiritual activities "self-expression." By this is meant acting as an agent for oneself rather than being acted upon; participating instead of merely looking on; becoming actively involved, as opposed to passively listening; creating rather than responding like a robot or a puppet to pressures, expectations, or stimuli from others.

Much of the world's work is essentially meaningless—mechanical, repetitious, physical, boring—involving no real mental exertion or emotional commitment, only robot responses. There is a great deal of research evidence to indicate that a mature and healthy personality seeks for purpose and meaning in his work and desires active involvement and participation as a total person. In other words, he seeks self-expression. Unable to find it in the kind of meaningless labor mentioned above, he often adapts by becoming apathetic, indifferent, and alienated. Work is seen by him as drudgery—as a mere means to an end that is to be avoided as far as possible.

We discover that this alienated individual, rather than striving for personal creativity and development in the other dimensions of his life, carries over his complacent and apathetic attitude and spirit into his personal leisure, family, and religious life. His total life slumps into mediocrity and boredom. He turns from himself, from his own unique and singular talents and capabilities. He is a clock-watcher all day; but once off work, he finds only boredom in many of his disorganized, purposeless, shallow activities. He tries one thing after another, but nothing seems to satisfy him. His rebellion against authority-enforced work discipline also evidences itself against almost every other form of organization and discipline, including that which might have been imposed by himself.

This unfulfilled person often prefers to sit back and watch others live. He spends endless hours in undiscriminating television viewing. Here the "one-eyed monster" can feed and brainwash him, think and feel for him, entertain and somehow hypnotize him away from what is happening to his life. He can watch others live in fancied circumstances, identify himself with the heroes, and sense all kinds of removed and vicarious satisfactions. Or he may resort to other compensating activities or escape mechanisms, such as alcohol, illicit sex, cheap movies and literature, or some other activity carried to excess. When he is asleep, he is half awake, and when awake, he is half asleep. He never is fully involved with life. Playing one imaginary role after another, he soon loses knowledge of his own role and experiences himself only as others want him to be. Meaningless chatter, gossip, and sarcastic humor replace genuinely rich interpersonal communication. But ungenuine communication is boring and forced, and therefore unpleasant and difficult. However, when alone, he is also bored. What a pathetic and too common plight!

This person's religious life is in itself mechanical and superficial—much of the time he is doing the right things for the wrong reasons. Familiarity with (rather than feeling toward) Church services provides him with relatively shallow satisfactions. If called upon to pray, he becomes fearful and more concerned with what others think of him and his prayer than with a real communication with God. Religious observances, for him, become a substitute for service rather than an inspiration to serve. To him, religion may be a weapon he can use to judge and condemn others, in order to let himself feel superior and exclusive.

This hypothetical example may or may not be extreme, but the fundamental idea is that an apathetic attitude tends to spread itself throughout all of one's life and associations, producing a kind of spiritual disease characterized by restlessness, loss of zest, self-dislike, general depression, sin, decay of the intellectual and spiritual life, etc. The individual in such a situation "regresses to a state of childish dependency and irresponsibility. With this regression comes an absence of initiative and that self-discipline which makes for effective personal relationships."

Once we are aware of the forces shaping us and of our own internal powers, we can begin to take charge of ourselves and to shape our own circumstances.

"Verily I say, men should be anxiously engaged in a good cause, and do many things of their own free will, and bring to pass much righteousness; "For the power is in them, wherein they are agents unto themselves." (Doctrine and Covenants 58:27-28.)

Deep desire and persistent work are demanded of us. We should search for work that provides a challenge to our unique abilities and interests, that presents an opportunity for self-expression, and that serves a purpose with which we can honestly identify ourselves. Work would then become an end in itself—creatively satisfying, recreative.

And even though every job has its monotonous, challengeless aspects, all of us have abundant opportunity somewhere, sometime in our lives to expand our interests, deepen our knowledge and understanding of those interests, and develop our skills and our abilities to participate actively in and to promote those interests—in short, to become "involved in life."

Use of Our Common Resource: Time

Time is an asset we all have in common and in an equal amount. Yet the wide variety in the use or abuse of this priceless resource is a startling fact of our day.

One person escapes from life and freedom and personal responsibility by conformity and by tranquilizing activities. But another person refuses these popular life-smothering sedatives and plumbs the deeper reaches of his own makeup to find phenomenal resources of intelligence, enthusiasm, ingenuity, creativity, and interests. He then engages in exposing himself and his talents, "in trying out," and in an industrious search for meaning, purpose, stability, and integrity in every aspect of his life. He is continually educating himself. His mind is active, informed, and curious; his body, responsive and well-disciplined; his emotion, loving and life-affirming; his behavior, genuine, spontaneous, and kind; his spirit and motive, noble and righteous.

In short, he is living the law of his own divine nature, the law of his spiritual birthright, the law he accepted and internalized in the premortal life, the law that the Lord is continually striving to write again into his heart and into his "inner parts." He is becoming the best he can because he must.

8

Seven Sources of Personal Security

Consider two ways of judging or valuing another:

1. *Extrinsic valuing*—comparing a person with another or against an external standard. For instance, Mark is not as good a student as his sister Alice. Or, Mark performs at the 85% level and therefore deserves a B in his studies. In both instances, the value is not in Mark—it lies *outside* him, in the comparison and in the standard.

2. *Intrinsic valuing.* Here we say that Mark has value inherent *within* him; as a person he has worth, apart from his performance, good or bad. If we do any comparing, we compare him only against himself or against his potential.

Both ways of judging or valuing have merit. We often use both simultaneously. But I suggest the *extrinsic* way is the most used and emphasized, to the detriment of the person.

Consider my reasoning.

From the time of birth a person belongs to one institution of society after another. Each one values or judges its members. These judgments accumulate and, taken together, tell or label or define just who the person is. This social definition may gradually become his self-concept, and a person's self-concept strongly influences his behavior. It becomes self-fulfilling. If he sees himself as inferior or irresponsible, and if he is continuously defined and treated that way, he will probably behave that way—that is, unless he places a different judgment or value on himself.

Now consider the institutions we join since birth.

The Family

The tendency to compare one child against another is a common practice used by parents. Discipline is often given out on the mood of the moment rather than on well-considered and communicated principles and rules. Individual differences are frequently ignored. Love, acceptance, warmth are often given conditionally, that is, if the behavior meets the expectation or standard. Judgment and rejection of the person often follow non-conformance.

Is there any wonder so many children doubt themselves and feel inferior and inadequate? They feel no value in them, only in what they do! And *that* is subject to the opinions and judgments of others, and opinions are fickle, being influenced by many different forces and standards. No wonder many feel anxious and fearful, and live to pretend, to impress. Their lives are buffeted by outside changing forces rather than being anchored by the changeless intrinsic value within. Development of a good self-concept is a vital function of the family. Recently, as reported in the February, 1968, issue of *Scientific American,* a group of psychologists, working with the support of the National Institute of Mental Health, conducted a series of studies in self esteem. The subjects were a representative sample of normal boys from middle-class, urban families and who were followed from pre-adolescence to early adulthood (an eight-year period).

They found that "the youngsters with a high degree of self-esteem are active, expressive individuals who tend to be successful both academically and socially. They are eager to express their opinions, do not sidestep disagreement, are not particularly sensitive to criticism, are highly interested in public affairs, and showed little destructiveness in early childhood."

Further, "they appear to trust their own perceptions and reactions and have confidence that their efforts will meet with success. They are optimistic and not self-conscious or pre-occupied with personal difficulties."

Some surprising factors brought out in these studies showed that there was *no* consistent relation between self-esteem and physical attractiveness or family social position or income level.

These subjects tended to gauge their individual worth primarily by their achievements and treatment in their own interpersonal environment and day-to-day personal relationships, rather than by general and abstract norms of success.

As they looked into the backgrounds of the boys who possessed high self-esteem, they gave three findings:

1. *Close relationships existed between these boys and their parents,* manifested by interest in the boys' welfare, concern about companions, availability for discussion of problems and participation in joint activities. The parents gave many other signs that they regarded their child as a significant person who was inherently worthy of their deep interest. Basking in this appraisal, the boy came to regard himself in a favorable similar light.

2. *Parents were less permissive.* They demanded high standards of behavior and were strict and consistent in enforcement of the rules, yet their discipline was not harsh. The boys with low self-esteem took the absence of rules and limits for their behavior as a sign of lack of parental interest.

3. *The family life had a democratic spirit.* The parents established the principles and defined the powers, privileges, and responsibilities of the members, but they respected the children's views, were open to persuasion, and gave the children a voice in the making of family plans.

The School

Almost from kindergarten, students are compared against each other. If graded on a curve, one gets a B because another got a D, and vice-versa. Yet the B student may be a "goof-off," a cramming artist with a lot of ability to find and take shortcuts, whereas the D student may be really producing in terms of perhaps fewer talents.

Again, no individual differences or potentials are considered when grading on a standard. Generally speaking, grades in school are given on an extrinsic basis, and perhaps this may be the best and most efficient way in terms of many practical realities in our present academic system.

But then in this system, what is a grade? A grade becomes more than an indicator of performance. It carries social value. The family and society reward and punish based on these grades. Opportunities are given or denied. Most importantly, when love and acceptance are offered or withdrawn on the basis of grades, the academic system itself contributes to'this socially rooted self-concept. The person who is told over and over again by various sources, "You are a D person. You are a poor student. You are irresponsible. You are stupid," tends to believe these things and thereby justifies himself in his "irresponsible, dumb, stupid" behavior. He lives up to this limited concept of himself, which acts like a straitjacket on his future efforts. His latent potential, which may be tremendous, remains latent. This is the plight of the underachieving student— good intellectual equipment with limited emotional circuitry (self-concept).

Social and Economic Systems

Generally, in social and economic institutions, worth is given on the basis of extrinsic value. Often a person's net work is equated with his personal worth. One may be grumpy and disagreeable with the elevator man or simply ignore him because he seems unimportant; but when the president of the corporation hops aboard, one's disposition and gentlemanly manner suddenly change. Material and social values become terribly important because they represent or symbolize or confer individual value. Or so many feel.

When we *borrow our strength* from the label on our shirt, sweater, shoes, or dress; from our association with a club, an "in" group; from our position of influence, power, and prestige; from our car, beautiful house, or other status symbols and trappings; or from our good looks, stylish clothing, fashionable appearance, clever tongue, or degrees and credentials, we do so in order to compensate from being impoverished and hollow inside. But by doing so, we reinforce our dependency on these symbols, on living by appearances, on extrinsic values, and we build weakness within.

The Church

Our theology and doctrine place great value on the individual—all individuals. We are taught to love the sinner while abhoring the sin. The Lord teaches us to leave the 99 and go after the one, that "the worth of souls is great in the sight of God." We are taught what we might call a "divine definition" of oneself.

In the Book of Moses in the Pearl of Great Price, God explained his relationship to Moses and told him that he was his son and was in the similitude of his Only Begotten, Jesus Christ. Later, when Satan came, in all his power—raging and demanding to be worshiped—Moses, with a correct understanding of who he was (a child of God) was able to rebuke Satan and cast him out through the power of Jesus Christ.

The universal appeal of the Primary song "I Am a Child of God" is basically an intrinsic appeal.

However, even some of us in the Church may use the Church in an extrinsic way to judge and reject. The very religion of love can be twisted and distorted by the unloving to justify their own seeming righteousness, to build a refuge around themselves, and to judge and reject all others.

Let me state here that I am *not* against extrinsic values. They serve useful purposes. For instance, I am convinced that the free enterprise system, with its free market, private property, and limited government concomitants, is the most effective and efficient economic system ever developed. Competition in any form of endeavor usually brings the best to the surface.

But what I am primarily against is the formation of a person's self-concept on the basis of these extrinsic values. I believe it should come primarily from an intrinsic sense of worth, a divine (as opposed to social) definition of oneself. The primary responsibility, in this regard, lies with the family, forged mainly out of the way the parents treat and regard each other and their children, as reinforced by the studies on self-esteem.

Seven Sources of Intrinsic Security

Parents can do a great deal to build in themselves and in their children a deep sense of internal worth, of internal security; the following suggestions may help in this regard.

1. *A Spiritually Rich Private Life.* Immersion in the gospel teachings, in the scriptures, and in daily prayer provides magnificent opportunity for the Lord to bestow on us a *divine sense of who we really are* and a *testimony of his gospel.* Jesus taught that those who keep the Father's commandments will receive the Father's love, and will abide in his love. (See Jacob 3:1-2; Mosiah 4:12; John 14:21; John 15:10.) I believe this to be the perfect source of a divine definition of oneself. The main source of distorting this eternal sense is personal transgression, for even though the Father continues to love us unconditionally, we may not feel that love. He may give the gift but we do not receive it. As the scripture says, "For what doth it profit a man if a gift is bestowed upon him, and he receives not the gift? Behold, he rejoices not in that which is given unto him, neither rejoices in him who is the giver of the gift." (D&C 88:33.)

2. *The Family.* The family is God's ordained unit or group to provide each of its members a deep sense of worth, of personal security. Parents need to spend time communicating with each other, which itself will feed the emotional roots of security, respect, acceptance, and love.

In addition to morning and night family prayer, and the weekly family home evening, parents should spend time with each child on an individual basis. This should be done frequently. Just before retiring at night may prove to be a good time—to sit, or lie down, next to a child and discuss that day and the child's feelings, concerns, and fears. I know of one mother who enjoys visiting with each child at night and asks them to tell her their happiest experience that day, along with anything else they wish to talk about. To merely be with a person and spend time with him conveys intrinsic value. Your child knows from watching you all day how much you value time. To listen, to attempt to understand, to be patient and kind and considerate take time. Thus, you communicate that you value him intrinsically.

To reprove with sharpness and then show forth an increase of love afterward communicates intrinsic love.

"Reproving betimes with sharpness, when moved upon by the Holy Ghost; and then showing forth afterwards an increase of love toward him whom thou hast reproved, lest he esteem thee to be his enemy;

"That he may know that thy faithfulness is stronger than the cords of death." (D&C 121:43-44.)

Security emerges largely from a sense of fairness and justice: limits clearly set, rules established, and discipline consistently applied, based on those rules and limits, not on the mood of the moment.

(The chapter suggesting eight principles of parenthood and character development and the one following it on discipline communicate my ideas on how a family and a home become vital sources of personal security, of intrinsic worth.)

3. *Nature.* Occasionally immerse yourself and the children in nature. Nature is very accepting and can bequeath its quiet strength to one who takes the time to feel and to appreciate. Nature teaches powerful lessons. There's no shortcut on a farm. Nature keeps careful books. Nature teaches honesty, which is called the foundation of all virtues. It's good for children to have chores in nature or in any area where natural laws plainly govern.

Animals are part of nature. Your good dog will jump up and love you even if you ιfailed today—he always accepts. A cat will sit quietly while a child strokes it and softly talks to it. Children gain some comfort, acceptance, and security from domesticated animals.

To absorb yourself in the magnificent beauties of a canyon, to spend a day on the beach or in the mountains or in any lovely setting, and to take time to meditate and drink it all in helps build an intrinsic sense of worth. There are few of us who cannot testify of this principle. Moses went into the mountains to pray, the boy Joseph Smith to the Sacred Grove, and the Savior frequently retired into nature to commune.

4. *Education.* I've been fairly closely associated with adult education programs for a number of years, and I'm impressed with their impact. Everything is changing so rapidly in the world; much of what we learned ten, even five, years ago is obsolete today. Science and technology have made incredible advances in most every field of endeavor. Too many simply aren't trying to keep up, yet vainly build their security on now-obsolete skills or knowledge.

It takes real effort to take a night class or a correspondence course or to go to an education week program or to do systematic reading. And travel is expensive. It's easier to watch television and just pick up a thing here or there. The human tendency is then to make excuses, to explain and justify. Yet the easy way in the short term is the hardest in the long.

I believe in a *system* of some kind for self-education. It doesn't have to be formal classes or courses. It may be an informal discussion group or a well-conceived reading program. But without some system or external discipline, most adults tend to give up after a good start on something and fall back to old ways.

Is the gaining of knowledge the main purpose of continued education? I don't believe so. The knowledge explosion is so vast and so rapid, no one, giving all his time, could keep up. If it's not knowledge, what then is it? To keep intellectually alive, to renew ourselves, to learn how to learn, how to adapt, how to change, what not to change.

We must develop a feeling and a competence *within* that we can "make a go of it" in any situation, regardless of what happens. One main source of this confidence and competence is continuing education.

Now, what about our children and the school? How can I, as a parent, help it to be a source of intrinsic security? As parents, we must *encourage our children in their school work to be very conscientious and systematic in their preparation, and then put value on their efforts.* We should reward and recognize real learning and not merely the grade. A student knows inside himself, to a considerable extent, how well he is doing. He may not know how well his teachers think he is doing, in terms of certain specified criteria, but on the more important matters—that is, his own effort, his daily preparation and honesty, his creative efforts, his concentration, his practical learnings, his development of understanding, and the joy and satisfaction of what he is learning—he knows perhaps better than anyone else. Put value on this. In the long run these things influence performance in life far more than grades will. This is not to say that grades do not have value, for they do, and generally speaking those who follow these suggestions will get the highest grades.

5. *The Church. Church activity and service are supremely important.*

Parents should practice and teach their children to do more than the minimum expected. They should exemplify the attitude of "How can I best serve?"—going the second mile—instead of "What's in it for me?" When a person gives *anonymous* service and goes the second mile, and no one knows save God and he alone, he grows in a sense of his own worth and value. And he receives the Father's commendation. (See Matthew 6:4.) This is divine definition, not social definition, of self.

When a person works diligently to help someone who may be disaffected, he is communicating value to that other, and he receives value in return.

Magnifying a priesthood calling, worshiping and praying with real intent (for the right reasons) are primary fundamental sources of an intrinsic sense of worth.

6. *Daily Work. Time must be taken for creative planning and for creative communication with key people.* Many people become bogged down in their work with mechanical details, and a lot of trivia, and they almost become automatons. Few people take the time to think very carefully about their assignments, to analyze the causes of the problems they deal with, to develop long-range plans of action to deal with them. This kind of reflection and planning takes initiative and imagination—in short, thinking, which is hard and an expression of individuality. But the dividends are rich in terms of building a sense of self-worth and self-power.

When we seek in a systematic way to educate ourself, by drawing upon both informal and formal sources, and when we creatively produce in our own work assignment, we discover that our job or economic security lies within ourself and not within our circumstances. There is no future in a job. The only future is inside oneself. We look inside rather than outside. We become producers rather than consumers of other people's production. Therefore, we have the security to go into new situations, to take on new challenges and job assignments. We know that we can come to grips with any circumstance and succeed.

The individual whose security lies outside himself can become almost desperate in an effort to avoid changing situations or circumstances, for this rocks the very ground of his being. Yet, that which he hopes is changeless is constantly changing. The individual who grows on internal intrinsic values is anchored to the changeless within himself and therefore can meet and adapt to any changing circumstance.

We must also plan into our schedule *creative communication with the key people in our lives* (uninterrupted blocks of time). We may give ourselves completely to our church job, to a stake board or priesthood assignment, and yet have shallow relationships with those closest to us—our wife, or husband, a child, a counselor, a fellow worker. The Lord spent the majority of his ministry with a few key people, his apostles. He established a strong, deep, unforgetable relationship with them. He loved them, taught them, served them.

To develop a close and open communication with those key people in your life is a rich and profound source of intrinsic security.

7. *Be True to the Light You Have Been Given.* This last suggestion deals with *integrity.* When we as parents live true to the light we have been given, and encourage our children to do likewise, then all of these suggestions or forces combine together and create within us a sense of peace and unity and wholeness—a sense of internal worth, internal security. Whenever we are untrue, this internal disunity puts us back onto the extrinsic treadmill, and unless we repent we will find ourselves anxious and fearful, often trying to become all things to all people. A life of pretense is a tortuous task. To live a life that is congruent and harmonious with Jesus Christ, our Savior and Redeemer, is the highest source of intrinsic security. ". . . and without compulsory means it shall flow unto thee forever and ever." (D&C 121:46.)

Ultimately, therefore, there is only one real and permanent source of personal security, which is completely interwoven with all these other sources. Our Lord speaks graphically of it at the end of the Sermon on the Mount.

"Therefore whosoever heareth these sayings of mine, and *doeth them,* I will liken him unto a wise man, which built his house upon a rock:

"And the rain descended, and the floods came, and the winds blew, and beat upon that house; and it fell not: for it was founded upon a rock.

"And every one that heareth these sayings of mine and *doeth them not,* shall be likened unto a foolish man, which built his house upon the sand:

"And the rain descended, and the floods came, and the winds blew, and beat upon that house; and it fell: and great was the fall of it." (Matthew 7:24-27. Italics added.)

9

Overcoming the Tremendous
Gravity of Habit

We were all transfixed by the lunar voyage of Apollo 11 and could hardly believe our eyes when we saw men walking on the moon. Superlatives such as "fantastic" and "incredible" are inadequate to describe those eventful days.

Where was the most power and energy expended on that heavenly journey? Going a quarter of a million miles to the moon? Returning to the earth? Orbiting the moon? Lunar and command module separation and redocking? Moon lift-off?

No, not these—not even all these together. Rather, it was on the lift-off from the earth. More energy was spent in the first few minutes of lift-off, in the first few miles of travel, than was used in half a million miles for several days.

The gravity pull of those first few miles was enormous. The earth's atmosphere was compressingly heavy. It took an internal thrust greater than both the pull of gravity and the resistance of atmosphere to finally "break out" into orbit.

Now for a moment let's look at ourselves and at our habits. Our problems don't stem from ignorance nearly so much as they do from disobedience of that which we know to be right.

For instance, how many of us regularly exercise? Few. How many know that regular exercise would be good for me? Nearly all. The problem does not lie in our ignorance but in our habits.

Ever resolved to break the overeating habit, only to disgustingly renew the resolve every other week?

Ever resolved to stop procrastinating? to write those long overdue letters? to get at your genealogy? to get going at those family projects?

What about your resolves to stop nagging your husband? to spend more individual time with each child? to have regular, well-prepared family home evenings? to control your temper? to make peace with that neighbor? to really magnify your Church calling?

Speaking of habits, what about the circular, self-feeding habit of making resolutions—then later breaking them—then remaking them, only to break them again. We begin to wonder if it's worth making any more.

Overcoming the Gravity of Habit

How can we break bad habits and form healthy new ones? The Savior gives us insight into the process in the following magnificent parable.

> "For which of you, intending to build a tower, sitteth not down first, and counteth the cost, whether he have sufficient to finish it?
> "Lest haply, after he hath laid the foundation, and is not able to finish it, all that behold it begin to mock him,
> "Saying, This man began to build, and was not able to finish." (Luke 14:28-30.)

Most of us are great starters and poor finishers. We begin to "mock" at ourselves, to lose faith in our ability to keep the promises we make with ourselves.

We simply do not sit down first and count the cost to see if we have sufficient to finish—sufficient desire, sufficient internal thrust. We try to lift off our launching pad without realistically calculating the "g's" (gravity pull) and the resistance of the atmosphere (our environment).

Billions of dollars, years and years of planning, work by thousands of scientists and engineers and by tens of thousands of technicians and workers—all went into the first successful moon walk. Everything was studied beforehand—every detail planned and programmed. The costs were counted. There was "sufficient to finish."

Habits have a tremendous gravity pull, more than most realize or would admit. Breaking deeply imbedded habitual tendencies, such as procrastination, impatience, criticalness, or living in the excesses or selfishness, involves more than a little will power and a few minor changes in our lives. We're dealing with our basic character structure (what we *are* inside) and need to achieve some very basic reorientation, or transformation, of values and motives as well as practices.

An Alliance With God

Furthermore, we can't fully overcome these habits and impacted tendencies by ourselves. Our own resolves, our own will, our own effort—all this is necessary but is not sufficient. We need the transforming power of the Savior, born of faith in him and his atoning sacrifice and of entering into a contract with him. In such a contract, made in ordinance work and in private prayer, we covenant, or promise, or witness to take upon ourselves his name and to keep his commandments. He, in turn, promises us to give us his spirit, which, if we are true to our promises, will renew and strengthen and transform us. In this way we combine our power with the power of the Almighty.

Before we renew our covenants in the sacrament, before we promise or resolve to overcome a bad habit and establish a new one, we should sit down first and count the cost.

If we realistically count the costs and then make a deep enough commitment, we, with the Lord's help, can overcome the gravity pull of habits and the atmospheric resistance of our environment with all its luring temptations.

It will be difficult at first, very difficult. Once we decide to change (to "lift-off" the earth or "to build a tower") we will have no freedom at first to do as we please (or what comes naturally) until new habits are formed and our desire for the old ways changed. We'll be doing things "against our will" for awhile simply because we know we should. It may not be too unlike the painful withdrawal process a drug addict goes through to "kick the habit," whether the craving is narcotics or alcohol or just plain food.

During the first few minutes in lift-off the astronauts were strictly controlled and were powerfully buffeted by the forces of nature struggling to keep man on earth. This is somewhat comparable to the pull of the flesh when our alarm goes off early in the morning. Unless we put "mind over mattress" and carry out the resolves made the night before, we will experience our first defeat that day. Not sufficient to finish. Mission aborted.

But if we overcome the pull and "get up and get at it," we will have won a victory. We kept our own resolve. We can then move to other things, for by small means great things are accomplished. Thus, even this "one small step" is also in another sense "a giant leap."

10

The Sacrament:
The Lord's Weekly Provision
for Self Renewal

"Dad, that's one of the best home evening lessons we ever had, but frankly, the sacrament has never meant that much to me. Why do we take it so often? Sometimes it seems like a meaningless ritual to me."

"Well, David, I fear that's the way it is for many of us. But, you see, we live in such a physical and material world, and we're often so materially protected and satisfied with ourselves, that we need a frequent reminder of Christ and the *real and spiritual purposes of life*. You notice the water and bread are blessed to our *souls*, not to our bodies, as at the dinner table."

"What do you mean—blessed to our souls? And why do we have two blessings, anyway?"

"Let me answer your second question first. The bread stands for Christ's flesh, which was broken when he was crucified on Calvary. Three days later he was resurrected and became immortal, meaning he took his body up again; his spirit and body became inseparably connected, and he will never die again. And, David, through this same miraculous power, you and I and all mankind will be resurrected and become immortal.

"Remember that scripture we memorized, the one summarizing the Lord's work and glory?"

"Yes, it was—'to bring to pass the immortality and eternal life of man.' " (Moses 1:39.)

"Correct, David. Now what does the bread stand for?"

"Christ's body—Calvary—the resurrection and immortality."

"Yes. The Lord has already completed one of his two purposes—the *immortality* of man. Now what is the Lord's second purpose?"

"To bring to pass the *eternal life* of man."

"This is where the water comes in, David. It symbolizes Christ's blood, which he shed in the Garden of Gethsemane and on Calvary for the sins of all men. This is called the atonement. If we have faith in him and repent completely of our own sins and promise him we will keep his commandments, he will give to us the Holy Ghost. Under this divine influence, as we keep our promises, we will be forgiven, cleansed, and sanctified from our sins.

"Then, if we stay true, when we leave this life we will feel clean and confident in God's presence. We will have a celestialized resurrection. This is *eternal life,* which is the second great part of the Lord's work and glory. So, David, the water stands not only for the atoning blood of Jesus Christ but also for eternal life."

"I understand that, but how could the Savior suffer for *our* sins?"

"I don't fully understand how he did it, but I do know it was real. He described this terrible ordeal in a modern revelation:

"Which suffering caused myself, even God, the greatest of all, to tremble because of pain, and to bleed at every pore, and to suffer both body and spirit. . . .' " (Doctrine and Covenants 19:18.)

"Son, this great atoning sacrifice of the Son of God is the heart of the entire gospel plan and the greatest act and gift in all human history; and to those who receive this transcendent gift, Christ becomes their Savior."

"Dad, what do you mean by 'receive the gift'? And what does all of this have to do with the sacrament anyway?"

"Many of us never receive the gifts given to us. For instance, have you ever given kindness to someone who would not receive your kindness or love?"

"Yes."

"Well, to receive this great act of divine kindness or love, we also must do certain things. [See D&C 88:33.] This is where the principles and ordinances of the gospel come in—including the sacrament.

"Now, let's think for a moment, son. Do you remember why you were baptized?"

"For the remission of sins. I also promised God I would keep his commandments."

"Correct. What about any sins you have committed since your baptism?"

"I don't know, except that I should repent of them."

"Yes. You see, when you were baptized you made a covenant or solemn promise with God to be true. And in return for your obedience, he promised you his spirit, guidance, and blessings. When you partake of the bread and water you renew your baptismal covenants, and if you honor these covenants the Lord will honor his. Your sins will be remitted or forgiven, and you will always have his spirit to be with you, just as the sacramental prayers state."

"You mean by partaking of the sacrament worthily I can be forgiven of my sins?"

"Exactly, and given great spiritual strength also. The late apostle Melvin J. Ballard testified of this:

" 'I am a witness that there is a spirit attending the administration of the sacrament that warms the soul from head to foot; you feel the wounds of the spirit being healed, and the load being lifted.'[1]

"David, my own experience has convinced me that when I partake of the sacrament worthily and 'with real intent,' I find peace and rest within my soul. Just as sleep unravels our weary bodies, so will worship and prayer, re-

---

[1]Bryant S. Hinckley, *Sermons and Missionary Services of Melvin Joseph Ballard* (Salt Lake City: Deseret Book Company, 1949), p. 149.

pentance, and covenanting 'with real intent' unravel our confused, doubting, weary spirits."

"Dad, how can I best prepare to partake?"

"First, son, look inside. Any hypocrisy there? pride? impurity? Pray for a sense of divine sorrow. Determine to forsake any and all forms of ungodliness. As you say, repent. Do you carry any grudges or have you offended anyone? Can you ask their forgiveness? It isn't easy. Doing these things may just about break your heart, but this is exactly the kind of sacrifice expected of us today—a broken heart and contrite spirit. It is a spiritual sacrifice as contrasted to the physical or blood sacrifice required of Israel prior to Christ's earthly mission.

"At the Feast of the Passover or the Last Supper, Christ himself administered the first sacrament and taught by example and precept his higher commandments of *humility* [see John 13:3-17] and *love* [see John 13:34-35], beautifully illustrating how we are to prepare and to partake worthily. Then he performed the last blood sacrifice by voluntarily giving up his own life."

"Just *how* do we covenant, Dad?"

"David, prepare yourself to promise or covenant hours or days before partaking. At the service sing the sacrament song with feeling. Listen intently to the words of the prayers. Mean every word. Remember the Savior and these truths. Then when you partake, literally within yourself, with your mind made up, promise the Lord, promise yourself, and promise the others there—in other words, renew your covenants—to take his name upon you, to always be a witness for him, and to keep his commandments."

"Dad, if we do this, what can we expect?"

"David, if you deeply and sincerely covenant, you will feel both unity and peace. Remember that private victories precede public victories. Christ's Gethsemane preceded his Calvary. Your own internal, private victory in the sacrament will entitle you to the companionship of the Holy Spirit, the only true source of personal security.

Anchored privately to true principles, you will then have public victories. Being true will bring self-respect. Your life will be calm and steady, and you will be aware of the presence of a real, though unseen, Friend.

"But if you just go through the motions, through 'meaningless daily prayer rituals' and 'weekly sacrament rituals,' you will find yourself compromising your principles and integrity under the buffeting pressures of life. You will lose both the companionship of the Spirit and your own self-respect. You will find yourself pretending, playing roles, focusing on clothes, looks, cars, and other material possessions, all in an effort to win the approval and popularity of others. But people's opinions are fickle and provide no security.

"David, most of the world is on this treadmill—thirsting for a water that does not satisfy the soul. Now, son, to come back to your very first question, 'Why *do* we bless the bread and water to our *souls,* not our bodies?'

"When we partake worthily, it actually does satisfy our *souls* and improve our living. Also, we become a witness for Christ."

III

UNDERSTANDING
AND EXAMPLE:
Succeeding With People

11

Diagnose Before
You Prescribe

Imagine. . . . You have been getting headaches and are having trouble with your eyes. You think you need glasses. You call on Stan, your friend, an optometrist. He briefly listens to your complaint and replies, "Yes, I'm sure you need glasses. Here, I've worn this pair now for 10 years and they've really helped me. They'll do the same for you, and I've got an extra pair at home. Take this pair."

You try them on. "But Stan, I can't even see as well as before," you report.

He assures you, "That's okay, it's just a matter of adjustment, of getting used to them. Before long you'll see as well as I do."

The foolishness in this scene is transparent. And yet, in every-day settings, prescribing (advice giving) before diagnosing (understanding) is most common.

For instance, you are trying to communicate with your daughter. "Come on, honey, tell me how you feel. I know it's hard, but I'll try to understand."

"Oh, I don't know, mother—you'd think it was stupid."

"Of course I wouldn't! You can tell me. Honey, no one cares for you as much as I do. I'm only interested in your welfare. What is it that makes you so unhappy?"

"Oh, I don't know."

"Come on, Mary, what is it?"

"Well, frankly, mother, I just don't like school anymore."

"What do you mean you don't like school! Everyone in our family likes school! If you'd apply yourself like your older sister does, you'd do better and then you'd like school. Time and time again we've told you to settle down. You've got the ability, but you just don't apply yourself."

After a long pause you begin again. "Now go ahead. Tell me why you feel this way."

Sometimes we train our children not to open up their problems with us.

First Seek to Understand

This tendency to rush in and "fix things up" with a lot of good advice is ever so common. It is easier and quicker to advise than to understand, but it doesn't work for two basic reasons. First, we don't yet understand and our advice may be way off the mark (as the optometrist's was). Second, the advice we give, however good, may be seen as a form of judgment, even rejection, because we never really took the time to listen in order to understand. To carefully listen is a powerful way of saying to another that we value him. The opposite can be very demeaning. Communication, in a sense, is like an iceberg. The verbal, or word, part is like the part of an iceberg that is seen above the surface of the water. Yet the great mass of the iceberg is under the surface and cannot be seen. So with communication. Most of it takes place in attitudes and feelings and spirit. We call this non-verbal communication.

When we take the time to understand and stay with it until the other feels that we do understand, we have communicated many things: we care, we want to understand, we respect their expression, we give them dignity and an individual sense of worth.

Communication lies more in feelings than in words. Don't you know some people you communicate with almost without words? You simply understand each other. You trust each other. You've had a relationship long enough to know what different things mean to each other. And aren't there others, perhaps even some in your family or in your work whom you see every day, with whom you have no communication, regardless of how careful you are about your words? Everyone on guard for fear of being made an "offender for a word"?

People spend a great deal of effort and energy (particularly is this true with youth) fighting for the feeling of being accepted and respected, for a sense of their own worth. If you grant them this sense of uniqueness and worth by sincerely listening in order to understand, you'll find that almost all of their fight will be gone.

Try it in the next argument you find yourself getting drawn into. You'll need to exercise a lot of self-restraint and patience. As you sense the other person becoming a little heated, stop and take the time to carefully express what he is trying to say. Stay with your effort until you are sure that he knows that you understand his point of view. Watch what happens. It will amaze you. You'll discover that most arguments are really not disagreements but are rather little ego battles and misunderstandings. If you find that there is an honest difference of opinion, you'll discover yourself disagreeing without being disagreeable. And you'll have a basis for further respectful discussion in the very area you found the disagreement.

Experiment at home with this principle and discover its value for yourself. You'll find it particularly effective with your teen-age children as well as with your husband or wife.

But remember, it will require patience and real sincerity. If you really don't care to understand but only pretend to, this itself will communicate itself. "White man speaks with forked tongue."

Now if you sincerely care to understand, you'll need to be open. You may change your understanding of the situation. This will require some internal security. It is important to prepare yourself by thoughtful meditation and perhaps prayer whenever you enter into one of these emotionally charged conversations, particularly with your own loved ones.

Think of the importance the Prophet Joseph Smith put on the promise of the Lord, contained in the book of James, that God would "not upbraid" him if he asked him for wisdom. Listen to the words of the Prophet himself:

"At length I came to the conclusion that I must either remain in darkness and confusion, or else I must do as James directs, that is, ask of God. I at length came to the determination to 'ask of God', concluding that if he gave wisdom to them that lacked wisdom and would give liberally, and not upbraid, I might venture." (Joseph Smith 1:13.)

To upbraid means to find fault with, to blame, or to reprove. I believe this tendency to upbraid is the main roadblock in communication between husband and wife and between parents and their children. People fear being judged and upbraided—particularly when they don't yet feel understood. It simply hurts. This is one of the reasons people pretend and play roles and say things they don't really mean, and hestitate to ask the questions they feel inside. As someone put it, "He thinks I'm stupid, so why open my mouth and remove all doubt!" We must learn to reward rather than punish people for their honest expression of ignorance and their request for help.

In addition to building harmonious relationships, let us look at the other reason why we must understand before we advise or judge. The reason is plain accuracy. Our advice, like the optometrist's, may simple not apply. Then if the person follows our advice and acts on our judgment, we are responsible. However, the opposite usually results. Until a person feels understood, he will simply not be influenced. Would you follow the prescription of the optometrist who didn't examine each eye?

To give another example, your child complains about not having friends at school. You advise, "Well, to have friends you must be a friend." Your advice may be good, but it may not apply at all. The real problem may be that your child is unhappy at school because he was caught cheating; but because he didn't have the courage to admit this, he substituted a safer reason.

Take another illustration. You're trying to teach in a home evening the importance of honoring the Sabbath day. No one is listening; the little kids are running about and contending; the teen-agers appear to be bored to death, even though they do have some real problems on the Sabbath day and some specific temptations they'd like to talk about; but they hesitate to do so for fear of being judged and upbraided.

Remember, the more emotional a problem is, the more time and effort you must put forth to understand. You'll need to listen with the third ear, the heart. A person needs to express himself freely and fully, without fear of ridicule or embarrassment or censure. He will likely then become open to influence and to reasoning. You may think you understand, and in fact even without listening you might actually understand what is going on, but the other person may not feel understood until he has expressed himself. To him, his problem is unique. It's different. And you just can't simply categorize and generalize.

You will find that it is not easy to understand before you prescribe. It is difficult. You risk changing yourself.

Perhaps we never fully understand another, but the effort to do so is highly affirming to the other person. The patience and restraint demanded flow out of emotional and spiritual strength. And you know where this kind of strength comes from.

It is ever so much easier to hand your friend or your loved ones your other pair of glasses that have fitted you so well these many years.

12

Understand the
Tenderness Inside

My, we had fun together—best fathers' and sons' outing yet! Gymnastics, wrestling matches, hotdogs and orangeade, and a movie. The works!

In the middle of the movie my four-year-old, Michael Sean, fell asleep in his seat. His older brother, Stephen (age 6), and I enjoyed the rest of the movie and then I put Sean in my arms, carried him out to the car, and laid him in the back seat. It was cold that night—very cold —so I took off my coat and gently arranged it over and around him.

On arriving home I quickly carried Sean in and tucked him into bed. After Stephen put on his "jammies" and brushed his teeth, I lay down next to him to discuss the night out together.

"How'd you like it, Stephen?"

"Fine," he answered.

"Did you have fun?"

"Yes."

"What did you like most?"

"I don't know. The trampoline, I guess."

"That was quite a thing, wasn't it—doing those somersaults and tricks in the air like that."

Not much response on his part. I found myself making conversation. I wondered why Stephen wouldn't open up more. He usually did when exciting things happened. I was a little disappointed. I sensed something was wrong; he was so quiet on the way home and while getting ready for bed.

Suddenly Stephen turned over on his left side, facing the wall. I wondered why and lifted myself up just enough to see his eyes welling up with tears.

"What's wrong, honey? What is it?"

He turned back, and I could sense he was feeling some embarrassment for the tears and his quivering lips and chin.

"Daddy, if I were cold, would you put your coat around me too?"

Of all the events of that special night out together, the most important was a little act of kindness, a momentary, unconscious showing of love to his little brother.

What a powerful, personal lesson that experience was to me then and is even now. It has helped explain, to me, at least, why people build defenses and often why communications between people break down.

This story is only one illustration of some universal lessons. Consider these three:

First, people are very tender, very sensitive inside. I don't believe age or experience makes much difference. Inside, even within the most toughened and calloused exteriors, are the tender feelings and emotions, the heart.

Second, we learn over time how to protect ourselves from getting hurt. We build defenses—sarcasm, cynicism, indifference, aggression, criticalness.

Children at first are completely open and trusting—and vulnerable. They too gradually learn how to defend themselves. They learn from getting hurt. Sometimes they care so much that their only defense is to say, "I don't care." Perhaps anger hurts them most. Often they'll fight back. Sometimes they must withdraw, perhaps into a blind apathy.

Third, "toughening our skin" may seem safer, but it may also hinder our growth and keep us apart as individuals.

I have a bum left shoulder from a boxing injury in college intramurals and must be somewhat careful in sports and rigorous work or it might dislocate again. This is very painful. Sometimes I briefly taste this pain just turning over the wrong way in bed. Therefore, when I ski, I ski in complete control. I overcompensate so I won't fall and take a chance. It just isn't worth it if I get hurt. But I never improve. I never get any better, and I've been skiing for years. My little children will be passing me shortly.

We can't grow when we're always protecting ourselves. Growth is positive; defenses are negative.

Many people, particularly family members, want to express warmth and affection freely to each other. They may not know how. They feel awkward. They may fear the consequences if they do. It makes them uncomfortable, too dependent, too vulnerable. It's turned on them before. "So why risk it again?" they reason, and they escape.

But what a tragic alternative! No honesty. No real understanding. Just surface communication, guarded communication. We keep ourselves from the very source of our deepest needs and satisfactions—the free, open giving and receiving of love in the family circle. This leads to dealing with each other "at a distance" (during TV commercials), to mask wearing, to making each other "an offender for a word," and to subtle forms of manipulation.

What to do? I offer one suggestion based on the above three lessons:

Realize and use the power of little acts of kindness and courtesy—when consistently given. This is true with adults, who often have learned best how to protect themselves behind social trappings and thought-out explanations. But it will make a big difference to young people, especially when they are at the various crossroads of their lives. I particularly emphasize the kindness of not rushing in and throwing around judgments and good success formulas—taking the time to understand, and then acting and counseling in terms of what we learn, in addition to what we already know.

13

Success With People

A world-famous graduate school of business administration, in an attempt to understand some of the prime
factors or ingredients that spell success in an executive
capacity, undertook an extensive research program that
covered several years. They arrived at this interesting conclusion: Two qualities among all others seemed to be
stated so often, so preeminently, that the research report
mentioned only these two qualities. First, and not necessarily above the other, is motivation. This is a many-
splendored term, including, of course, determination,
initiative, and the desire to assume and act on responsibility. The second is the ability to get along with other
people. These qualities are more of attitude and of personal characteristics than of knowledge and technical
skills, and they are more abstract and intangible than perhaps some of the other qualities we may think of as
being the determinants of success in executive capacities.

Building upon the basic assumption that the study
and skill of human relations or the ability to get along
with others is of supreme importance for all of us to understand and practice, I should like to briefly discuss
what I consider to be two basic or cardinal concepts of
human relations and to subsequently elaborate on them.

The first is the concept of understanding human
behavior. Why do you behave as you do, and I as I do?

Once we can gain an understanding of behavior, we will come to see why individual personal differences exist. This is a fact we intellectually accept, but accepting it emotionally is an altogether different matter. We need to respect these individual differences and allow for them and not expect immediate and constant perfection of ourselves or of anyone else, because the very process we are going through in life is one of maturation, of trial and error, of experience, and of perfection. The implications of this concept are vast and far-reaching.

The second concept builds naturally on the first and entails two facets: a recognition of and an appreciation for the basic individual differences in people, and an understanding and a testimony of the basic divinity within all people. We are all children of God. Coupled with this concept, I add the necessity of creating and maintaining a climate or an atmosphere in our working and personal relationships that will be both productive and satisfying. Such an atmosphere is more valuable than all the techniques, gimmicks, and manipulative devices we might attempt to use in influencing other people and in soliciting their friendship and support. This atmosphere or climate is of supreme importance and cannot be overemphasized.

Now to consider these two concepts in order:

1. The first is *understanding our behavior*—why we behave and act as we do.

Basically, behavior is based upon need. We are motivated to satisfy particular needs that reside within us consciously or unconsciously. The first such basic need is biological or physical—for instance, hunger. "Man does not live by bread alone," but he does live for bread alone when there is no bread. Brigham Young was quoted as advising the elders not to preach the gospel to a hungry person, but to feed him first and then offer the gospel. As our hunger is satisfied, we are then desirous of satisfying other of our needs.

113

Another example: if I am denied air, I will fight for it; I will obtain it in any way possible. Once I can breathe easily again, the fight for air no longer motivates me, at least not consciously. If I am in physical danger, my only interest and motivation is safety. Once safe, I seek other things.

A second basic need that resides in all of us is a social need—to have a sense of belonging, to have opportunity to express friendship and love, and to receive friendship and love; to have an association with other people and to feel an acceptance socially.

The third, and a higher level need, is the ego or psychological need. I break this down, for purposes of this discussion, into two areas: self-esteem, or that which we think of ourselves, our own self-confidence, independence, sense of achievement, feeling of competence and of knowledge, etc.; and what others think of us—a desire for reputation and for status among our fellow men, a desire to obtain a sense of recognition, a sense of appreciation for work well done and for the efforts that we put forth, and to receive the respect that we feel we deserve. These needs are basic in all of us.

The fourth need we could term the self-fulfillment or spiritual need. Within each one of us there is a basic spiritual anxiety to return to the celestial presence of God, from whose presence we have come. Until we realize the ultimate potential or possibility that we have within us, i.e., the spirit within us, we will never be fully satisfied. We may have an abundance of this world's goods but remain without satisfaction because possession of things alone does not satisfy our spiritual anxiety or fulfill the ultimate potential or capacity that we have as human beings, as children of God, spiritually begotten of our Father in heaven.

Whenever any of these needs are deprived for one reason or another, there is consequent behavior. The satisfaction of certain needs may conflict with the satisfaction of other needs. If perhaps I seek a satisfaction of a self-fulfillment or spiritual need, I may have to deny a physical need or a social need. Perhaps one of the ego needs conflicts with the other. This is often the case. This internal confusion often creates a very real conflict or stress situation. When a person strives for popularity with other people, for reputation and status, he may have to sacrifice his own self-esteem, his self-respect. He may "give in" on his principles, for instance, and then may feel that he is not true to himself, although he has gained the followership or the friendship of other people. So the true test of life—or one aspect to it—is, which needs do we choose to satisfy? Sometimes we have to sacrifice one in order to obtain the other. We know that the ultimate criterion in making such choices and discriminations was given to us in the revelations of the Lord —and that is, to differentiate between that which is ultimate, eternal, and incorruptible as opposed to the temporary, transitory, and corruptible. One's character is formed by the myriad of decisions, large and small, made in one's life. So we see here a hierarchy of needs.

Another helpful concept in attempting to understand behavior is the concept of threat. A person has certain beliefs and feelings about himself, and these are very near and dear to him. He also has needs, beliefs, and feelings about other people, about ideas, about things. Gradually these are less and less important to him. The most important, or the closest things to him, are his beliefs about himself as a good parent, a good priesthood holder, or whatever the case may be. This we would term the self-image or the self-concept. Whenever this self-concept is threatened or whenever these beliefs about ourselves are put in jeopardy, one of three phenomena results:

1. Fight. We fight or resist in one of several ways—physical, mental, verbal, etc.
2. Flight. We strive to get out of the presence of the atmosphere that is threatening to us.
3. Rationalization. Often in embarrassing or threatening situations we will manufacture reasons,

either real or fanciful, in justifying and defending our positions and behavior. These mental callisthenics reduce the threat and often remove it altogether.

Building upon these understandings, let us now move on to another key idea in understanding human behavior and individual differences.

Different people see the world from different frames of reference. I am sure you will agree that this is a well-tested and proven fact. I had a very memorable and significant experience at the Harvard Business School in which the professor demonstrated clearly and eloquently that two people can see the same thing, both claim it was something different, and yet both be right. He brought into the room a stack of large cards, half of which had the image imprinted upon them of a young girl and the other half with the image imprinted upon them of an old lady. He passed to the right side of the room the cards with the image of the young girl, and to the left, cards with the image of the old lady. He asked us to look at the cards and to concentrate upon them for about ten seconds, then to pass them back in. He then projected upon the screen a picture combining both images, neither one more preeminent than the other. He asked those who had studied the image of the young girl, "What do you see?" Almost to the man they said, "We see a young girl." To the left side of the room he asked the same question, and they said, "An old lady," again almost to the man.

The students then started to converse back and forth. The professor asked one student to explain what he saw to a student on the opposite side of the room. Gradually as they talked back and forth you could see emerging a tremendous breakdown in the communication. Eventually one student caustically said, "You old fool, can't you see that is an old lady?" The other one argued back equally sure of, and adamant in, his position. All of this occurred in spite of one exceedingly important advantage that the students had—they knew another point of view did in fact exist, something many of us would never admit. Yet only a few students endeavored to see this picture from other frames of reference. After a period of time and futile communication, one, pointing to the screen, said to another, "I think that is the old lady's necklace." The other one said, "No, that is the young girl's mouth." Gradually as they calmly discussed different points, the images of both came into focus. However, when we looked away and then back, we would only see the image that we were conditioned to see in a ten-second period of time.

What about the conditioning of a lifetime? The influences in our lives—the church, the social activity, our families, our school, friends and associates, and the other many environmental influences—have made their impact upon us and helped to shape our own frame of reference, our own point of view. You can easily understand why we run into a tremendous barrier in the communication process. It depends upon the point of view, the frame of reference; therefore, it behooves each one of us to draw from this a valuable lesson that we must first seek to understand others as they understand themselves, to see the world through their eyes, to stand in their shoes, that we may understand why they behave as they do before attempting to evaluate, to judge, or to condemn. "Judge not, that ye be not judged." (Matthew 7:1.) It is not only wrong to judge but we are incompetent to do so, because we are often totally without understanding of the many, many factors that help to formulate a man's point of view or frame of reference that directly affects his behavior.

I hope that this assists in giving us an understanding and an appreciation of and respect for individual differences. We all have basic needs, but the environmental influences and other conditioning factors tend to have us satisfy the needs in different ways, to see things in different ways.

2. This brings us to the second concept regarding the kind of working climate, based on human understanding, that is most productive and satisfying. While building

upon our superstructure of the hierarchy of needs and individual frames of reference as we have constructed it so far, we should attempt in all our relationships with other people to establish a climate of approval and of acceptance of people as they are, so they do not have to pretend in our presence to be someone they are not. To do this we need a sense of self-esteem, the feeling that we are true to ourselves, and that we have value apart from our performance or our particular point of view. Let us learn to disassociate the person's point of view and his performance from the person himself. This is basic. If he does not feel accepted, he becomes threatened and defensive; and in such a situation there is no learning, no growth, no progression, no development.

Perhaps the attitude might be expressed in this way: It is like admitting the person to the human race. "I accept you as an individual person, as a child of God. I may not agree with your ideas. I may totally disagree with your ideas—but you, as a person, I accept and respect."

The lesson for us as students of human relations is to attempt to develop empathy—the ability to see the world as others see it, to cease judging and work from an accepting position. This creates the atmosphere in which others will listen to constructive criticism, in which they will begin to grow and develop. The great obstacle to communication is the tendency to *constantly* evaluate or moralize with others, creating in them a fear to speak or to act outside of the puppet-like response we create and often desire.

The great key to this communication process is to learn to listen, and to listen attentively and with understanding, to listen acceptingly to the other person's point of view. This then creates the atmosphere of love and approval.

We should avoid the tendency to manipulate people, to pull strings, to verbally make it possible for others to think that the ideas came from within them when they were in reality our ideas. People do not like to be manipulated arbitrarily or have some type of an authority pull strings and verbally run them down any alley they wish them to go. They resist this. Sometimes they never find out what we did or how we did it. But what do we think of others if we attempt to use them or manipulate them into our way of thinking, even though they never find it out? Do we recognize that they are children of God? Would Jesus assume this type of attitude? Would he act in this manner?

On the other hand, insofar as the organization permits it, instead of attempting to manipulate people, we should attempt to gain their consent or participation in the decision-making process, particularly when it involves their own lives or jobs or activity. We should be genuine and sincere in asking them to help and to participate, especially when they want and expect to. Though the ideas finally agreed to are not what we might consider the ideal, if we have their support and cooperation, and if it involves no sacrifice of a basic principle, I am sure that we will go much further in the achievement of our goals and in our personal relationships in any endeavor we both seek to promote than we would if we were to ramrod and manipulate our ideas down the throats of others. I am suggesting that we need to weaken our habits and attitudes of labeling, of judging, of rejecting, and of manipulating, and substitute for them strengthened tendencies to understand, to accept, and to work participatively with others.

Summary

Let us realize as executives or as workers in any endeavor in any organization that people are the most important thing in this world. They are the greatest creation of God. The gospel and the Church are means to the end of development and perfection of these people. The Lord said, "This is my work and my glory—to bring to pass the immortality and eternal life of man." (Moses 1:39.)

He gave the gospel as the way of life or the means to assist in this great process.

Man's own exaltation and perfection is our goal. Let us never lose sight of this. In all of our relationships let us realize this and allow it to shape our attitudes and our strategies. And we will find that if we can achieve this atmosphere wherein these basic human needs are being met, that the group and organizational goals and purposes will be achieved at a higher level than ever before. When personal needs and goals are identified with organizational goals, both goal attainment and human satisfactions, being interrelated and interdependent, will together reach new heights. Trouble begins when we put our entire emphasis upon the achievement of group goals or standards and forget the indispensable need to do it in ways that will satisfy the basic and high-level human needs in all of us.

The Golden Rule is perhaps the finest expression of the human relations concept. Paul in First Corinthians, Chapter 13, speaks of love, the key to success with others. Much of what we have been discussing here is science, but the greater part of getting along with other people is found in the art or the attitude of love. It is the basic love within you and me that is the determining factor as to whether we can be successful with this knowledge and understanding in achieving our goals and in maintaining happy and productive relationships with other people. Learning and practicing the basic human relations skills and attitudes is often a long, hard, and frustrating process, but it is worthwhile, very satisfying, and always in the long run immensely rewarding in making this world a better one and a happier one for all.

14

The Process of Rebuilding
Relationships

To rebuild broken-down relationships, we must first of all study our own hearts, to discover our own responsibility, our own faults. It serves no useful purpose to study others' hearts and thereby to judge and criticize them for their failures and irresponsible acts. It is easy to stand at the sidelines and pick at others' weaknesses. This process serves only to feed our own pride and to justify ourselves. Pride is the leaven of envy and strife.

The Savior taught us to cast the beam out of our own eye first, and then, and only then, shall we see clearly enough to help our brother cast the mote out of his eye. This takes honesty and courage to really look into our own hearts and find the keys that we must turn to begin the process of rebuilding. But there is no other key we can turn. In spite of how much we would like to, we cannot turn someone else's key. He must turn his own. Our greatest help to him is to turn ours.

Desire—the Most Fundamental Key

To rebuild a faulty relationship, we must really want to do so. This desire must be very real and very strong. It must be realistic and vibrant enough to pay the price in longsuffering and self-sacrifice, time and patience, and honest, continual effort. Many desire the great blessing of a beautiful relationship, but they do not desire it enough to obey the law upon which that blessing is predicated. The Lord teaches us forcibly that if "we obtain any blessing from God, it is by obedience to that law upon which it is predicated." (D&C 130:21.) Inevitably the test of obedience becomes one of sacrifice.

There is no shortcut or simple solution or easy answer. There is no simple formula to rebuilding relationships that have taken weeks or months or perhaps years to deteriorate. It involves the eternal law of the harvest—we reap what we sow, no more and no less. The significance of this cannot be overstated, because many have lived for years on a diet of easy answers and panaceas, shortcuts, and simple formulas. In many areas of their lives they have learned the technique of "getting by"—in school, in business, in church work—or acquiring a kind of superficial success through a fairly simple and painless route. They usually discover later, to their own disillusionment, that their success was as empty and as hollow as the methods they used to achieve it.

Farmers have learned to live the law of the harvest. They know that unless they sow in the spring, they will not reap in the fall. No matter what else they know, or what else they do, they simply cannot violate this basic and immutable law. Athletes learn the same thing—often the hard way—that unless they are in condition and "practiced up," they simply cannot expect to compete and to win.

This is also true of all relationships. Unless there is a basic sowing of those seeds which foster a harmonious relationship and the purposeful destruction of those seeds which undermine and destroy such relationships, there will be no reaping. Relationships must be built conscientiously. They must be worked at constantly. Let no one deceive himself on this point.

Now, as we look at those relationships we want to rebuild, or to help others rebuild, let us ask ourselves honestly, is our desire strong and deep and abiding? Do we honestly accept the law of the harvest?

Three Fundamental Laws in Rebuilding Relationships

The Lord taught us to love and serve him and our neighbor with all our heart, might, mind, and strength. We can distill from this all-embracing, magnificent teaching three fundamental laws to obey in rebuilding relationships. First, the "law of Moses"; second, the law of preparation; and third, the law of Christ.

The *"law of Moses"* interpreted herein is essentially the law of personal discipline. The real law of Moses was this also, for it "served as a schoolmaster to bring people to Christ." Unless a man learns to govern and control himself and become his own master, he is continually subject to the fickle forces of life and the approvals of others, and will find it impossible to "turn himself over" to the government of God and to be a willing and obedient servant. Until he is his own master and leads himself, he cannot lead others.

In relationships, this means we must learn to discipline our tongues, to control them, to bite them occasionally rather than to say the unkind thing. We learn as President McKay did: "I learned, when I was tempted to say the unkind, thoughtless thing, to put my tongue way back in my mouth and clamp my teeth down on it; and each time I did that, it was easier the next time not to say the unkind, hurtful thing." Next time you want to criticize a leader or a teacher don't. Next time you want to answer a "cheeky" teen-ager sarcastically, don't.

The "law of Moses" in rebuilding relationships teaches us to discipline our perception—that is, to look for those qualities in others that are good, desirable, and lovable. We must often do this purposefully: resist the tendency to focus on the undesirable and unlovable. We must concentrate and practice, practice, practice. This kind of discipline may run counter to our faultfinding habits and to our past labels on individuals, but nevertheless, if consistently and properly applied, this law of discipline, of the "law of Moses" in relationships, will gradually bring us to Christ, or to the laws of Christ's gospel, wherein are found the higher spiritual qualities of mercy and forgiveness, justice, and "love unfeigned."

The second law is the *law of preparation,* or to love and serve God and neighbor with our mind. This involves using our intelligence. Think through the process which has brought about the deterioration. Study the broken laws on both sides. Think and rethink. Reflect and meditate. Read, study, and prepare.

Intelligent relationships must be based upon planning and preparation. We cannot blunder into other people's presence, particularly where bad feelings exist, and expect to enjoy peace and good communication, any more than we would blunder into the presence of the Lord without the true attitude of prayer and expect to feel his beautiful sustaining Spirit.

Study the prayer relationship to discover a beautiful insight into the process of rebuilding relationships. To pray effectively, we must prepare our prayers, our attitude and spirit. Without such preparation of desire and feeling, prayers become mechanical and ritualistic, mere lip service. People lose faith in these kinds of prayers, for they feel as if they are speaking to the wall or simply praying to those who are listening, "for effect." This kind of praying affects people's faith in God, and even in themselves—that is, in their own sense of sincerity and integrity and inner unity—and, as a logical consequence, this will inevitably affect their faith in others.

But rather, before our prayers, let us say to ourselves, "What is it I really want? What is it I really am grateful for? To whom am I talking? What is my relationship to him?" These questions, honestly put to ourselves, may lead us to make reconciliation, so that we can seek forgiveness from the Lord before we will feel to make our sincere requests. We may even discover that we had no real intention at all of obeying those laws upon which the blessings we seek are predicated. But let's take a prayer we were prepared for, one that was worshipful and sincere. Did it not change us? Did it not give us a new frame of mind? Did it not increase our desire to serve the Master and to be kind to our neighbor?

When we pray from our heart, not from our lips, we discover a beautiful and vibrant inner power, and then with a prepared frame of mind, we can go about rebuilding our relationship. Before we visit with the other person, we should think about the visit, think about the worth of the other, and appreciate his or her noble qualities. This simple mental exercise itself will go far in making our re-contact effective. We will communicate from our heart, not from our lips alone.

The third law is the *law of Christ*, which involves mercy, forgiveness and love, humility, faith, repentance, covenant-making (baptism and/or sacrament), and the gift of the Holy Ghost. If we have obeyed the first two laws —the "law of Moses" in relationships (that is, self-control, self-discipline in talking, in perceiving and responding), and the second law (the law of preparation and planning —creating that attitudinal frame of mind which is conducive to harmonious and unified relationships)—then we will literally be brought to the law of Christ, which is the highest law, necessarily built on the other two and embodying both. It might be considered the law of the heart or of the spirit.

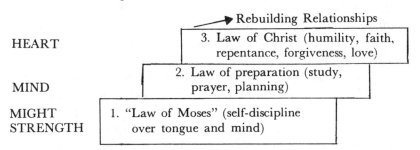

To achieve this law, we must have *honesty and humility*. Honesty in a large and kindly spirit says, "Let's talk things over. There's no value in pretending that things are okay when down deep we both know they're not. You and I know there isn't the kind of unity and harmony with each other that we need. Let's get these matters out on the table and talk about the real things that are affecting our relationship. We can't do this work if we're carrying personal grudges and unkind memories."

Then, on top of this honest conversation, humility says, "I am sorry. Forgive me. I have judged you wrongly and harshly. This past year I thought you were always trying to find fault with me. But I recently discovered that this wasn't the case at all. I have misjudged you, and I want to grow to love and appreciate you, and if I've ever been a stumbling block to you, please forgive me."

Pride is the opposite of humility. It refuses to acknowledge fault. It is boastful and pretenseful, selfish and grasping. It rationalizes and justifies. It is also the opposite of honesty with self. If a man is dishonest with self, he cannot be honest with others. When one pretends to another, both wear masks, and the whole relationship is built on a false foundation.

Now let's study those relationships that we want to rebuild. How can we set up a situation where we can have an honest conversation with a good spirit present?—not an angry, critical spirit, but a kind and respecting spirit in which we can mutually explore the points of difference between us and can look into the situations in the past that have developed antagonism? We may want to discuss our present feelings that seem to affect our relationship. Admittedly, this is a difficult and humbling experience, and we must prepare for it.

Remember that sometimes we have to resurrect the past in order to rebuild the future. Old grudges and sour memories stay with people and feed upon themselves and poison. If the spirit is right, they must be discussed with the Lord and with each other, in order to "clean the place up" so that a new and true foundation can be laid. We will discover that shallow attempts at peacemaking may calm the waters at the surface, but not the unruly turbulence underneath. The true peacemaker is not a superficial peacemaker but rather comes to grips with the real underlying forces. Sooner or later they'll crop up anyway. It's best to deal with them now. But both parties must genuinely want to do that. One cannot force it upon another, for a person trying to force another person into an honest conversation will only stoke up the existing fire.

Sometimes an appeal to a third party helps. This person can serve as an arbitrator or a discussion leader or a catalyst, and can help provide an accepting atmosphere in which feelings can be honestly and fully expressed, without fear of ridicule or criticism or "carrying it too far." Perhaps one of the local church leaders or a friend who is mutually respected may serve this useful role. His calling would be one of helping each to be understood and of creating an honest and frank, yet kind and responsive, atmosphere.

Starve the False Foundation and Feed the True

A relationship that has been based on false principles —that is, dishonesty and pride, pretense and surface peace —will inevitably have its facade shorn away and its faulty foundation exposed the day the storm comes. The storm will come in various ways—criticism, situations where one's motives are impugned or integrity doubted, unexpected visits from leaders, a feeling of not being understood or appreciated, time pressures, suddenly enlarged responsibilities, crises, and deadline dates. Sometimes trouble and difficulty in other areas in one's life will flow over into church work; the winds and waves will batter viciously. Eventually, every foundation will be tested for what it is, and those relationships which are built upon true foundations—upon the principles of Christ's gospel —will stand. All others will be washed out into the sea, to one degree or another. Let each person, therefore, examine each relationship, to determine the nature of its foundation. Husbands and wives must do this. Parents must do it in analyzing their relationships with their children. Church officers and teachers must do it to understand their relationships with other officers and teachers, with their leaders, and also each individual in their class.

Let's avoid two mistakes: first, that of feeding a true foundation without starving the false one, and second, that of merely starving a false foundation without feeding the true one. Both processes must go on simultaneously; for instance, if we have a relationship that has been based on pretense and mask wearing and insincerity, with criticism and faultfinding behind each other's backs, then stop the faultfinding and the pretending. Then it may be necessary to have an honest conversation, and even to be humble enough to confess our own fault and to ask forgiveness and then to grant forgiveness—whether asked of us or not. Then continue to live those three basic laws —the "law of Moses" and of preparation and of Christ— so that sincerity and genuineness and kind acts characterize the new and developing relationship.

Be patient. Relationships take time to rebuild. They cannot be rushed. We cannot overload the circuit by pushing things, or we will short-circuit it. The relationship is in its infancy, and it will mature gradually and naturally, just as a child grows—gradually and naturally—unless its anxious parents tend to push that growth or become critical because it doesn't come fast enough. Each must acknowledge the right of the other to grow at his own pace. Each must respect the other's feelings.

Practice of these attitudes and skills may seem awkward at first. Just as our first attempt to teach felt awkward, or to give instruction at a large dance felt awkward, or to ski or play tennis or the piano for the first time, there is always an awkward period when the skill must be developed through practice. But those who are impatient, trained in the short-cut philosophy of life, don't like this awkward phase. It feels unnatural to them. They sometimes claim it makes them feel insincere and hypocritical, and then they give up the practice.

Take an individual who finds it difficult to express warmth and appreciation. He feels love, but it's hard to express it, and he feels it's sometimes dangerous to express it because of possible mistakes and blunders, just as in playing tennis or playing the piano for the first time, so he ceases the practice, saying, "I don't want to be insincere." To this degree every learner is insincere because he feels awkward and unnatural. But sincerity is not defined by past habit. It is defined by feeling and desire. As long as we feel a warmth and appreciation, we should express it. The expression involves practice, and it will be hard at first, but as President Heber J. Grant stated, "That which we persist in doing becomes easier—not that the nature of the thing has changed, but that our ability to do has increased."

A starving man feels hungry and seeks desperately for food. Any habit will seek food for survival, including the habits of faultfinding and backbiting and criticizing. Often the only source of unity between two individuals is their criticism of a third. The relationship will hunger for such food if it is deprived. It's important to accept this hunger, to live with it for a while, until the new food begins to bring its own kind of satisfaction, to establish new habits—habits of right thinking and kindly acting, the habits of looking for the good in people, the habits of listening respectfully to them.

The old man must die so that the new birth will take place. The old foundation must be torn down so that a new one can be erected. There are death pangs, and there is the travail of the birth—the new birth. This is part of the dynamics behind the principle of repentance.

To rebuild badly deteriorated relationships is not easy, but it is much easier to accept fundamentally that it is not easy, and that it will require sustained and sincere and real effort, than to think that one good "make-up period" will do the job. The foundation may be temporarily rebuilt and seem strong and good, but if it is built again on false principles, or not continually worked at, then another storm, in some way, someday, will come and wash it back out into the sea.

The usual tendency is to judge and reject when people do not live up to our expectations. Take the students in a class. It's easy to accept them when they behave in good and lovable ways, but what is our reaction when they become unlovable? Is our attitude one of acceptance—not of their behavior, but of the person— or one of rejection? Can we say, "There, but for the grace of God, go I"? When someone confronts us with hostility, do we fail to develop a counter-hostility and then try to understand how he feels? To accept others as they are is to respect them as moral equals, to appreciate each person's personal worth, to recognize fully everyone's right to be different and to be himself, to feel kindly disposed toward him, interested in him, desirous of knowing him better.

This is not the law of the world. The Scribes and Pharisees accepted their own and rejected all else. Christ's law is a higher law—the law of the second mile, of turning the other cheek, of loving one's enemy, of praying for those who persecute and despitefully use us. Why? Why should one love the unlovable? Because of the intrinsic worth of each individual soul as a child of God! Because of our faith in their innate, Godlike potential! To treat people in terms of this potential is to help them to fulfill it. To judge and reject them serves to freeze this potential within them.

For instance, take Tom, a "cut-up" student in a class. Do we notice how he responds to moral judgments and rejection of others with aggression, hostility, and resentment? It seems to fire him up so he can get more laughs and recognition from the other students. In this mood he doesn't have the desire or the capacity to change. Moreover, as one person said, "The mutually hostile feelings completely block the only kind of communication that might lead to mutual understanding. The situation tends to deteriorate rather than to improve when there is rejection. It is unpleasant and disturbing to be rejected. It is deeply satisfying to be accepted." Accept Tom as a person who has a problem. Try to build a relationship with him—an individual one, based on true principles and on unguarded and genuine communication. He'll open up with us if he trusts us not to betray him; and as he opens up, because he knows we really like him, he'll have the courage to look honestly at himself and his behavior, and he'll learn from his experience and from us.

Understand People—Don't Label Them

Think of an individual with whom we have a poor relationship. See if our mind doesn't immediately give us labels that we attach to him—cold, indifferent, dominating, hypocritical, insincere, ambitious. What is he? Think of all these adjectives as labels. Are we sure we understand what he is? Have we ever tried to understand him and to see the world from his point of view? To do so will be difficult, because we'll have to listen, and this will take some real *humility*. If we listen, we may change, and this will take *courage*. We also have to believe that a good purpose will be served, which will take *faith*.

Very few people have ever really experienced the feeling of being completely understood. When they experience it, it can become one of the richest feelings they have ever had. Truly, to listen to another with understanding requires a sincere desire plus practice, practice, and more practice, but it amounts to about the richest form of human affirmation and acceptance there is.

It is amazing to see the power in honest listening. Many deteriorated relationships can be rebuilt through the process of sincere listening—listening that strives to understand. If we work on the assumption that people behave as they do for a good reason and that from their point of view they are right, and if we strive to understand their point of view, we will inevitably find both of us moving a little closer to each other. We will discover that many of our earlier disagreements were misunderstandings, and with the others we will "agree to disagree agreeably."

One who has successfully rebuilt a relationship that had deteriorated will also discover all his relationships improved, including the one with himself.

15

Be A Light, Not A Judge

The wife is upset because her husband just doesn't seem to spend enough time with her. No communication anymore. The husband is irritated because his wife doesn't understand the pressures on his life. She doesn't appreciate what he's trying to do. Their son Bill is frustrated because he can't take the car when he wants it. And all these time restrictions really get to him!

Daughter Susan wishes her parents would get off her back over the way she wears her hair and the length of her skirts. And, would you believe, she can't date until she's 16!

Marvin, a college student, simply can't understand why the Church doesn't take a stand on more social issues. Sacrament meetings simply bore him—"so irrelevant."

These complaints aren't so abnormal. Think about some of yours. Don't you sometimes feel that if such and such a person would change, things would surely work out better for you? If only your boss would really recognize your ability and use you properly, what a contributor you could be! If only your wife would understand more and nag less. If only your husband would sense your need to get out of the house and to have some adult conversation. If only the Sunday School teacher would stop talking about her own life and get into the doctrine.

Notice the underlying thread in this complaining, murmuring, and stone throwing. If only others would change, or if the circumstance would change, then I'd improve. I'd change. Things would go well again.

In a very real sense this kind of thinking brought about the crucifixion of the Savior. The people of that day, who ultimately crucified him, also looked for the situation to change "out there." Their Messiah was to come in great power and glory and overthrow the Roman taskmasters and enthrone Israel into its rightful place again. This is somewhat comparable with many of today's protests—others are to change, the government should do this or that, the establishment better "get with it or else," the youth should learn the lessons of life and appreciate what we have given them, etc., etc.

But the Savior taught a hard doctrine, perhaps the hardest doctrine of all. It is the doctrine of repentance. It is the doctrine that says that I must change in order to help change the world. It is the doctrine that the only revolution with any permanent value is the one that takes place in the breast of man. It is the doctrine of being "born again." Basically, it is the doctrine of accepting responsibility for one's own life and situation and for our attitude toward whatever happens to us.

Mote-Beam Sickness

The Savior asked,

"And why beholdest thou the mote that is in they brother's eye, but considerest not the beam that is in thine own eye?

"Or how wilt thou say to thy brother, let me pull the mote out of thine eye; and, behold, a beam is in thine own eye?

"Thou hypocrite, first cast out the beam out of thine own eye; and then shalt thou see clearly to cast out the mote out of thy brother's eye." (Matthew 7:3-5.)

Great truths are given to us here. First, there is a strong, almost universal, tendency to find the fault in another; that is, the mote that is in our brother's eye.

Second, when we focus on this mote, his fault, we don't focus on the beam or fault in our own life.

Third, in this spirit we often try to correct another. It doesn't work. We may have a correct opinion but our spirit is wrong. Then we hurt, reject, offend, and threaten. Spirit, or attitude, communicates far more powerfully than opinions or gilded words.

Fourth, because of the beam in our own eye, we are unable to see clearly. Our judgment, or opinion, may be entirely wrong. We may be merely projecting our own weakness and calling it his or hers. We may mistake introspection for observation. Perhaps this is what Paul meant when he said:

"Therefore thou art inexcusable, O man, whosoever thou art that judgest: for wherein thou judgest another, thou condemnest thyself; for thou that judgest doest the same things." (Romans 2:1.)

How widespread is this mote-beam sickness! Perhaps we are all afflicted by it to some degree. The doctrine of magnifying our own stewardship is the only medicine that will bring about a permanent cure.

In other words, to improve a situation, *you* must improve. To change your wife, *you* must change. To change the attitude of your husband, *you* must change your attitude. To win more freedom, *you* must be more responsible, must exercise more discipline. To raise obedient children, *you* and *I* must be more obedient to certain laws and principles.

This is not to say that we should altogether ignore the faults and weaknesses of others or that we should be blind to injustices in a situation. But it is to say that the very first step we take in improving any situation is to work on the injustice or fault in our own personal life, which helps remove the beam from our eye. "And then shalt thou see clearly to cast out the mote out of thy brother's eye." We then become a light, not a judge.

We might be terribly concerned about the various injustices in the nation, or an institution, but how just are *we* in raising our own children? Is *our* discipline consistent, based on well-established and well-communicated principles and rules, or is it based on the mood of the moment? One moment permissively indulging them, the next moment arbitrarily restraining them? Are we upset with the hypocrisy of others? Do *we* live what we profess?

"Judge not that ye be not judged. . . ." (Matthew 7:1.)

Again, what is the medicine that will cure this mote-beam sickness? It is a principle, the understanding of which will eliminate the confusion as to when we are to judge and when we are not to judge—the principle of stewardship.

The principle of stewardship is the principle of focusing on your own responsibility, on your own assignment, whatever that might be. You so focus on your duty as to magnify it, that is, to do more than is normally expected, to make more out of it than existed before. For instance, as a husband you focus on your responsibility of being a noble example to your children and a kind, understanding companion to your wife. You are the patriarch of the family; and if you live and seek for the Lord's direction and help, he will inspire you with righteous judgment. You are called to exercise such a judgment, just as a bishop does over his area of stewardship and as our prophet does over his area of stewardship.

Cain became so bitter over Abel's righteous stewardship that he neglected his own, and in his insane jealousy he murdered his brother.

Peter counseled wives who had the word and whose husbands did not obey the gospel that if they wanted to bring their husbands to the word, then they should do it without the use of the word. (See 1 Peter 3:1-6.)

There are young people who would win ever so much more right and privilege and trust from their parents if they would be diligent and cheerful in doing their work and obeying their parents. I've personally seen scores of young people get permission to join the Church from parents who initially said no, by simply not arguing or preaching or contending at home and by cheerfully and quietly doing more than what was asked of them. It takes time and it takes patience, but the power of example is the highest source of influence.

All of us are interested in things outside of our stewardship, and we should be, but the most important way to do anything about them is to magnify *our own* stewardship. This builds trust and confidence and our responsibilities and opportunities to influence increase. "Well done, thou good and faithful servant: thou hast been faithful over a few things, I will make thee ruler over many things. . . ." (Matthew 25:21.)

Take a magnifying glass and notice how it enlarges that which it is placed over and how blurry your peripheral vision is. Now remove the glass. Observe your tendency to look all around the thing you focused on earlier. Where a person focuses on his own responsibility, he becomes relatively unconcerned with other people's stewardships. But when he doesn't magnify his own stewardship and is not a light himself, he looks at the stewardship of everybody else and becomes a judge.

All of this is a simple, almost self-evident principle. But I believe few of us really live it. Do a little introspection and find your own tendency. Once we can accept this principle, it is amazing how clear and simple becomes the path of duty and how freed we are from the habit of finding fault elsewhere and excusing ourselves, justifying, explaining.

The wise Solomon put the matter this way: "Keep thy heart with all diligence; for out of it are the issues of life." (Proverbs 5:23.)

The highest form of influence is to be a model, not a critic; a light, not a judge.

16

The Key to the Ninety-nine Is the One

After a zone leader's meeting in the mission field, one of the missionary leaders approached his mission president and expressed appreciation for the meeting, and then made a rather strange remark. "For the first time since I have been in the mission field, I can believe and accept your expression of appreciation and affection for me."

"Why would you say that, Elder? You have been out here eighteen months. What is it that made you feel this way now?"

"Remember in the meeting when we were talking about that elder in that far-off city, and how his zone leaders gave such a critical report of his rebelliousness and slothfulness?"

"Yes, I remember that."

"Well, I sensed as the report was being given, and as the other elders chipped in their two-bits on this elder, that you sincerely cared for him as a person."

"I do sincerely care for him. I am concerned."

"But it was more than that. As you questioned the zone leaders back and forth, I felt you were really looking for a way to help him, and that you really cared for him, if you know what I mean."

"I'm not sure I do know what you mean. Besides, why would this make such a particular impression upon you?"

"Well, that's the very point. You sincerely do care about us as individuals and want to help us. You see, I am rebellious too—only you don't know it. Whenever I am around you I am always on my guard and trying to make the best impression. But many times I get very rebellious inside myself, and so critical about my companion, about mission rules and about a lot of things. But I just never let on as that elder does.

"So all through these months when you have expressed your affection for me, and when you have congratulated me on my work, inside I kept saying to myself, he doesn't really know me. If he really knew what I was like, he wouldn't say that. But this afternoon when you didn't join in on some of the sarcasm and laughter over this elder's antics, I felt that even if you did know what I was really like you would still have sincere regard and care for me too. I am so glad I had that experience in the meeting. Otherwise I wouldn't even have the courage to tell you what I've just told you. I would have been too afraid of disappointing you and of opening up too much of myself. But now I feel you would accept me and try to understand and to help."

To the mission president this sobering experience taught him an invaluable principle of human influence—that the way to inspire and preserve the many (the 99) is in the treatment given to the one. Going after the one "lost sheep" results not in neglecting the 99, but in effectively reaching them.

Test it for yourself. What happens inside you when someone in your company maliciously rips into another? What happens inside you when a teacher is caustic and sarcastic and always trying to give the clever, cute answer? Are you willing to open up and expose your thinking and feeling to such a one?

What happens inside you when a leader confides in you about one of your fellow workers in a critical way, or when you see a leader behind the scenes making arbitrary decisions—manipulating the lives of others—and then in public expressing sincere interest in their views and feelings?

Such leadership communicates powerfully the insincerity and egotism of the leader. It also tells you what your limits are. You had better watch out—you may be the next one to get it! How do you know he doesn't confide in others about you behind your back? that you are not being manipulated also?

It is impossible to violate a true principle of justice and honor toward one without, in this sense, violating it toward everyone else.

Now consider the opposite. What happens in you when you see a teacher or leader respectfully listen to another or go out of his way to serve another, particularly someone who might be a little obnoxious or rebellious or indifferent? Does it not communicate worth to you also?

What happens inside you when this teacher or leader refuses to gossip, label, stereotype, or slander another— someone freed of the need of sarcasm, or cutting humor, of cynicism? Aren't you more willing to trust him, to open up with him, to seek help with your problem from him?

What about our children? Could it be that the key to influencing all of them lies partly in how we treat one of them, particularly the most difficult one, in the presence of the others?

Is the Lord also teaching us that in some sense all of us are lost sheep?

Considering which commandments or teachings we measure ourselves by, aren't we all somewhat inactive in the Church, and, therefore, in need of each other's encouragement rather than labeling? One person may be inactive in his church attendance, or in keeping the Word of Wisdom, while another is inactive in living the law of love or the principle of forgiveness.

Test this principle by using it. Do it at home, in the classroom, in the office, in the planning session, over the pulpit. Think about the one, talk to the one, regard the one, serve the one. If you are sincere and constant, you will discover that gradually your influence with the many will be magnified.

The key to the 99 is the one. Or put in another way, the key to the group is the one individual.

17

Two Principles in
Motivating Others From Within

I. *Involve Them in the Problem*

Parents, teachers, leaders, and employers are all concerned with how to get others to feel and act responsibly.

I suggest one principle that can be highly effective in developing a sense of responsibility: involve the people in the problem and then work out the solution together.

I give two personal illustrations. First: one night I was visiting alone with my oldest daughter about some of her problems and feelings and concerns. After I listened for awhile, she then asked me if I had any problems I wanted to talk about. I decided to open up with a problem that had irritated my wife and me for sometime—that of getting the children down and in bed on time with pleasantness so they have sufficient sleep and we can have a little time for ourselves.

What happened amazed me. She asked a few questions about the problem and sensed my concern. And then she came up with some of the most ingenious ideas and suggestions on what might solve it. But, more importantly, she herself became involved in the problem and this developed in her a sense of responsibility to help in the solution. Since she is my oldest child and has good influence on the others, her responsible involvement literally solved most of the problem.

Prior to this visit we had only "talked solutions" to our children and, consequently, we had retained the responsibility to implement them. And this was the problem!

Second illustration: I want my two cars in good running order, without having to worry or take time to check up or follow through. That was my problem. What to do?

Again, the principle: involvement. So I frankly shared my problem with the manager of a service station I had patronized and expressed my trust in him and his judgment.

The moment he felt involved in my problem, he became responsible. And how responsible he became! He took care of my cars as if they were his own—personally servicing, making preventive check-ups, giving me the "best deals" on purchases. Result? Low-cost, trouble-free service without time or worry on my part. The key? My service station man developed a moral responsibility when I trusted and involved him.

An MIA teacher used this principle one night in her class. She felt physically ill and was struggling with the lesson. The students were noisy and irresponsible. She didn't quite know what to do, so she candidly shared her problem, including how she felt at that moment. Her students immediately became responsible and carried on beautifully, receiving only occasional direction from their teacher, whom they had sit in the back. Once involved, they became responsible. Once responsible, they became part of the solution rather than part of the problem.

The most enlightened leaders and business managers throughout the country have been adopting this very principle in one way or another. They have learned that it is only when people are sincerely and meaningfully involved that they are willing to commit the best that is within them. When a person identifies his personal goal with the goal of an institution, an enormous release of human energy, creativity, and loyalty results.

Why does this principle work? Most know inside what is right, but often they do not feel responsible. However, when they are trusted enough to hear some of the facts of a problem situation that includes them, along with the feelings and anxieties of those who are affected by it, then they want to help, to respond. This honors them, and they feel to give their best ideas, their cooperation and support.

But when the solution to the problem is given along with the facts, they feel robbed of the opportunity to do something good on their own, to use their own initiative and creativity, to act rather than to always be acted upon. Thus the responsibility stays with the one proposing the solution.

Consequently, many parents find themselves carrying the responsibility to get their children to bed on time, up on time, to the table on time, to school on time—things that the children can do for themselves if they really want to and feel responsible.

And for the same reasons many teachers and leaders find themselves needing to always check up, to threaten, to motivate externally. They have never learned how to develop internal motivation.

There are certainly many problems and many situations in which parents or leaders or teachers simply do not have time to involve the people. Moreover, the solution often has already been decided upon, and any attempt at involving or democratic problem-solving would be ritualistic and insincere—and eventually would boomerang.

However, when the principle of sincere involvement is used in situations of vital and personal interest to the others, a trust develops in the fairness and wisdom of those making some unilateral decisions, and the willingness to cooperate and obey, even without understanding, generally follows. In a sense they say, as did Adam, "I know not, save the Lord commanded me." (Moses 5:6.)

Experiment with this principle. It will take genuine humility and honesty, and it must not be used to manipulate someone into coming around to your own viewpoint or decision. You must be open and influenceable; then, ironically, you will also discover an increase in your own power to influence.

Remember this—when the nature of the solution requires the cooperation, commitment, and involvement of others, then you had better involve them in the problem in the first place.

II. Trust

He was just a little boy. Only six years old. And that's a mighty big job—to have full responsibility for a yard that size!

What an interesting three-step process this determined dad went through to teach his son responsibility.

Step 1—training. He spent considerable time over a two-week period, training his son in exactly what the job entailed—turning on sprinklers front, back, and side each day; hand-watering the shrubs and areas not reached by the sprinklers; and picking up any clutter. Not much, really, but quite a bit for a six-year-old. The boy chose this job himself one family home evening when all the jobs were being volunteered for or assigned.

Step 2—committing. In the middle of the second week of training the father said, "Son, next Saturday I'm going to ask you if you will fully take this job of keeping the entire yard green and clean just as we've been doing together. It won't be my job anymore. It'll be your job. If I have time, I'll help if you ask. I don't care so much how you do it or when you do it. All I care is that the yard is always clean and green. Okay, son?"

"Okay, dad."

That following Saturday the boy, after another visit on all that was expected, committed himself to take the full responsibility of keeping the yard clean and green.

Step 3—becoming a source of help. The father returned home from work the following Tuesday and noticed paper strewn around and the lawn becoming slightly yellow. All he needed to do was to take two steps away from the car and turn the water key, and most of the large front yard would be watered. How simple! How easy! But he knew that if he did so he would take back the responsibility he had given. And his son would have been delighted—for he obviously enjoyed playing with his friends more than tending the yard.

But he stuck to his guns. He did nothing. He said nothing.

The next night things looked worse. His son simply wasn't doing his job. The clean, manicured yards of his neighbors were an embarrassing contrast to his own cluttered, yellowing yard. He thought of the expense if things began to die. He even wondered if he hadn't given too much responsibility for one so little. But again he determined that the character growth of his son was more valuable than things, and he refused to take over.

He asked his son if the two of them could walk around to see how things were going. The son agreed. After he sheepishly walked around the yard, he finally exclaimed, "Oh, Dad, it's so hard!" to which the Dad responded, "Anything I could help you with? I have a few minutes."

"Oh good—wait there," his son instructed, running into the house. When he reappeared, he had two sacks, and he directed his father to clean up a portion of the front while he took the other. A few minutes later the son took the father's sack, thanked him, emptied it in the garbage can, and turned on the front sprinklers. Look at who was beginning to direct whom!

Within two more weeks that son really felt the responsibility. He knew that if he didn't do it, no one would. He knew that his father depended on him—trusted him—and he was not going to let him down.

It became "his" yard. His brothers and sisters had better watch out if they "threw stuff" around the place!

He was supervised by his own sense of responsibility, his conscience. There was no need for the father to judge or supervise, coddle or threaten, or worry when away on trips.

It is not always this easy or this simple, but there are some significant principles involved in this homely but true story for us all. Look again at the three steps.

1. The training process is essential.

Most parents or leaders fall short in this training and delegating process. They reason that it's just too time consuming, and they assume the assignee clearly understands what the assignment is and will want to do it well. Both assumptions are often wrong. Then, in the long run, this supervisor spends much more time in externally motivating and in clearing up misunderstandings, which often spawn worse problems, such as strained relationships, personality conflicts, and bad morale.

2. A point of mutual understanding is reached in the training process when the assignee commits himself to do the job. If the training is well done and the communication two-way, this commitment will be honest, deep, and realistic and will internalize the source of motivation or supervision from then on. If the training is rushed and the communication one way and guarded, then the commitment will be shallow and easily uprooted with the first obstacle or storm. Then the supervisor will become critical and find it ncessary to "hover over" and to motivate with social rewards and punishments.

Thus, he has essentially taken back the responsibility —or, better put, he never really delegated it in the first place.

3. Once a commitment is made, the supervisor or leader becomes a source of help, not a judge. If the assignee is falling down on the job, the supervisor's attitude is one of trusting, of "How can I help?" An assignee may ask for more training or he may ask for a new job or assignment, honestly admitting this one is too much for him.

These three steps are interwoven and feed back and forth on each other. Successfully performing them requires considerable character strength, faith, and patience in the leader or parent.

Many lack such strength, and many assignees and children are so conditioned to irresponsibility and to hovering supervision that this trust philosophy of motivation cannot always be immediately implemented. Again, it will take time and character strength.

Trust is the highest form of human motivation.

IV

COMMUNICATION:
A Two-way Process

18

With God: Prayer

Prayer, or communicating with the Lord, is in many ways similar to communicating or talking with another person. Let us explore five of these ways and then consider six principles of prayer.

I.   Any true communication is a two-way process.

It is a dialogue, not a monologue. We all experience from time to time how unsatisfying and boring it is to have a conversation with someone when there is nothing of mutual interest. Words may be exchanged but meaning is not. One might pretend to listen but not really listen. Eventually this will become evident.

But whenever we experience a genuine talk with someone, even though it may be about a subject of little importance, if both are interested in it, how satisfying such a communication is. It is not the importance of the subject so much as the depth of interest that matters. For instance, two individuals may find questions of war and peace in the world, although terribly significant, of little interest, while the subject of how to tie a fly for fly fishing may unite and even enthrall them.

Thus, in a communication with the Lord, the first requirement before it will be a two-way process is that we have a *genuine* and *real* interest in the things that the Lord is interested in.

When that interest is mutual, a dialogue will naturally take place. Otherwise a one-way, mechanical effort or monologue—almost like going down a check list out of a sense of duty—is inevitable.

II. Communication is mutual understanding.

That is, persons need sufficient dialogue back and forth with each other as to be certain that they understand each other. With the Lord also, our communication should result in mutual understanding. We must become open and honest in our expression of feeling and thought, in our effort to understand ourself, to be understood by the Lord, and to understand him. If we are not sufficiently open and honest with ourself, we may not be ablt to distinguish between a self voice of doubt or fear or hope or guilt—or whatever it may be—and his voice. Then we will not be able to understand him and his will for us. Therefore, there will be no mutual understanding, no communication.

III. True communication results in mutual influence.

When people truly understand each other, they are open to each other's influence; but until a person feels understood, he cannot be influenced, because he feels that whatever is told him doesn't quite pertain to him in his own unique situation. For instance, suppose your child is sick and you desperately telephone your doctor, but before you feel you have accurately described the symptoms, he gives you a prescription and some advice. You can't help but feel some distrust toward this advice. It wasn't based upon understanding.

Does this mean that communicating with the Lord is a process of mutual influence, that not only I am influenced by the Lord but that the Lord is also influenced? Yes, I believe it means exactly that. The scriptures are replete with examples of how the Lord's behavior toward us is influenced by our behavior toward him. He indicates that he works with us and through us according to the level of our faith. (See Ether 12 and Moroni 7.) If we have a higher level of faith, we become just that much better—

a willing, obedient servant, one with whom he can work and whom he can use to serve his divine purposes. Therefore, our belief in him, our trust in him, our faith in him, as well as our doings and actions, influence his behavior toward us.

IV. The crucial dimension is the relationship.

Another highly significant way in which communicating with the Lord is similar to communicating with other people is that it is not so much a matter of words as it is of relationships. All of us have been in situations in which, because relationships were strained, we had to be very careful about the words we used for fear of giving offense, causing a scene, or being misunderstood. In such situations, how easy it is for further misunderstandings to take place. People become suspicious and distrustful, making a man "an offender for a word" instead of attempting to gather in the meaning of his words.

Each of us has been in situations in which the relationships were so unified and so harmonious we could almost communicate without words. In fact, there was so much mutual understanding and good feeling that we didn't have to watch our communication technique at all. Sometimes people can almost grunt and nod with each other and still have an understanding. I've been in situations in which my relationships were so well established that one word or even a nod or a smile would communicate a world of meaning. I have also been in other situations in which the relationship was not so established and a chapter of words wasn't sufficient to communicate meaning. People who work with words are called semanticists, and one of the basic rules is that "meanings are not found in words—they are found in people."

The important thing in all of this as it relates to prayer is that our communication with God is more a matter of our relationship with him than the words we might use.

The Savior in both the meridian dispensation and this last dispensation explicitly condemned those who draw near to him with their lips but are far from him with their hearts. In other words, they may say they are interested in the Lord's things but their heart is on other things. The relationship is strained. They are like strangers with each other. "For how knoweth a man the master whom he has not served, and who is a stranger unto him, and is far from the thoughts and intents of his heart?" (Mosiah 5:13.)

V. The key to the relationship is trust.

Trust is born by having had experiences with each other that are trustworthy or honorable. If I make a promise to a person and don't keep it, then I don't feel good toward him or myself. When I walk down the street, I try to walk on the side opposite him. If I see him, I don't look in his eye. There has been a strain, and a literal, though unseen, barrier has been erected between us. If I repent and go to him to seek his forgiveness and try to make reconciliation, I can do away with that barrier. If I try to rationalize within myself—that is, if I tell myself rational lies, such as that he was untrue to me at such and such a time, so it doesn't make any difference if I don't keep this particular promise—then I will erect a barrier between us, a barrier that will be inside me.

Therefore, in summary, *prayer must be a two-way process resulting in both mutual understanding and mutual influence, and it is a matter of relationship, not words, born of having trustworthy experiences with each other.* This now leads us to the discussion of six vital principles of prayer or divine communication. By using your imagination and changing the words somewhat, these same six principles would pertain to human communication.

Six Principles of Prayer

Principle No. 1: Preparing.

Take out your Pearl of Great Price and read the Joseph Smith story. You'll discover that this young man of 14 years of age had, perhaps unknowingly, made a tremendous preparation for his first vocal prayer with God, which resulted in the transcendent vision and appearance of the Father and the Son and which opened up this last dispensation. Read carefully his words. As you do so, think of all that his mind might have been going through:

"During this time of great excitement my mind was called up to serious reflection and great uneasiness; but though my feelings were deep and often poignant, still I kept myself aloof. . . . In process of time my mind became somewhat partial to the Methodist sect, and I felt some desire to be united with them; but so great were the confusion and strife. . . .

"My mind at times was greatly excited, the cry and tumult were so great and incessant. . . .

"In the midst of this war of words and tumult of opinions, I often said to myself: What is to be done? . . .

"While I was laboring under the extreme difficulties caused by the contests of these parties of religionists, I was one day reading the Epistle of James. . . .

"Never did any passage of scripture come with more power to the heart of man than this did at this time to mine. It seemed to enter with great force into every feeling of my heart. I reflected on it again and again. . . .

"At length I came to the conclusion that I must either remain in darkness and confusion, or else I must do as James directs, that is, ask of God. . . .

"So, in accordance with this, my determination to ask of God, I retired to the woods to make the attempt. . . .

"After I had retired to the place where I had previously designed to go, having looked around me, and finding myself alone, I kneeled down and began to offer up the desire of my heart to God. . . ." (Joseph Smith 2:8-15.)

What a tremendous process of mental and emotional preparation this young man went through! He developed both a strong desire to ask God for wisdom and the faith that he would receive it.

Four important activities are helpful in this preparation process:

a. *Study the scriptures.* The scriptures contain the mind and will of the Lord, and if we sincerely and conscientiously read them in an effort to understand his mind and will, not just for the people of ancient times, but for us of this time, we gradually, in a sense, put on a pair of glasses. When we wear glasses, we look through lenses that affect all that we see. If we were to look through an eternal lens at temporal and wordly things, we would see them in an entirely new perspective. If we have the words of eternal life flowing continually over our minds because we diligently search the scriptures, we are, in a sense, looking through glasses with eternal lenses. We begin to think and feel and see things differently. Scripture study is one of the finest disciplines an individual can cultivate.

b. *Meditation.* President David O. McKay has called meditation the language of the soul. To take time to reflect and contemplate and think deeply about the things of God, our relationship with him, and our real deep needs, perhaps in an attempt to *distinguish them from our wants,* is a very subduing experience that prepares the mind and heart for prayer, which President McKay has called "the conscientious moments of meditation."

c. *Fasting.* This is an excellent way to prepare if it is done in the right spirit and if it is accompanied with meditation, prayer, and scripture study. Fasting subdues the spirit and makes an individual humble, open, and teachable, and aware of deep spiritual need. It serves as a purifying and sanctifying activity, both physically and spiritually, when done with real intent.

d. *Repentance.* Oftentimes, in preparing ourselves to worship and to pray to God, we become aware of some deficiency or sin that leads us to repent. If we have offended someone, we make reconciliation. We seek forgiveness. Of course, prayer will help us to fully repent, but often before we can pray sincerely we need to get our heart and mind freed of some static.

These four activities—diligently searching the scriptures, meditation, fasting, and repentance—cause us to become vitally interested in the things the Lord is interested in, and thereby prepare the heart and mind for two-way communication, which is embodied in the next three principles: expressing, listening, and committing.

Principle No. 2: Expressing.

We begin our communication by thanking the Lord

from our heart for his blessings. If we have adequately prepared ourselves, this expression of gratitude is deeply felt and sincerely given. If we have not adequately prepared ourselves, it might be wooden and mechanical. We also (from our hearts) express our needs, our feelings, and our requests for help, direction, guidance, and comfort. In short, we ask for the Lord's blessings. I personally believe in the importance of being very *specific*, both in the things we thank God for and the things we ask him for. To me, at least, this has helped to achieve a deeper level of sincerity, feeling, and concentration in prayer. Example: "We thank thee that our prayers were answered and Martha's operation was a success." Or, "Help us to know how to give our son Johnny a better concept of himself. Help him to feel our love and support." Or, "Please help me to gain control over my temper. I feel I lack influence with my children because of this."

I believe that *the Lord deals with his children largely in terms of their needs as he perceives them,* rather than their wants as they might perceive them. God's will is found in man's real needs, while man's will is generally embodied in man's wants.

The Lord's Prayer is a magnificent example of the general areas of *need.* First, our relationship with our Father in heaven is indicated, as we say, "Our Father which art in heaven." We give to him all of our allegiance, our loyalty, and our total being, so we say, "Hallowed be thy name." We desire to see his will done on earth and to see ourself as an instrument in that process, so we say, "Thy will be done in earth, as it is in heaven." We are aware of our temporal needs, which enable us to exist and enjoy life, so we say, "Give us this day our daily bread." We are in need of harmonious relationships with our fellow men and the inner peace that comes from forgiving and being forgiven, so we pray, "And forgive us our debts, as we forgive our debtors." We have a great need to lead a pure, clean, devoted life of service and to give the honor to the Lord, to recognize him as the source of our power, and to avoid the evils of the world; therefore we pray, "And lead us not into temptation, but deliver us from evil: for thine is the kingdom, and the power, and the glory, for ever. Amen." (See Matthew 6:9-13.)

A person may *want* to be delivered from hard work, maybe from suffering, but perhaps the growth or need of the character demands exactly these things. A young person might want and therefore will pray to be helped in school even though he did not do his own part in homework, but he may *need* to learn that if he doesn't sow he won't reap. This may be a hard and a bitter lesson, yet it is a necessary one.

If the Lord has said, "Your Father in heaven knows your need before you ask him," to me this implies that we should attempt to think and pray in terms of our needs and that if we adequately prepare ourself, we might come to understand more fully our needs or at least his will for us.

Principle No. 3: Listening.

If communication is to be two-way, it must be literally just that. As in any conversation, we talk, then we listen, and then we express ourselves again in terms of what we heard. If in our conversation we pretend to listen but continue talking along the lines we are interested in, giving no response to that which has been said to us, it is a monologue. Listen to young children; you will hear them carry on these collective monologues.

Susie: "I'm going to the zoo. As soon as my daddy comes we will go."

Mary: "Do you like my red shoes? They are new."

Susie: "I've been to the zoo before, when I was little, only I can't remember."

Mary: "My Mommy said I could choose the color of shoes I like."

Susie: "There is a real tiger and an elephant too. As soon as my daddy comes we will go."

Everyone talking and no one listening. Sometimes older people do the same thing, except they pretend to listen; they are actually forcing themselves *to be quiet* as the other person talks, while in the meantime they are preparing their next speech.

How do we listen to the Lord? In a sense, think of the heart as the ear or the listening instrument of the spirit. From my study of the scriptures, I am convinced that the heart is exactly that and the Lord's voice is the still, small voice of our own conscience that speaks to our heart. President McKay has said that *the Holy Ghost speaks through the conscience* of members of the Church who are in the line of their duty. This still, small voice can pierce to the core and center of a person's soul. It is sharper than a two-edged sword, but it must be carefully listened to, and a person must be in tune in order to hear it. ". . . and he hath spoken unto you in a still small voice, but ye were past feeling, that ye could not feel his words. . . ." (1 Nephi 17:45.)

The Lord indicated in the Book of Revelation that he is always willing to come in and speak to us if we are willing to hear and hearken.

"Behold, I stand at the door, and knock: if any man hear my voice, and open the door, I will come in to him, and will sup with him, and he with me." (Revelation 3:20.)

He didn't say, "I stood at the door." He said, "I stand at the door." He didn't say, "The prophet (or the bishop or the president) hears my voice." He said, "If any man hear my voice, and open the door, I will come in to him, and will sup with him, and he with me."

I believe that most of us, particularly those who are members of the Church, have an internal, moral guide and compass that literally speaks to us most of the time. I believe that all men have some divine spark that becomes a divine conscience (the spirit of Jesus Christ). A person might also develop a social conscience out of his environmental upbringing, but I believe the divine conscience may be separate from this. The divine conscience might be dulled and numbed by transgression and the traditions that form the social conscience, but for almost all people, if they are willing to listen, there is a still, small divine voice that speaks to them deep inside. If they would follow that light, they would receive more light, and the voice would become more clear and plain and understandable to them. And the scripture tells us that the light would grow brighter and brighter, "line upon line, precept upon precept."

In the *Adventures of Huckleberry Finn,* Huck said:

"It made me shiver. And I about made up my mind to pray and see if I couldn't try to quit being the kind of boy I was and be better. So I kneeled down. But the words wouldn't come. Why wouldn't they? It weren't no use to try and hide it from Him. . . . I knowed very well why they wouldn't come. It was because my heart warn't right; it was because I weren't square; it was because I was playing double. I was letting on to give up sin, but away inside of me I was holding on to the biggest one of all. I was trying to make my mouth say I would do the right thing and the clean thing. But deep down in me, I knowed it was a lie, and He knowed it. You can't pray a lie. . . . I found that out."

In a sense, Huck Finn was listening to this still, small voice, his conscience, which revealed to him his dishonesty and hypocrisy. He obviously was in need of more preparation, of making his mind up about a few things.

In other words, carefully searching the scriptures, meditating, fasting, making reconciliation, confessing— these activities are often necessary before a person will be open enough to carry on two-way communication with the Lord.

Over the last few years I have experimented, while speaking to various audiences, with this principle of listening. I have asked people to take a minute to meditate on some of their own spiritual needs, to listen very carefully to the still, small voice of their own conscience regarding things they should do to draw closer to the Lord or to their husband or wife, or the things they should do to more fully magnify their church calling or their priesthood. I have asked them again and again if they could recognize and hear or feel a distinct voice, not in their ear but in their heart, giving them specific guidance and counsel—in fact, perfect guidance that they absolutely knew they needed and should follow. The inevitable response has always been that the people do hear (feel) this voice, that it is distinct and discernible, that it subdues their spirit, and that they recognize their need.

I will never forget my most memorable, inspirational experience with this principle of listening to the still, small voice. I was representing our Church at a "Religion in Life Week" at the University of Arizona at Tucson. A Jewish rabbi, a Catholic father, a liberal Protestant priest, an orthodox Protestant priest, and a Mormon elder had been invited to represent their various religious faiths and introduce their viewpoints to problems and issues of current interest. This was part of an attempt by the university to bring a religious dimension into the classroom and into the social clubs.

On the second night I was invited to speak at a sorority-fraternity exchange at a sorority house on the subject of "the new morality." The house was packed with about one hundred and fifty young people. They were sitting in the front room, in the dining room, in the hallway, and up the stairs. I had a terrific sense of being overwhelmed and surrounded, and I felt very alone.

The "new morality" is a situational ethic based on the idea that there are no absolute truths and standards but that each situation must be looked at in terms of the people involved as well as other factors that might be present. I put forth my point of view and my conviction that there is a God, that there are absolute truths and standards that have been revealed, and that the "new morality" is merely a rationalized old immorality. I sensed throughout my entire presentation considerable resistance and disbelief. When it came to the question and answer period, two articulate students began to express themselves strongly in favor of this situational ethic of the "new morality." One was particularly effective and persuasive and acknowledged to the entire group that he knew it would be wrong for young people who were unmarried to live together as man and wife; he said that he wasn't advocating any evil thing, but that love is so sacred and so beautiful, if an unmarried man and woman truly and deeply loved each other enough, then premarital relationship would be logical and right.

Though I sensed considerable support for this point of view, I continued to express my beliefs and quoted some scriptures to support them. I sensed there was little faith in my scriptural support, and to many of these students I was pretty much "out of it." I tried to reason that terrible consequences resulted from breaking the law of chastity. The particularly persuasive student on the front row agreed and indicated that the individuals involved were to be careful and responsible and unselfish but certainly not to be prudish. I asked him directly what would happen if a person were to take poison unknowingly. Would it not still bring on terrible consequences? He answered that it was poor analogy; that I wasn't giving enough value to the freedom that genuine love grants.

I remembered praying inwardly for some help and direction, and I came to feel that I should teach the idea of listening to the still, small voice of the Lord, of their conscience. I quoted the scripture earlier mentioned, Revelation 3, and indicated that if they would listen very carefully, they would hear a voice. It wouldn't be audible, and they wouldn't hear it in their ear, but they would hear or feel it deep inside, in their heart. I challenged them to listen, to meditate very quietly, and I gave them the promise that if they would do this, they would hear or feel this voice. Many sneered and jeered at this idea.

I responded to this ridicule by renewing the challenge: I asked each person to try it for himself, and if each person did not hear such a voice in one minute, the group could immediately dismiss me and I wouldn't waste any more of their time. This sobered them, and most appeared willing to experiment. I asked them to be very quiet and to do no talking, but to listen internally and ask themselves, "Is chastity, as it has been explained this evening, a true principle or not?"

The first few seconds some looked around to see who was going to take this business seriously, but within about twenty seconds almost every person was sitting quietly and appeared to be very intent in thinking and listening. Many bowed their heads. After a full minute of this silence, which probably seemed like an eternity to some, I looked at the individual at my left who had been so persuasive and vocal and said to him, "In all honesty, my friend, what did you hear?"

He responded, quietly but directly, "What I heard I did not say."

I turned to another who had been disagreeing and I asked him what he had heard.

He answered, "I do not know—I just don't know. I'm not certain any more."

One fellow stood up spontaneously in the rear. "I want to say something to my fraternity brothers I have never said before. I believe in God." Then he sat down.

A totally different spirit came to that group, a spirit that had distilled gradually and silently during that minute of silence. I believe it was the spirit of the Lord or the spirit of Jesus Christ that they felt inside. It had some interesting effects upon them. For one thing, they became subdued and quiet and rather reverent from then on. For another, it communicated worth to them. They became less intellectual and defensive and more open and teachable. I believe it also met a real need and confirmed some hopes and perhaps convicted others.

It was easy to teach from then on. I felt as if seed was falling on fertile soil. I was enabled to bear witness of the living Christ, the restored gospel of Jesus Christ, and the divinity of the Book of Mormon as concrete evidence of this restoration. I invited many to come out to the Institute of Religion, and later inquiry indicated that they had. I was able to loan some copies of the Book of Mormon. Many stayed around afterward merely to talk about this matter and other spiritual and religious matters. I discussed this experience with an institute teacher the next day and he had almost an identical experience that very night.

I sometimes think we attempt to make what is simple

and natural into something that is complex, mystical, and mysterious. If we would spend a little more time meditating and listening, we would receive some immediate and perfect moral guidance, the following of which would lead us into further light and guidance, and many of our other needs and problems and queries might be answered. But when we wait for a mysterious kind of spiritual intervention to answer a far-out question or to give us guidance on a really pressing problem, but are unwilling to be true to the light we have at the present, I think we deceive ourself. God does not work this way.

A short time ago I visited with a student who asked me, his past mission president, for counsel and advice regarding a crucial decision he was to make. He didn't know whether to go on to graduate school and get married or to go into military service and delay his marriage and then go to graduate school later.

The more I got involved in the details of the alternatives, the more I sensed my own ignorance and inability to give good counsel. I asked him if he had "inquired of the Lord" about it. He said that he had and that he had done so frequently. I asked if he had listened carefully to the guidance he was receiving in many other matters, as magnifying his priesthood and keeping the commandments on a daily basis. He knew immediately what I was speaking about and acknowledged that he really hadn't been nearly as faithful as he ought to be. I then asked him if he wasn't really trying to find a shortcut by coming to me or to others for counsel, rather than living the law of the harvest in obeying the light he had been given, by being true to his present assignment and stewardship, and also continuing to inquire of the Lord over this matter, believing that God would give him guidance in his way and in his own time. He acknowledged that he was seeking a shortcut, that he was really aware of what he needed to do, and that he was also aware that if he did it, he would receive the guidance he needed.

Now what would be the next logical step after listening and hearing the still, small voice give us guidance and direction in terms of our needs on these vital matters? If we are truly engaged in two-way communication, in a sincere dialogue, and if we have expressed ourself and then listened, would it not be logical and natural to respond in terms of what we have heard? Wouldn't it be logical to tell the Lord that we would obey the guidance he had just given; that we would be true to the light we had just received?

Principle No. 4: Committing.

Once we listen and hear the still, small voice, then we must promise or commit ourself to obey it, to do that which is counseled.

This is often a difficult principle or stage because it implies that our mind is made up, whereas many times it simply is not. We know what we should do, but as the saying goes, "There is a lot of slip between cup and lip." The doing of it is another matter, and we hesitate to promise or commit ourself that we will, in fact, do it, when we are inwardly hesitating and uncertain as to whether we really will or not. Consider these examples.

> *Express:* "Heavenly Father. I don't seem to have any influence on my teen-age daughter. Please help me to have a better relationship with Annette. This is such an important period in her life."
>
> *Listen:* (What principle is this blessing predicated upon?) Is Annette *really* that important to you? Is there any double-mindedness in your life? Are you willing to take the time to develop this relationship for which you ask? Are you willing to even give up other things that matter less in order to achieve this?
>
> *No Commitment:* "Bless me to have a desire to get close to her and spend time with her so that she will know of my interest and love and concern for her welfare."

Commitment: (going on) "I will make a point to talk to her privately every day this week, and spend the afternoon with her and the family on Saturday instead of going golfing at the country club."

* * * * *

Express: "Heavenly Father. Please help me with my new calling as a stake missionary. Bless me to be effective with the discussions and bless our contacts, Mr. and Mrs. Holbrook, that they will keep their commitment and read the Book of Mormon this week as they promised to do."

Listen: Is there any power in your teaching? Can you expect the Holbrooks to keep their promise and read the Book of Mormon, when you have repeatedly promised your companion and stake mission president you would master the six discussions and twenty-seven basic scriptures and you still haven't done this?

No Commitment: "Please help me to get my discussions and scriptures memorized so I can be a better stake missionary."

Commitment: (going on) "I promise that beginning tomorrow I will get up an hour earlier and memorize the basic scriptures and conclusions in discussions three and four."

Again, the overriding importance of Principle No. 1, adequate preparation, becomes evident. If the preparation is deep and meaningful enough, then to promise and commit, having made one's mind up, will be a logical and natural step. If, however, the preparation is superficial and mechanical, or eliminated altogether, then the committing step or principle will loom as a huge, forbidding obstacle.

I believe that the principle of making commitments is central to the entire gospel plan. Another more sacred and spiritual name for a commitment is a covenant or an oath.

We are the covenant children of the Lord. Abraham made a covenant with the Lord, and the Lord, in turn, covenanted with him to bless his posterity in certain ways. Those who are either the natural or adopted offspring of Abraham and Israel may partake of these blessings through their own renewing of the covenants.

A covenant is a contract entered into by two parties and binding upon both. In the waters of baptism we enter into a covenant or promise to keep the commandments of the Lord. He, in turn, gives us a promise that if we are true to our promise, he will give us peace in this world and eternal life in the world to come. The Holy Ghost is sometimes called the Holy Spirit of Promise, which plants in man's breast a conditional promise of eternal life, regardless of the problems and afflictions that may dog his path in this world. It is my understanding that if a person is sufficiently faithful and proven in this world, the time might come either in mortality or in eternity when he will be given an unconditional promise of eternal life. I understand this to be making one's "calling and election sure."

The sacrament renews the covenant of baptism, which has in it the two-way contract or promise. We promise, or witness, unto the Father to take upon ourself the name of Jesus Christ, to keep the commandments he has given to us, and to always remember him; he in turn promises that if we do so, we will have his Spirit to be with us.

In the theologies and philosophies of men, this covenant-making philosophy has largely been either eliminated or distorted. Generally speaking, salvation is offered for a confession alone either to Jesus or to a priest, and covenants contained in ordinance work become no longer necessary for salvation. In the Book of Mormon, we are told that many plain and precious things have been taken out of the Bible and that "also many covenants of the Lord have they taken away. And all this have they done that they might pervert the right ways of the Lord, that they might blind the eyes and harden the hearts of the children of men." (1 Nephi 13:26-27.)

If Satan could eliminate or distort the concept of making covenants, he would achieve his end, for covenant making is a vital part of the divine system ordained in the premortal life for the growth and development of God's children toward eternal life.

Why is it so vital?

We are all conditioned heavily by our past experiences. These influence our present reactions and behavior, and therefore they influence our future, because our present becomes the future. If we become enslaved to our past habits and conditioning, this process will be self-reinforcing and circular and we will never be able to arise out of it.

But if we become enlightened and knowledgeable about what we should do, and we learn to marshal all of the forces within ourself, within our heart and our mind, and make a commitment in the present with the full knowledge of what cost and sacrifices that commitment may mean, all the forces within and without us will be unified, and the blessings of heaven will be secured upon us so that we can break loose of the tremendous gravity pull of the past and of past habits.

The successes of the Apollo trips to the moon highlight the influence of gravity and the power necessary to overcome it. Years of effort and billions of dollars went into the preparations before lift-off. It is impressive that most of the power expended on the celestial journeys took place at the beginning, at the time of lift-off, in breaking loose from the gravity pull of the earth. Once the rockets were freed of the earth's gravity pull, it took almost no power to move around the earth in orbit, to kick out of orbit and move to the moon, to separate the lunar module from the command module, to return to a quarter of a million miles to the earth. In fact, one of the astronauts, when asked how much power was expended when the lunar module separated from the command module to go down and survey the moon, answered, "Less than the breath of a baby."

So in life, if our commitment inside can be deep enough, and our awareness of the costs and sacrifices involved realistic enough, we can break loose of the past; and even though the energy and power necessary to do this are tremendous at the beginning, once we have broken loose of past habits and traditions and environmental influences, which have so conditioned and enslaved us before, we then have almost unlimited freedom and power to accomplish many things. True freedom, therefore, is internal, not external, as often defined by the world. *External freedom* is opportunity or the availability of alternatives to choose from, but *internal freedom* is the capacity and willingness to make such choices. A person who is heavily conditioned to one response to a particular situation has no internal freedom. He is a slave to his own passion or appetite.

All of this points up the tremendous value of making commitments or covenants with the Lord. Daily, private prayer is an ideal time to review our promises and commitments and enter into a new commitment that day to follow the counsel given through the still, small voice. The Lord has told us in our day that we are to enter into promises or vows and covenants on the Sabbath Day, but also that they are to be offered up in righteousness on all days and at all times: "Nevertheless thy vows shall be offered up in righteousness on all days and at all times." (D&C 59:11.)

My experience with this promising phase of the prayer process has taught me that it will bring more reality and sense of responsibility and honesty and true humility than can come in almost any other way except, perhaps, by the sheer force of circumstance.

A husband kneels next to his wife in prayer, praying for the blessings of peace and harmony in their home. While he prays with his lips, his heart, the "ear of the spirit," has heard the still, small voice tell him that he hasn't been as kind and considerate and understanding as he should have been toward his own wife, next to whom he was kneeling that very moment. While all blessings from God are predicated on obedience to his laws, he was seeking a blessing but was unwilling to do his part to earn it. Perhaps out of pride and stubbornness, justification and rationalization, he hasn't allowed this still, small voice to really have place in his heart and result in two-way communication. He has continued the monologue in a mechanical way, praying for the Prophet, for the general and local authorities, for national leaders, for soldiers, for missionaries, for loved ones, etc.—almost like going down a checklist, fulfilling a sense of duty before hopping into a nice, warm bed. This is hypocrisy. It is prayer without real intent. It brings its own kind of internal dishonesty and deceit, which is a form of damning or condemnation.

"And likewise also is it counted evil unto a man, if he shall pray and not with real intent of heart; yea, and it profiteth him nothing, for God receiveth none such." (Moroni 7:9.)

But if, instead, while praying with his wife, he were to hear that still, small voice tell his heart that the law upon which the blessing of harmony and peace in the home is predicated is that he himself become an example and a model of gentleness and understanding and kindness, and if he had the spirit of humility and adequate preparation in him, he could listen to what the Lord is telling him and acknowledge it, then seek his wife's forgiveness and His forgiveness. Then, having made reconciliation, he could enter back into the divine communion or dialogue and promise to be more kind, gentle, and considerate.

Unless we are willing to obey the law, should we ask for the blessing? Is that not an attempt to seek a shortcut, to avoid the responsibility, and thus to thwart the Lord's principle of growth?

I personally learned this principle while working with missionaries and doing missionary work. When we earnestly sought the Lord to help us find a family we could teach the gospel to, and when we thought very carefully about the law upon which this blessing is predicated, we would then ask ourselves if we were willing to obey that law. If we were unwilling to make such a commitment, then it was better not to seek the blessing but rather to seek another blessing, perhaps lesser, that we were in need of and to obey the law on which that blessing was predicated.

Feeling and thereby promising to obey the law on which the blessing is predicated caused a level of unity and harmony inside ourselves and between companions we had not known before. We moved forward then with real sincerity and integrity and obeyed that law, and we learned how the Lord works: he performs his work and his miracles through the instrumentality or agency of his servants. If he has a servant he can trust, that servant will be used in the Lord's way. One who can make commitments and keep them is the true servant of the Lord and can become a powerfully effective influence and instrument in his hands for the blessing of many lives. But when we hesitate and vacillate in uncertainty and indecision and fear, unable to make a commitment or a promise because of our past experiences and habits, we cannot be effective servants of the Lord. We are too much servants or slaves to our own futile ways, to environmental pressures, to our passions and appetites and unrighteous desires. How can the Lord use such a one?

We developed a motto in our mission that somewhat capsulizes this philosophy. Until a person can honestly say, "I am my own master," he cannot say sincerely and realistically, "I am thy servant." In other words, until a person has great self-control over his body, his passions, his appetites, and his desires and is willing to submit them to the Lord's spirit and will, how can he be an agent or servant of the Lord and follow the Lord's whisperings and directioning? Thomas Huxley described such a true person as one "who is full of life and fire but whose passions are trained to come to heal by a vigorous will, the servant of a tender conscience."

This process of making a resolution and subsequently breaking it can itself become a habit and can destroy the ability to make resolutions, so that the very thought of entering into honest promises or covenants becomes uncomfortable to us, as we are aware of our own weakness and inability to keep our promises. Or we might make them lightly and mechanically, without any real meaning and conviction behind them, and then break them, but remain unaware of the consequences. Or we might make them with other people and then when circumstances change we break them and rationalize, hurting our relationship with those people. Making covenants is a boon or a curse, depending upon the integrity of the person making them.

The Lord, in a magnificent parable, teaches a great principle:

"For which of you, intending to build a tower, sitteth not down first, and counteth the cost, whether he have sufficient to finish it? Lest haply, after he hath laid the foundation, and is not able to finish it, all that behold it begin to mock him, saying, This man began to build, and was not able to finish." (Luke 14:28-30.)

Part of the preparation process is to sit down first and count the cost. Part of the process of meditating and listening in prayer is to count the cost to see if we have sufficient to finish the job. If we feel we do, we commit ourself. If we do not, then we might commit ourself to something for which we do have sufficient to finish—something of lesser importance perhaps, but a beginning step toward that of greater importance. Great things are accomplished by small means. "A thousand-mile journey begins with a single step."

I found that missionaries who were struggling with various kinds of problems, particularly relationship problems with their companions, first needed to conquer some basic schedule and physical problems before they could move on to these higher problems. I encouraged them to enter into covenant, but only when they were sure they would honor the covenant; and they were never to make a promise they would not keep. But they needed to begin making promises and keeping them. Then their sense of integrity and internal unity grew, and they developed the capacity to make higher promises.

I believe that the temple endowment is a magnificent illustration of this principle. Covenants are central to this sacred, eternal ordinance. Almost all else seems to revolve around them.

Principle No. 5: Believing.

The Savior told his disciples on both continents, and in both the meridian dispensation and the last dispensation, that whatsoever we ask the Father in his name, that is right for us, believing that we will receive, he will give it to us.

"And whatsoever ye shall ask the Father in my name, which is right, believing that ye shall receive, behold it shall be given unto you." (3 Nephi 18:20.)

"And if ye are purified and cleansed from all sin, ye shall ask whatsoever you will in the name of Jesus and it shall be done.

"But know this, it shall be given you what you shall ask. . . ." (D&C 50:29-30.)

To my understanding, the Lord is telling us that our attitude or frame of mind, heart, and spirit is of crucial importance in releasing the true power of prayer. While this seems obvious, I believe it not to be very common. Too often we place our faith in the seen realities rather than in the unseen God and his promises to us. We then call ourselves realistic, but with the Lord nothing is impossible: if the thing we request is right—that is, if it is wise from the Lord's point of view, even though all the seen realities might shout at us that it cannot be done— and if we pray in faith, believing that it can be done and that it is right, and then put ourself in alliance with God in doing our part, the Lord will work his miracles. I have come to believe from my own experiences that many times faith in the Lord Jesus Christ just begins when "it cannot be done," when all of the seen realities combine together to hedge up the way, and people mock and ridicule. The doubts of the cynic are self-fulfilling and support his cynicism, just as the righteous hopes of the believer are also self-fulfilling.

So in prayer: If preparation is adequate, if there has been sincere expression and listening and committing, then the person who prays should go forth in a believing attitude, knowing that the Lord will grant the blessing requested if it is right and if he does his part. One person plus God comprise a majority, for God is all-knowing and all-powerful. A miracle to us is to him the operation of a higher natural law. When the brother of Jared held up those sixteen stones, he did it in mid-air but in a believing attitude, and in a sense he testified to God that he knew God had the power to touch the stones and make them "shine forth in darkness." The Lord did so. The brother of Jared then asked to see the Lord himself. The Lord asked him if he believed the words that he would speak. The brother of Jared testified that he knew that God was a God of truth and that he did believe, and the Lord showed himself to the brother of Jared. (See Ether 3.)

I believe that if parents will continually pray in faith, in the believing attitude, knowing that, if it be God's will, he will bring down a special blessing or opportunity into the life of one of their children, this will take place. But if these same parents offer such a prayer but don't really believe in their hearts, they frustrate the very laws upon which the blessings or requests are predicated. The Prophet Joseph was told by James that he should "ask in faith, nothing wavering. For he that wavereth is like a wave of the sea, driven with the wind and tossed." (James 1:6.)

Principle No. 6: Doing.

If I keep my promise and if I am true to the commitment made in prayer and then report back at night on my stewardship or my assignment for that day, I will feel inside myself a sense of integrity; the Lord will be telling me that he is pleased with my work.

If I go through all of the other steps but neglect the sixth and last step, I will find myself unable to go through all of the steps again until I have repented and prepared myself for two-way communication. If I go through all of the steps with the exception of commitment, I will find that my "doing" step will be rather easily uprooted by the pressures of environment and the pull of habit and personality. If I do not adequately prepare myself and attempt to go through the rest of the steps, my commitment will be shallow and I will not be a doer. I need to prepare. I need to commit. I need to do. They serve and reinforce each other. The hand cannot say to the foot, "I have no need of thee."

If I do not live true to the light that I have been given, to the still, small voice of my own conscience, to the voice of the Lord, to the oaths and covenants I have made, then I lose my internal source of light and I become buffeted by the fickle pressures of circumstance and personality. But if I do live true to that voice and to that light, then I will have an internal source of light that will be my source of guidance and comfort and direction; it will be like an anchor and, as the scripture says, "without compulsory means it shall flow unto thee forever and ever."

This is how the Savior can literally become the light and life of our personal lives. We are not a hearer only, but a doer. We acquire an internal anchorage, a personal relationship with the Lord Jesus Christ, and then he literally becomes our guide and our comfort. "The Lord is my shepherd; I shall not want. He maketh me to lie down in green pastures . . . he restoreth my soul."

These six principles of prayer—preparing, expressing, listening, committing, believing, and doing—comprise a whole gospel way of life, oriented and centered on God and his Son Jesus Christ.

The doing phase or the doing principle, in a sense, becomes the first or preparing principle for two-way communication.

19

With His Children:
The Spiritual Roots of Communication

In a recent interview I heard the voice of a distraught and tearful mother. "Oh, what can I do? What can I do? My daughters are leaving me."

"What has happened?"

"My daughters don't want to live with us anymore. They're going to the university and they're becoming involved in all of the activities there. They are beginning to stray from the teachings of their youth."

"Are they going to church any longer?"

"No."

"Can you communicate with them?"

"No. We haven't been able to talk together for a long time now."

"Does their father communicate with them?"

"No. There's a real break there. And now they want to take their own apartment and live away from home and go to the university. I don't know what to do. I have prayed about it. I'm just beside myself with worry." Many of us who are parents of teen-agers become very much aware, over the years, of the tendency to lose our influence with our children. Teen-agers tend to listen more to the group to which they belong—to their friends—because their friends seem to understand them and sympathize with them. And therefore we, as parents, gradually find that as our children become more and more independent and free, our influence on them lessens. When we begin to see them taking a lower road, we naturally have great anxiety. We want to know what we can do. In our eagerness to do something, we often rush in and take emergency measures. We might even take an extreme measure and give strong counsel or reject certain kinds of behavior. As we do this, our children may withdraw a little more from us, and rather than come toward our counsel they sometimes move away from it. They may even begin to "use" (by turning against) the very things we have taught them—the gospel and the Church, for example —as weapons with which to strike back at us.

It seems to me that there is a common denominator in all of these situations and problems. I became aware of this common denominator while serving a mission in Ireland and watching the lives of several hundred missionaries as they came into the mission field. We also watched the process of conversion in the lives of hundreds of people. As mission president, I wrote each of them asking the reasons for their joining the Church.

Again and again I came to sense, as a result of these experiences and communications, that a common denominator seemed to lie beneath the attitudes and the behavior of almost everyone. For lack of a better term, I call it insecurity or self-doubt. With such feelings, a person doubts his own ability, his own basic worth and righteous capacities.

How do people handle such self-doubt? In various ways. In the mission field, for instance, nonmembers could escape it by simply saying to the missionaries, "I don't want to hear any more." They had tasted enough of it to realize that there was something there that might require a change within them, so they would withdraw or fight against it. Many times we would find individuals who really did not want to live the Word of Wisdom, but they masqueraded their reasons: "I just can't accept Joseph

Smith and the supernatural revelations he claimed." But again and again when we asked those who came into the Church to look into their hearts and examine the real reasons why they joined the Church and why they perhaps hesitated for a period of time, they responded by admitting that they had earlier doubted themselves. People were not doubting the Church—they were doubting themselves!

We discovered that an individual would know the Church was true only to the degree he or she was true to the Church. By being true to the Church, there seemed to be an unlocking from within of a divine sense or a testimony—a conviction that came from obedience.

Once we learned this transcendentally vital lesson, we stopped trying to convince people by persuasion, reason, and the use of scripture alone, for this approach stirred up their self doubts. Instead, we encouraged investigators to obey, to change, to repent, to pray, to live a commitment, to attend church, to study the Book of Mormon. This approach, when followed, minimized self-doubt.

Some missionaries were sent to a new city to open it up. If one of the missionaries had been bruised in his life —hit too much by criticism, rejection, or maltreatment— he tended to become defensive in order to protect himself. The fastest way to escape the responsibility of finding and teaching was to reject the city and say, "It can't be done there. There's no one there who's really interested. The people are already too committed to their own religions." Or an elder could even reject his own companion, because if he were to open up with his companion and have an honest relationship—a true, genuine communication—he might be hurt, or so he felt. Such people are not quite sure whom they can trust. They have likely trusted before, perhaps, and it ricocheted on them. They were hit, and people who are hit continually get bruised and naturally grow defensive—and learn to keep up their guard.

These are some ways of handling insecurity: avoid

situations or responsibilities that may reveal one's self-doubting and insecurity; either move away and escape, or fight, criticize, and find fault with others—leaders, programs, or self—to avoid confronting the real problem inside.

An enormous responsibility rests upon us to communicate effectively, and because of this responsibility, self-doubts and insecurities within can rise to the surface until one of the two approaches is taken: escape and withdraw; or fight, criticize, and find fault. Find the mote (weakness) in your husband's (or wife's) eye and focus on it until that view obscures the view of the beam (weakness) in your own eye. This makes it almost impossible to clearly see or to effectively give help. Or withdraw, saying, "I don't want to communicate. I have nothing to say— nothing to talk about." That is an escape! Or else compensate for your insecurity by focusing on security from the outside—clothes, styling, and membership in select groups—inwardly saying, "These things can compensate for my own feeling of insecurity and make me feel adequate and more secure."

I suggest that none of this works upon the roots at all. None of it works with the underlying causes of strife or of peace. I suggest that the world doesn't know fully what those roots are—those deep spiritual roots which, if exercised, fed, and nourished, could bring about a great internal feeling of security and peace so that, in turn, out of that internal strength and anchorage will flow the ability to be a peacemaker in our relationships with others, particularly when the storms descend.

In my judgment, too much of present-day thinking regarding communication is based upon a sunshine philosophy. When the sun is shining and things are going wonderfully, people can communicate easily, naturally, and effectively, but the moment the storms descend (and they descend almost every day on all of our lives in one way or another—at least little storms: conflicting expectations, economic pressures, conditions of stress, time pressures, etc.), we lose our temper, shout out, condemn, do some things that we would never think of doing when the sun is shining.

But sooner or later the storms come. Then our self doubts surface and relationship problems commence and communication breaks down.

Henry David Thoreau, the great natural philosopher, wisely stated, "For every thousand people hacking away at the leaves of evil, there is one hacking at the roots." What are those roots and how can we stir them deeply within us? Let me tell you a story and see if you can discover what those roots are. One night as a young family were on their knees in family prayer, the eight-year-old son said, "Does Heavenly Father really love me?"

The father assured him, "Yes, he does. Pray to him from your heart."

The children had been taught to pray privately but also to pray as a family.

"Does he really love me?"

"Yes."

"No matter what I do?"

"Yes, he loves you all the time. If you ever do naughty things, he even loves you then, but he wants you to change and do good things."

As the parents rose to leave the bedroom, the little boy started to cry and said, "Oh, Mommy! Can we have a talk?"

"Yes, son."

So they went into the other room and for about an hour and a half they visited together. And he began to open up and tell his mother about what was happening in his life.

For about three or four days prior to this little visit, the young boy was having all kinds of problems in the home. He would take out his hostilities on his little brothers and sisters; he would shout; he would wake up angry in the morning, very disturbed, and would disturb the entire family. There was strife in the home, and he was the author of much of it.

His parents could not understand all of this.

But during the talk, he said, "Mommy, I'm doing something naughty in school. Do you promise you won't tell Daddy?"

"Yes, I promise, son. But maybe you'd like to tell him."

"Oh, no!"

"What is it?

"Well, we started to get into this one subject." He then told about a subject he was studying in class. He continued, "And as we started to get into it, the other kids were really good at it and I wasn't. I didn't know much about it. The rest had taken this subject before, but I had never studied it before. Whenever the time would come to work on this subject, I wanted to ask the teacher to help me, but everyone else knew it and I didn't, so I felt awfully stupid. I didn't want to ask her. I was frightened to ask her. I asked her once and she was mean toward me, and so I wasn't going to ask her again. So . . ."

He then broke down, "Oh, Mommy, can I tell you this?"

He had to have reassurance that what he would say would not bring his mother's disapproval of him as a person. When he felt sufficiently assured, he said, "I'm cheating, Mommy, I'm cheating. And now I've cheated so much that the teacher thinks I'm one of the best students in the class. I just have to keep it up or else she'll know I've been cheating."

He confided in his mother the various devices he had used to cheat—looking at a book, looking at someone else's paper, and even pretending to go somewhere in the room to get some chalk and other materials while looking at some answers on the way. He had to calculate all this.

He said, "I know I've been baptized. That's why I haven't even wanted to go Primary and Sunday School lately. I haven't felt good within myself. And, Mommy, that's why I haven't prayed from my heart, because I knew I was doing wrong. I don't know what to do, Mommy."

Soon he got sufficient courage to tell his father, and later he went to his teacher and confessed what he had been doing. There was a marked change in him after this repentance. He would wake up with peace within him. No longer was he the great troublemaker and strife producer with his brothers and sisters.

Now if you were to tell someone that the reason this little boy was having such a problem in the home was because he was sinning, they would probably say, "Oh, get off it. To say that little eight-year-old boy was sinning [and that was the core of the real problem] is foolish. You need to communicate with him more and to give him more love because he is feeling a lack of security. Give him more security, more affection, more understanding. It is just a phase."

That is good counsel, I admit. But, nevertheless, the root of the problem lay in his own transgression. As long as that internal strife was there, the eight-year-old merely carried it into the lives of others. When he resolved that internal problem, he had peace within himself and he carried peace into the lives of others.

James the apostle asked, "From whence come wars and fightings among you? come they not hence, even of your lusts that war in your members?" (James 4:1.) He suggests that conflicting loyalties and passions within are the cause of human strife. In other words, the real root of peace and effective communication when the storms of life descend is obedience to divine law. This is not the easy answer—in fact, it is the hardest answer of all and yet the truest, for it overcomes self doubt.

We had problems arise one time in our mission between the mission board and the district board. They were "warring" with each other. Some on the mission board felt that the district board would not cooperate and follow the program they had been given, and the district board felt that the mission board was too authoritarian, too dictatorial. There were many communication problems that went on for months.

We worked on the problem for a while, but we only worked on the surface. We would often counsel: "Let us be one. If we are not one, we are not the Lord's." Then all would momentarily be inspired, but within a few days something else would creep up to confirm some earlier suspicion, and the communication problem would arise again. Whenever the storms would come, the program would fall apart again; but when the sun was shining, everything seemed fine.

"Problems are rooted spiritually, and they begin with me." I had to start with myself, and it was a very hard, demanding experience. When I looked into my own heart, I could see that in many instances, in trying to resolve this problem and to work with it, I had not communicated properly. I had not taken the time to build certain relationships that were important. My planning was not as careful or as long-range as it should have been nor had I been as dedicated in my efforts to communicate respect and love to the members of the various boards. Therefore, before I went to a meeting with the boards, I asked our Father in heaven in the spirit of fasting and prayer to give me the courage to look into my heart and to acknowledge sincerely my own failings in the meeting itself. I did look and so did they, each in his own turn. I had never had an experience quite like that. When each man looked into his own heart and saw the beam within his own eye and confessed it, he committed himself to removing it rather than focusing upon the mote in his brother's eye—"He that is without sin among you, let him first cast a stone. . . ." (John 8:7.) And from then on the roots were being stirred and worked upon. We were repenting—we were deeply changing—and the communication naturally became a peaceful one.

One day a branch president called me and said, "I quit. I can't take this anymore."

"What's happening?"

"Do you know that the district president is actually coming into my branch and interviewing my people and asking them about me and then criticizing?"

"No, I didn't realize that."

"He's undermining my entire branch. There's no use in my going on at all. I quit. I resign."

"Did you know the district president is actually interviewing the members of my branch and criticizing me, both in the way I run the branch and the way I raise my family? I feel completely undermined. I can't take it anymore. I quit, that's all."

"It's difficult, president, to talk over the telephone. Can we get together so we can really talk it over?"

"What's there to talk about?" he replied. "Do you sustain him or me? I've just had it."

"We've got to discuss this together. We don't want this to hurt your branch."

"Hurt my branch? It's already hurt it, and frankly it's upset my wife and family terribly. I guess I've lost my temper a few times around here. Frankly, nothing's going right. Even my kids are upset, and my wife feels just the way I do. We've tried our best, but now we want out!"

"May I visit with you tomorrow? I'm on a mission tour right now. I could certainly come to your home when we return in two days and we could then visit together."

"There is nothing to visit about! Don't you accept my word for it? Is he right or am I right? Whom are you going to stand behind?"

I tried to reason, but reason and emotion are two different languages. Until I accepted how he felt and did not try to answer all his emotion with reason, he continued to pour forth emotion. As soon as I accepted how he felt, he became reasonable.

Eventually, after I listened to this branch president's full story, he agreed to have a personal visit on the matter and to fast and pray, along with me and his wife, in preparation for our visit.

Two days later, on completing my mission tour, I called at the branch president's home. The cordial greeting, in contrast to the heated phone conversation, evidenced some mellowing. However, just as soon as we discussed the real problems and what this other church leader had allegedly done, apparently over a period of several months, all the old feelings of justifying bitterness erupted through the surface again. Both parents poured out the venom.

After further discussion, I read from the Doctrine and Covenants wherein the Lord taught the doctrine of forgiveness.

"My disciples, in days of old, sought occasion against one another, and forgave not one another in their hearts; and for this evil they were afflicted and sorely chastened.

"Wherefore, I say unto you, that ye ought to forgive one another; for he that forgiveth not his brother his trepasses standeth condemned before the Lord: for there remaineth in him the greater sin.

"I, the Lord, will forgive whom I will forgive, but of you it is required to forgive all men." (D&C 64:8-10.)

I asked the branch leader, "Would you go to this brother and ask him to forgive you?"

"What do you mean," he replied. "Him forgive me? You've turned this whole thing around. It's for him to seek *my* forgiveness."

"Let's read this scripture again," I pleaded. "The Lord here decries the hurtful effects of the unforgiving attitude more than the acts that prompted it."

"Oh, I couldn't do it. Not sincerely. Could you, honey?" he said, turning to his wife.

"I'll say not!"

"You can do it. You are disciples of the Son of God, not of this world. He taught us to go the second mile, to turn the other cheek, to forgive 70 times seven, if necessary. I can check into this problem myself, but you need to get this bitterness, this poison out of you. It's afflicting you, just as the scripture states, and hurting you, your marriage, and your family far more than anyone else. If you pray earnestly for the Lord's spirit and spiritually prepare yourself to receive it, the conviction and courage to seek forgiveness will come."

After an extended discussion of what it means and costs to be a disciple of the Son of God, they expressed belief and agreed to seriously seek forgiveness.

A few days later he came to the mission home and with tears in his eyes related what happened.

"My wife and I did prepare ourselves. We began to see more clearly what had happened, not only about the problem we spoke of but also about a lot of other problems we face. President," he said, "I now know what it means to have a 'broken heart and a contrite spirit.' I have never seen my own sins so clearly. We came to feel only sorrow, and we sincerely wanted to ask forgiveness."

"What happened?"

"When we called on him he seemed distant and cold, but then we sincerely and humbly asked his forgiveness for our bitter feelings over all these months. He then broke down and said, 'Oh, it isn't for me to forgive you. It's for you to forgive me.' President, our souls became knitted. I love that brother now. We understand so much more now. I guess I'm just beginning to understand what it means to be a disciple of the Son of God."

Much of the world's counsel and solutions to the communication problems between people—and the strife in families, between husbands and wives and parents and children—are superficial. They are not based upon a fundamental understanding that transgression lies at the root of strife and that the only way to work upon that root is through faith in the Lord Jesus Christ, repentance, covenant making in the waters of baptism, at the sacrament table, and in the temple where there are several essential covenants—each one, in turn, giving the power to obey the higher one. If one is obedient to a lower covenant, more light and power is given. Then comes a higher covenant, until eventually a person is taught how he can return to the presence of God and how he can commune with him here and now.

Jesus Christ is the way. If a person tries to take any other way but through him and his holy gospel, he becomes a thief and a robber on his own soul. He has deceived himself. There is too much aspirin-thinking or symptom-handling concerning communication problems and too little willingness to look deeply within and to acknowledge where the root of the fault or error might be. Then out of that deep humility and honesty a spiritual well will overflow with love, sweetness, understanding, respect, and courage.

We live twenty-four hours a day. Could you use one hour or just one-half an hour seeking the presence of the Savior of this world? If you really knew that five per cent of your time would influence the other 95 per cent of your time, that even your sleep would be more peaceful, more restful, and your communications would be more authentic and peaceful, particularly when the stress conditions come—if you knew really that you would be more successful in 95 percent of your life by being true in five percent of your life, would you neglect or superficially use that five percent? I don't think you would.

A suggestion: Learn in a daily way to stir yourself spiritually. How? Get to know the standard works and love them. Feel the pulse of the Lord through them. Find out how he thinks and how he feels. Get to know Christ. Memorize his teachings. Let the "solemnities of eternity" distill upon your mind. Let not your inner security come from outer status symbols, from efforts to impress others, from clothing or looks, but instead from a real deep, honest, spiritual communion. Those who commune with God can communicate with self and others under conditions of stress. Those who do not so communicate find that when the environment presses upon them and people judge or reject, they usually fall apart because there is no strength within.

I testify out of my own experience that if we will have that kind of an honest, prayerful, studious experience every day and covenant with the Lord to be true to him, we will find a well of water coming up within us replacing self doubt with a deep internal strength and anchorage. We may have to repent sometimes and confess, we may have to break our heart—but that is the nature of the spiritual sacrifice required of us today. The deepest need in this world is to be born again, with Christ becoming the Father of that second birth. This, to me, is the spiritual root of communication.

20

The Two Languages: Logic and Feeling

A stake leader, on entering an MIA dance, was approached by a group of irate teenagers and asked why they could not participate in some of the extreme modern self-expression dances.

The questions were put forward more in the form of angry statements, and it was obvious that these teenagers were dead serious. A flood of these kids immediately surrounded the leader and barraged him with their questioning, insistent demands.

"We don't participate in this kind of dancing because it is not consistent with the high standards of the MIA program."

"Why isn't it? What's wrong with it? There's nothing wrong with it any more than there is wrong with jive or jitterbug, and you permit that!"

"Well, these dances involve more self expression, and besides—"

"Oh, go on. You can get as much self expression in any kind of dance. It is merely up to the individual."

"But that's not really the point, either. The point is that these dances are crude and often very suggestive and—"

"Only suggestive to those who think that way. We don't, and we want to dance that way."

"Well, the MIA is trying to set a high standard in dance, as well as in everything else."

"High standard, huh? We think cheek-to-cheek dancing is just downright suggestive. It's far below even our own standards."

"But—"

"And furthermore, we think that the way we twist and shake is just a lot of fun, and we—"

The leader, feeling a challenge to his own authority, angrily and summarily cut in, "I don't want to talk any more about it. The Church policy has been laid down, and that's that! The Church teaches us not to smoke and drink—you don't smoke and drink. Now the Church teaches us dance standards to maintain. If you accept the Church, you should accept those standards."

One teenager chirped in from the outer ring of the evergrowing cluster of kids surrounding the leader: "Do you mean that if we don't dance like you want us to, we can't associate with the Church?"

"Now, I didn't say that. I meant—"

"Well, that's what you said!"

"That's not what I meant. I meant to say that this Church is run by revelation and that the purpose of it is to set a high standard to all the world, and this especially applies to our youth activities. You've accepted other standards of the Church. Why is this one such a hard one to accept? Besides, you shouldn't be questioning these things. What your leaders say should be enough for you. Now, *that's* what I mean, and I don't want to talk anymore about it!"

At that, the leader tried to break through the grumbling crowd, which had somewhat broken into small arguing, contending groups, each taking different sides of the question.

The leader felt bad. Not only had he failed to get his point across, but he had also got a mean spirit in him in the process of trying. He had felt his own authority questioned and disrespected, and he had let loose on that spirit, and those kids, particularly the ones closest around him, had felt it and had had good reason to disrespect him.

Immediately out on the dance floor the kids started twisting and shaking and twitching. It was a kind of mutiny. The stake leader could partly understand the rebellion from what had happened before, but this made him even angrier, and the desire came within him to close down the whole dance and call it quits. Just then, a young girl who had been close to the stake leader and who had confided in him on several occasions came up to him and said, "Do you mind if I ask you a question?"

"What is it, Judy?" snapped the leader.

"What can we do?" she answered sincerely. "What can I do? I want to do what you say, but I don't know these other dances. Besides, I'm scared."

That last statement was so honest. It stuck like a lump in the leader's throat. He could give no answer. He asked himself, What can I say? I can't just tell her not to be afraid. Maybe these kids really don't know how to do these other dances. They certainly involve a lot more instruction, and when I think about it, they also involve more social skill, the ability to talk to each other while they're dancing, and these kids are new at this. Some of them aren't even members of the Church. Maybe we're just expecting too much. What can I say to Judy? Not to be afraid? But she is afraid, and she's honest. I wonder if I'm that honest. Aren't I afraid? Afraid of my feelings, my own authority, afraid to have it questioned, doubted?

"Well, Judy, let's talk about it for a minute. Come over here and sit down."

Judy and the leader went over to the side and sat down; and for the first time in this entire squabble, two people began to listen to each other. Neither tried to play a role or to put up a mask or a facade. There was no anger, no hostility or defensiveness. In their place were sincerity and honesty. Neither felt that his or her point of view was the only one. that he or she was right and all else was wrong. Therefore, no one felt bludgeoned into consenting. There was a feeling of acceptance between Judy and the leader as they talked. They accepted each other. They accepted the fact that they thought differently and felt differently. They respected each other. They continued to talk, Judy giving her reasons for her feelings, and the leader giving his for his feelings and the policy of the Church. They found that the earlier fear they had both felt seemed to vanish. They felt rather sustained and strengthened by each other—merely because in their honesty they accepted each other's feelings, each other's expression. Once Judy felt that the leader respected her feelings, she seemed to have the power to deal with them herself and to look objectively at them. Gradually they changed.

Once the leader felt that Judy wasn't questioning his position or that of the Church, he felt sustained and wanted to listen; he wanted to understand. And because he did, he learned. He learned a great deal. He learned about methods and proper timing. He learned about education and instruction. He learned the absolute futility of using the mind to dominate the heart. He learned that there are two languages—the language of logic, the "shoulds" of this earth, and the language of sentiment, how people feel, how they really feel. He learned that people behave more on the basis of how they feel than how they think. He learned that unless there are good feelings between people, it is almost impossible to reason intelligently. He learned that fear is a knot of the heart, and to untie these knots is a matter of relationship—of sincere, genuine, honest, affirming relationship. It is not so much a matter of intellectual understanding at all! Reason didn't seem to stand for much, but acceptance did—acceptance of others, acceptance of the fact that they're different, that from their point of view they are right, acceptance of the value of their feelings, that they truly do feel these ways, and that this isn't so wrong—to feel.

The leader learned that both he and Judy changed,

that both grew and both learned. He wanted to undo the harm he had caused. It seemed vain, considering there were so many involved. Some had already left the dance in disgust. Others were twisting in rebellion, and others were carrying angry feelings in their hearts. The leader went up to one of the chief spokesmen of the group and said, "May I speak with you a minute, Tom?"

"Yes, sir."

The leader drew Tom over to the side, put his arm around his shoulder, and said, "Listen, Tom. I'm sorry for the way I acted out there. Boy, I really got to feel mean inside me. Will you forgive me? I was only trying to explain the policy of the Church."

Tom answered, "Me, forgive you? It's more we need you to forgive us. We know we're wrong. We know what we should do, but I guess we just don't know how to do it. It's not that we don't love the Church or not believe it's true; we just got mad and rebellious. We felt you questioned our acceptance of the Church. It's not that at all. We know it's right, and we really know that the high dance standards are right. They're reasonable. Sometimes, you know, you get with a group of people, and its spirit kind of comes over you, and you stop thinking very straight. You know what I mean?"

"Sure, I understand, Tom. I understand. Thank you, Tom. I'm glad we talked. I'll see you later."

The leader returned home with his mind and heart full of questions. Mainly the questions were about himself. His accepting, honest relationships with Judy and Tom seemed to give him a kind of courage to look at himself and face clearly some pretty fundamental questions. He asked himself, "How much do these kids really mean to me? How important are they? What is the best way to introduce these changes? I guess the 'How' question is just as important as the 'What.' Maybe even the 'Why' question must be answered to them. Why do we assume so much about these people, thinking that if they just accept the doctrine of the Church, the way of life will be easy to accept?"

In his self ponderings, the leader could see how clearly it was that human experiences and human relationships formed the foundation for spiritual experiences and divine relationships. He could see ever more forcibly the central truth in the gospel that love is the most powerful and all-embracing principle of all, and that unless there is love, then faith and hope and knowledge and all else are useless. The leader could see clearly that unless people feel that they are accepted and that they have a right to express their feelings without fear of embarrassment or ridicule, that all they will do is react and rebel and struggle for their identity—fight for their individuality.

The leader could understand that these people tended to act on the pressure of the moment, and that a sense of belonging in the group seemed all-important to them. He could feel with more persuasiveness than ever before some of the real forces that lower moral standards and which force group conformity and a weakening of individual character and integrity.

Oh, so clear were many of the earlier problems in MIA becoming! For the first time, he thought, I understand why we had a difficult time introducing the new stake schedule with some of the wards. I can even understand why the Barlows and the Monsons didn't want to get into MIA work when they were called. Why haven't I listened more? Why haven't I accepted people more? Why don't I try to understand more? What's happened to my patience?

Looking into this mirror and asking questions of himself and talking it over with his wife and a very loyal and dear friend, the leader discovered that he, too, had feelings and tended to act upon them, rather than merely upon the "shoulds" and "logics." He discovered also that if he could learn to *communicate with himself honestly and to listen to himself acceptingly* as he just had done, he would find it gives him a sense of security and peace and inner strength and helps him to communicate better with others and to understand and accept them more also. He could see there's a time for the mind to rule and a time for the heart to rule. He could see that you cannot place a priority on thinking over feeling, or a "should" over a "want." One may be right, but the other may motivate and dominate, and unless people feel accepted, they seem either to want to run away from these responsibilities or to fight and criticize.

The leader reflected on the entire situation and decided that he would act on the assumption that these young people did believe in the Church and they wanted to do what was right. They had some real fears and self-doubts, feelings of inadequacy, and they needed help, patience, and someone to show them the "hows," someone to listen to them and to appreciate them for just what they were, rather than just to judge and evaluate and moralize and preach to them.

It was one of the greatest experiences and lessons of the leader's life, but he has since found that he must relearn it every day, for if he is a good observer of others and of life, it will be taught to him every day.

Fear Dies and Faith Is Born in the Atmosphere of Love and Acceptance

One day a BYU professor visited with one of his students in a religion class. The student had just received a very low mark on a test and was discussing it. In the course of discussion, the student began to reveal some of his real feelings about the class and about religion in general. The teacher probed a little and then opened up a Pandora's box.

"I hate this religion class. They made me sign up for it on registration day. I didn't know what I was getting into. I can't see why they make you take religion classes. I thought religion was supposed to be a matter of one's free agency—not force. My Sunday School teacher told us that force came from Satan, not God, and yet I'm forced to take this religion class. I've had religion jammed down my throat for so many years, and I'm just fed up."

The teacher wanted to explain the reasons for the school policy and program, to point out, "Can't you see that this is all for your own good? You didn't have to come to this university. This is a church university, and when you decided to come, you agreed to live and learn within its framework." But the teacher had an intuitive feeling that this boy had had this type of lesson taught to him dozens of times over the years, and that if he too tried to teach it at this moment, after his emotional tirade, it would be another form of rejection—rejection in the name of the eternal "shoulds," in the name of religion. But rejection and true religion—the religion of love— seemed opposite to each other. Furthermore, the teacher didn't feel personally threatened because his class was so criticized and condemned by the student. He felt only to accept the feeling and to listen. He said, "William, I'd really like to understand how you feel. Which way are you going to your next class? Can we walk across campus together?"

William immediately felt somewhat disarmed and even felt a sense of importance, that the teacher really wanted to listen, that he was sincerely interested in him and his feelings.

As they walked across campus, William continued to pour out to an accepting ear feelings he had held within himself for a long time. All the fight was gone, and within a few minutes, as they neared their next class, he started to express his positive feelings about the class and how he knew, "These religion classes really serve a good purpose, and I really know they're best for me, but when I got that low grade, I just couldn't accept it. I had to fight in some way. I can see now that I've fought my parents. I actually am purposely doing things contrary to the Church because I knew that would hurt them the most. But I felt that they had hurt me for so many years by using the Church against me, I guess I just wanted to get back at them."

Over the next several weeks the teacher and his student had several more talks, with the teacher mostly listening at first and the student doing the talking, and ironically he changed and grew by just listening to himself in the presence of someone who would accept him. He seemed to acquire a courage and a strength that enabled him to unlearn many of the bad lessons of his life and to act on some new ones. He gradually became one of the best students in the class and seemed to have a completely different attitude about religion. By the end of the semester he called the religion "his," instead of merely "theirs" or "yours."

Important Concepts

1. *Human relationships and experiences are the predicate for divine relationships and experiences.* People's concepts of God and his attributes are largely the projection of their own experiences—happy or bitter—with the authority people of their lives. In spite of what they intellectually agree to, or even verbally teach, many feel that God cannot be trusted, that he is unforgiving and unloving and is only to be feared. For this reason, they're afraid to pray to him sincerely, to really express how they feel. They would rather tell God what they think he wants to hear. Their prayers become phony and insincere; they feel hypocritical; they don't like to pray, except to relieve a sense of duty. Their prayers are merely mechanical ritual—expressions from the lips. Someone may teach them to pray sincerely from the heart. They may even feel momentarily inspired and resolved, but often when they get back into the posture of prayer, the old and niggardly experiences narrow their conception, and they feel rejected and unloved and pray again from their lips.

2. *People behave more out of their feelings than out of their thinking.* Motivation comes primarily from the heart, not from the mind. Many people intellectually know that the gospel is true, but they won't obey it unless they feel strongly about it—feel more strongly about it than they do about other things. There are many competing activities and influences to the church program, and each of

these plays its role in everyone's life. Our youth will follow the church program if they "feel good" about it and "feel good" about themselves in it. Not only must they feel good, but they must also feel stronger and better about it than about any other source of loyalty, influence, and enthusiasm.

It is very important for leaders and teachers to understand this. Otherwise, they may find themselves working on the assumption that by merely telling people what they should do and how they should behave, this is sufficient to motivate them to behave this way. It is sufficient with some—those who have internally committed themselves to the "shoulds" of religion—but certainly not with most. A leader must give of his faith in and love for the youth, so that they "see themselves" in the religion and feel adequate and good about this. Then he can begin to teach them the "shoulds." Once he has the relationship established, they see him as a trusted friend, one who accepts them as they are; then he can teach them almost anything, however demanding, and he will be amazed at their positive responses. But until he has this relationship formed, his teachings may be utterly disregarded and ignored or even rebelled against.

Then, unless the leader or teacher is understanding and internally strong, he may take this indifference and rebellion personally and will lose faith in them and in himself. From then on, he might himself obtain only shallow satisfactions from his church job and may live up to the letter but not to the spirit of his calling and he will gradually find himself more interested and more involved in other endeavors that carry richer personal rewards to him. Then *his* leaders may wonder what has happened to him, and instead of trying empathetically to understand and accept his feelings by listening to him without judgment, they begin to preach the "shoulds" to him, the logics, only to find the same responses of the youth repeated at his level. Then they will lose faith in him, and perhaps in themselves, and communicate this lack of faith, no matter how they try to hold it or conceal it. It becomes a self-feeding cycle.

3. *If leaders and teachers in the church will learn to live the laws of love, they will encourage their people to live the laws of life—that is, to live the "shoulds," to behave as they should behave.* The laws of love essentially amount to accepting people as they are, listening to them with understanding, respecting their feelings, patiently and caringly building relationships, and then beginning the teaching process—both by example and by precept. If, however, the teachers and leaders disobey the laws of love, by constantly preaching, moralizing, judging, and rejecting, or by manipulating people, masterminding them, double-talking them, or whatever reduces a person to the level of a "thing," they will encourage disobedience to the "shoulds" or the laws of life.

4. *Several important gaps must be bridged:*

(a) The long term spiritual picture (eternal gospel plan, church teachings, church standards) and the shorter term emotional picture (group pressures, fears, and self-doubts, need for immediate satisfactions).

(b) The communication gap between the youth (feeling of not being understood, appreciated, accepted) and their leaders and teachers (moralizers and preachers of logic and "shoulds").

(c) The gap between what the teachers and leaders profess with their lips regarding the laws of love and how they actually behave in living these laws of love.

The leader or teacher must work on (c) first and build within his own life a true relationship with the Savior and derive from that relationship a kind of strength and anchorage and courage that will give him the power to bridge the second gap, the communication barrier. (See John 15:12; Jacob 3:1-2.) He will have an easier time to accept and understand feelings when he doesn't take expression of negative feelings as a personal insult to his own position, competence, or authority. By caring, understanding, and building an honest and accepting relationship, he will give the courage, strength, and anchorage to the youth to act upon the longer range "shoulds," upon the logics of religion, rather than upon their shorter range emotion—the sentiments of life—usually controlled by their needs to belong to their peer groups. (This concept is illustrated and discussed in greater depth in chapter 23: "Communicating With Our Youth.")

5. Sentiment often is wisdom. Men assume that logic is a greater value than feeling. This assumption is often incorrect. The heart is often much wiser than the mind. A person must learn to listen to his heart, to take counsel from his conscience, feelings, and intuition, as well as to use his mind.

Sometimes there is a higher value placed on logic or what is practical or "masculine," and a lower value placed on sentiment or what might be considered a more emotional or "feminine" approach. Such a notion, if continually followed, would stifle most of the creativity and spontaneous enjoyments in life, and rather than leading to wisdom, it would lead to a kind of imbalance and a distortion of life.

What does this mean to you as a teacher or a leader? It means essentially to listen to your intuition, to consult with your heart, to give full opportunity to those in a group, who simply "feel" a problem or "feel" the situation or "feel" right about a particular answer, to express themselves. There are times when it would be wise to act contrary to logic and to definitely place the higher value on feeling. One of the saddest mistakes some continually make is to disregard those who "think with their heart" because they cannot express themselves clearly, logically, or with intellectual persuasion. Often their logic is a higher logic, for they feel with their heart, and in many situations, particularly where the human element is strong, these feelings may be much more trustworthy and dependable than the cold and clear logic of a "practical" person. It has been said that we must think with our mind before marriage (eyes wide open) and with our heart after marriage (eyes half shut). There may be truth to this idea in other aspects of life, including church work. However, at the highest level of maturity, there is no difference between logic and sentiment.

The youth of the Church will identify with the church program, and with its leaders and teachers and also its values, if they feel understood and respected in their own personal world and accepted for just what they are. Many of them are plagued with self-doubts, fears, and uncertainties, and unless they feel this understanding and acceptance, these fears may drive them from the Church—not so much because they doubt the Church or the "shoulds" of the Church, but because they doubt themselves.

Let every leader and teacher ask himself four questions and consider the answers given herein:

1. What is the greatest thing in all of the world? A child of God, a human personality.

2. What is the greatest way to bless this child of God, this human personality? The gospel of Jesus Christ, as found in the living programs and doctrines of the Church.

3. What is the greatest and highest law in the gospel? The law of love. Upon this law hang all the other laws.

4. What is the finest expression of the law of love? To accept and respect another person, in all his uniqueness, just as he is, which includes what he may become.

V

Self Discipline:
Applying True Principles to Life

21

To Parents:
Eight Principles of Parenthood and
Character Development

Principle No. 1: Commitment to the Family

President David O. McKay has stressed that "no other success can compensate for failure in the home." Other leaders have counseled that the most important work we will ever do in this life is in the "four walls" of our own home.

The church, over the last several years, through the correlation programs, has placed increasing emphasis upon the family, on the home, and on the responsibilities of parents. Ward teaching was "escalated" into home teaching. The family home evening program has become one of the most emphasized programs of the Church. Our leaders have counseled us that the purpose of the Church, through the auxiliaries and the quorums, is to strengthen the home, to build an eternal family capable of exaltation and eternal life. The role of the father as the head of the home has been stressed again and again. He is the patriarch of the home.

All of this renewed emphasis is coming at a time when the home and the family are being ravished and buffeted on every side by almost every institution of society and by all of the evil machinations of Satan.

Our direction and counsel is God-inspired, and every father and mother in Zion needs to awaken to all that is happening around us and to the will of God, which has been so clearly manifested through his servants in meeting the situation. It is a revelation to us today, and we ignore it only at our peril.

Therefore, I suggest that the first principle on the subject of parenthood and character development is an honest, clear recognition of the transcendent importance of parenthood responsibility and a personal commitment to this vision.

The family is the first obligation in the Church, and if an active church worker will prayerfully and conscientiously organize his affairs, the Lord will give him the power to magnify his (her) calling as a father (mother) and as a church worker.

While many of us might give lip service to the importance of parenthood responsibility, often we will give our prime energy, enthusiasm, time, and loyalty to our professions or occupations or to other good and worthy causes. We will approach our secular work with careful planning, using the best systems, keeping careful records, spending time to analyze the problems; but with the character development of our own children we might go on day in and day out without any real analysis or planning or record keeping, without any intelligent system.

The enemy of the best (the home and the Church) is often the good (other good causes).

We often think that the family problem is one of time —that there are only so many hours in the day and so many important things to be done, and we simply don't have the time to do them all. We rationalize by saying, "All well and good, this talk about getting better organized, but when this night is taken for this, and that night for that, and these two nights for that, it just simply comes down to the fact that I hardly have any evenings for my own family."

Though I acknowledge and sympathize with this reasoning, I do not believe that time is the main problem. I believe it is the excuse. I think the main problem is twofold: first, a lack of real commitment to the vision behind this emphasis on the family, and second, the lack of internal discipline to act accordingly. The Lord has told us that he will make our backs equal to their burdens. If we will obey true principles, take the time to prayerfully search the scriptures to maintain the larger eternal vision, and carefully plan and organize our days, and then work our plan, most of us will literally be amazed, even astounded, at what we will be able to do and accomplish. (See D&C 90:24.)

There are specific things parents can do to teach responsibility, respect, virtue, obedience, work, and other gospel principles. But first they must really commit themselves to parenthood responsibility as their highest one, and must be willing to give their best time, their best thinking, their highest loyalty and enthusiasm and dedication to this task. They will need to analyze carefully and to pray specifically for the growth and development of each child, perhaps to keep careful records, to take special pains to have frequent communication with each, to give proper recognition for performances and achievements, to utilize daily contacts and chores and teaching moments around the home as vehicles to build character—in short, to put more value on character development than on comfort, convenience, pleasure, or material values. "When one puts business or pleasure above his home, he that moment starts on the downgrade to soul-weakness." (President David O. McKay.)

As with all other things, there is no shortcut to this process of character development. There is only one law that governs—"the law of the harvest." We will reap what we sow. The wheels grind slowly but exceedingly fine.

Principle No. 2: Stewardship

Parents are stewards for the children born into their family. They need to render an honest accounting on this stewardship. Their children are actually begotten children of God, the Eternal Father, and are to be raised by his eternal laws and principles.

Both the father and the mother have separate stewardships, both of equal importance, either incomplete without the other. They must learn to live and work together under the most holy and strict laws of heaven: unity, mutual consideration, kindness, cooperation, and harmony.

The father, particularly one who holds the Melchizedek Priesthood, is to obey God. He needs to use his own priesthood to bless his family in righteousness. He must be careful to avoid the almost universal tendency to exercise unrighteous dominion and to force, coerce, or demand that his wife or children obey him, for if he does not himself obey the Lord, and live by true principles, the whole patriarchal concept will be distorted and the children will grow up in an atmosphere of fear, suspicion, criticism, and inconsistency, and will thereby be encouraged to adopt the value systems of the world. (See D&C 121:34-44.)

"Likewise, ye husbands, dwell with them according to knowledge, giving honour unto the wife, as unto the weaker vessel, and as being heirs together of the grace of life; *that your prayers be not hindered.*" (1 Peter 3:7. Italics added.)

Husbands, what it is that most enthuses you and excites you and taps your deepest loyalties and your best enthusiasms? Whatever it is, in a very real sense, is your god, your object of devotion. If your god is truly the Lord, then you will be magnifying your stewardship, but if your god is your profession, your work, your possessions, your sports interests, your social image and pleasures, your political allegiances, or anything that is created, the whole concept the Lord has given us of the family will be distorted. Your wife and your children will have a difficult time following such an unworthy and inconsistent example. Your wife's sense of personal security will be weakened, and her own ability to give herself properly to the children will be lessened. In a very real sense you are her mainstay and support in life, and if you are lukewarm or untrue or unworthy, she will be undermined, and in time you will sorrowfully reap the harvest you have sown.

"They seek not the Lord to establish his righteousness, but every man walketh in his own way, and after the image of his own God, whose image is in the likeness of the world, and whose substance is that of an idol, which waxeth old and shall perish in Babylon, even Babylon the great, which shall fall." (D&C 1:16.)

The wife is to obey her husband in righteousness, which I believe includes her righteousness, for she is not to be his judge. If she attempts to be his judge and to obey that which suits her fancy and withdraws her support or obedience when she disagrees, or if she competes with him for leadership and direction, the patriarchal concept will be distorted. If she "punishes him" in one way or another when he's "off base" in her eyes, it is likely that he will feel that he has atoned and no longer has to change or repent. The wife is called to love and to sustain the husband, and I believe nothing will do more to encourage and chasten him in his own stewardship than consistent acceptance, unconditional love and sustaining. If he is absolutely unworthy, or consistently makes unrighteous demands, then she might counsel with the steward over him, the bishop, but she is not to be his judge and punisher.

Both Paul and Peter have given excellent counsel to wives along this line.

"Wives, submit yourselves unto your own husbands, as unto the Lord. For the husband is the head of the wife, even as Christ is the head of the church: and he is the saviour of the body. Therefore as the church is subject unto Christ, so let the wives be to their own husbands in everything." (Ephesians 5:22-24.)

"Likewise, ye wives, be in subjection to your own husbands; that, if any obey not the word, they also may without the word be won by the conversation of the wives; While they behold your chaste conversation coupled with fear. Whose adorning let it not be that outward adorning of plaiting the hair, and of wearing of gold, or of putting on of apparel; But let it be the hidden man of the heart, in that which is not corruptible, even the ornament of a meek and quiet spirit, which is in the sight of God of great price. For after this manner in the old time the holy women also, who trusted in God, adorned themselves, being in subjection unto their own husbands: Even as Sara obeyed Abraham, calling him lord: whose daughters ye are, as long as ye do well, and are not afraid with any amazement." (1 Peter 3:1-6.)

Children are to obey and honor their parents. Children first need examples or models to follow. They need understanding and respect; they need clear limits, well-established rules, and consistently applied discipline. They need explicit teaching and testifying; they need order, system, and regularity; they need work and responsibility, and to give an accounting; they need time for fun, free expression, and good humor.

I have come to believe from my own experience, as well as my observations of others, that children tend not to obey their parents when the father does not in truth or in deed obey the Lord, and/or when the wife does not in truth or in deed obey her husband, and when the parents do not have this vision of the patriarchal family concept and/or at least a deep commitment to their parenthood responsibility.

Principle No. 3: The Emotional Climate of the Home

The most significant aspect or characteristic of a true gospel-oriented family is reflected in the emotional climate of the home. You might call it "the feeling tone." By far the most important factor in setting this feeling tone is the depth of harmony and unity between the husband and the wife.

President McKay has had much to say on this subject. In general conference on April 7, 1963, he said: "Our homes radiate what we are, and that radiation comes from what we say and how we act in the home. No member of this Church—husband, father—has the right to utter an oath in his home or ever to express a cross word to his wife or to his children. You cannot do it as a man who holds the priesthood and be true to the spirit within you by your ordination and your responsibility. You have to contribute to an ideal home by your character, controling your passion, your temper, guarding your speech, because those things will make your home what it is and what it will radiate, . . . and every Latter-day Saint home should have it.

"[We have today] greater responsibility than ever before, as men of the priesthood, as women of the church, to make our homes such as will radiate to our neighbors harmony, love, community duties, loyalty. Let our neighbors see it and hear it. Never must there be expressed in a Latter-day Saint home an oath, a condemnatory term, an expression of anger or jealousy or hatred. Control it! Do not express it! You do what you can to express peace and harmony, no matter what you may suffer."

In a priesthood session, October 2, 1954, President McKay counseled: "Say nothing that will hurt your wife, that will cause her tears even though she might cause you provocation. Realize that those children are your eternal possessions, treasures of eternity. Do not dare to set an improper example toward them. You are men of the priesthood and you are leaders. You should control yourself. He is a weak man who flies into a passion, whether he is working a machine or plowing or writing or whatever he may be doing in the home. A man of the priesthood should not fly into a passion. Learn to be dignified. You cannot picture Christ flying into a passion. Indignant with sin? Yes. Overturning the money changers when they insulted God and defiled the temple—yes; but so dignified and noble that when he stands before Pilate he makes that leader say: 'Behold the man.' "

In the *Church News* of October 8, 1961, President McKay is quoted as saying: "Many a woman's heart is broken because a man has not learned to subdue that part [temper] of his nature. Many a husband's heart is broken because a wife has not learned to hold in subjection her temper, or her thought and feelings. A little thing you say? Analyze it, and you will find that yielding and not controlling your temper brings many an unhappy hour in your home."

Husbands and wives must learn to talk through their differences and difficulties rather than either taking them out on each other or withdrawing into a silent sullen world of quiet anger and self-pity.

Principle No. 4: Desire and Time for Husband-Wife Communication and Planning

We can all become so busy following such hectic schedules, tyrannized by the telephone, meeting the small crises, that we may go for days without any deep meaningful communication with our husbands or wives. There is some communication all right, but it is often rather superficial and focused upon just the practical necessities of day-to-day life. Every person needs someone else to whom he can speak freely without fear of censor, embarrassment, or ridicule of any kind. People need to feel understood, and that comes from being genuinely listened to.

We are told in the scriptures that the spiritual creation preceded the temporal creation, and that the spiritual thought or ideal is to underlie all temporal concerns and actions. This points up the need for the husband and wife to sit down together and to carefully plan or, in a sense, spiritually create their own world. Planning isn't easy. It requires thinking, and many of us are often too lazy to do any creative thinking and planning. Yet planning is of overwhelming significance in any endeavor of life, and certainly it must be in the most important endeavor, that of successfully raising a family. It must play a vital, central role.

Such planning involves carefully discussing and analyzing the problems in the home and the process of growth and development of each child, and seeking to understand some of the elements and characteristics of various age levels so that realistic expectations might be set.

If parents find it difficult to find the time in the natural course of events for deep, meaningful communication and creative planning together, involving the Lord, who is the other member of this eternal partnership, they should determine to set aside specific times and to hold them inviolate. Parenthood is our highest responsibility. Why shouldn't other things "go by the board," if necessary, in order to maintain deep, meaningful, two-way rapport and understanding and to reap the incalculable benefits of careful, creative planning?

Principle No. 5: Communication With Children (Teaching, Training)

The only real way to build a relationship or to strengthen a relationship that has been strained is on a one-to-one basis—to go to that person to make reconciliation, to talk the matter over, to apologize, to forgive, or whatever it might take.

Over and over again I find with my own six children this lesson being taught: When I take a child aside from the others, go where there is some privacy, and give full attention—be completely present—it is literally amazing how effective my teaching, discipline, or communication can be. But when, out of a sense of time pressure and practical necessity, I attempt to teach, discipline, or correct when others are present, how ineffective I usually am. Why is this so? Because a one-to-one personal relationship is highly respecting and affirming of the worth of the other, whereas a social situation is charged up with many other emotional variables and factors that play upon people's hearts and responses.

In social situations people often learn to play roles. They are fearful of being too open and vulnerable, afraid they might get hurt. They have been hurt before, and they have learned to defend themselves, to cover up. Their responses are more contrived and artificial than they are sincere and natural. Pride strongly enters in. But this is not the case in a personal one-to-one situation, particularly where real time is taken to build rapport, either before or during the discussion of the problem at hand.

One Saturday morning I was sitting quietly in my

office preparing for a meeting when my wife called, in a rather desperate voice. I asked her what was wrong. She said, "Just listen and you'll know." She lifted up the phone and I could hear screaming babies, quarreling children, and television cartoons. What a nightmare! She asked: "Stephen, can't you come home and help me? Here it is 9:00 and I've got an appointment downtown at 9:30 and I'm not even dressed yet. This place is bedlam."

I answered that I was preparing for a meeting and simply couldn't come home and help; then I proceeded to give some advice. (It is always easy to sit in a cool, quiet place and give advice to those who are out in the dust and sweat of the arena.) I first asked her to get our oldest daughter, Cynthia, to take over, because she is very conscientious and responsible when she makes her mind up to be.

My wife's response was: "She won't cooperate at all. She hasn't done a stitch of work, and I can't get her to help at all."

I knew immediately what the problem was. Cynthia had not made up her mind—probably had her own reasons. Probably one of those reasons was that my wife had not taken the time to listen to Cynthia or to meet a special need or problem that Cynthia had. So I said: "Sandra, take Cynthia into the study for no more than one or two minutes and listen to her. Find out what is bothering her, and I assure you that will solve your problem."

"I don't have time to do that. I have just got to get going."

Then I said something that has come to be meaningful to us both. "Too busy sawing to take time to sharpen the saw?"

She immediately sensed what I was saying and said, "Okay, I'll try," and hung up. Later she reported what had happened. She left the bedlam and took Cynthia into the quiet of the study. She said: "Honey, I'm sorry I haven't paid any attention to you this morning. What is it that is bothering you?" Cynthia answered that she felt her mother had not been fair in granting a particular privilege that one of the other children had had the day before, and that when she had tried to talk to her about it, she at first had been ignored and then later had been treated as an interruption.

Almost as soon as the problem was out on the table, as soon as Cynthia was sure that her mother understood, inwardly she was assured that something fair would be worked out at a later time, Cynthia said to her mother, "Go on, Mommy, change your clothes. I'll take care of the kids."

I am convinced that many of our children know what they should do, but their minds are not made up to do it. People don't act on what they know. They act on how they feel about what they know and about themselves. If they can come to feel good about themselves and about the relationship, they are encouraged to act on what they know.

Admittedly it takes some time and patience to "sharpen the saw," but I am convinced that in the long run—and sometimes in the short—it saves time and a lot of nerves.

Principle No. 6: Be Willing to Pay the Uttermost Farthing

Consider the Savior's teaching from the Sermon on the Mount:

"Agree with thine adversary quickly, whiles thou art in the way with him; lest at any time the adversary deliver thee to the judge, and the judge deliver thee to the officer, and thou be cast into prison.

"Verily I say unto thee, Thou shalt by no means come out thence, till thou hast paid the uttermost farthing." (Matthew 5:21-26.)

Sometimes in our hearts we know we have crossed the sensitive line and hurt or insulted or offended another person or a child of our own. We may have felt justified at the time—they may have deserved this treatment—but from the Savior's standards as given in the Sermon on the Mount, we learn that we are not to react to the treatment of others but rather to act from within, based on his divine value system. We are to overcome evil with good instead of paying it off.

Therefore, when we hurt another person (and some people actually sadistically get a delight from this at the time), we should go to him and acknowledge it and seek his forgiveness. This, in my opinion, is paying the uttermost farthing, if it comes out of our heart and is not used merely as a manipulative technique.

I found the efficacy of this principle in my own labor with missionaries who were low in desire and irresponsible in performance. I remember one elder who wasn't rebellious; neither was he very enthusiastic. He would just barely go along. I had him labeled thus in my mind, and for a number of months, every time I saw his face and name on my wall board, I would think of him in this way. In the monthly interviews, even though on the surface I would appear interested, under it all he was labeled and categorized in my mind, so in a sense my sin was of omission rather than of commission.

Eventually I reached the point where I knew I had to take some initiative myself and do something else that might help him "get on fire." Once he began to open up, and said something like, "President Covey, I know you have a lot of good ideas and advice for me, but could you kind of listen to what I feel like and what my problems are and help me from there?" I did what I could at the time but his sincerity was so transparent and my inability to remove myself from the label I had about him so set that I needed more time to prepare. In the intervening time I carefully introspected and came to be aware of how I had labeled him and how this label had tended to be a self-fulfilling prophecy. People tend to become like you treat them or like you believe them to be.

I decided I needed to "pay the uttermost farthing," to use the Savior's expression. I went to this missionary, opened up what I believed had happened and how I had played my role in contributing to this situation, and sought his forgiveness. He broke down and acknowledged his role in things also. He paid the uttermost farthing also, in a sense. Our relationship began on a new base at step one, but for the first time it was thoroughly honest. Both of us began to build with each other, and he would use me from time to time as a sounding board to thrash out a lot of his feelings, both negative and positive. Gradually he "came to himself" and began to build internal controls; then he performed magnificently in finding and teaching families, and he finished his mission supremely happy.

With my own children I have needed to use this principle. I have crossed over the sensitive line and disciplined out of an angry mood, and I knew I wounded feelings. My pride, for a while, has often kept me from paying the uttermost farthing, but eventually I know I must swallow my pride and specifically describe how I offended, then express my sorrow and apology, and seek forgiveness.

What happens when a person pays the uttermost farthing? Assume, to begin with, that relationships are hurt and strained and that you are at least partly responsible. If you merely try to be better and not to confess and ask forgiveness, the other person will still be suspicious. He has been hurt and wounded, and therefore his guard is up. He will be defensive and suspicious of your new behavior, your "kind face," wondering what might happen next. Your improved behavior and manner do not change his distrustful perception. Nothing you can do will change it, because you are behind bars and walls in a prison of his own making (in his mind). The bars and walls are the mental and emotional labels that he has put upon you and that give him some feeling of security (in knowing not to expect much from you). It is only by a complete, full, and specific acknowledgement of your own failings or sin, whether of commission or omission, that you will pay the uttermost farthing. This same principle applies in seeking the Lord's forgiveness. We must hold nothing back—

must hide nothing—and must surrender completely and totally to his will, his way, and his power.

Principle No. 7: The Prayer of Faith

Sometimes the relationship is so strained, the other individual may not even allow you to pay the uttermost farthing. There may be absolutely no communication of any kind. Often parents are concerned and heartsick about one of their children who is living away from home and totally under the influence of the world. They feel they have tried their best, but they don't know what to do. Many realize past mistakes—neglecting, offending, not understanding, or whatever—and have even attempted to pay the uttermost farthing, but still there is no change. The influence sources on this wayward or indifferent son or daughter simply do not lie with the parents any longer, so it seems. Now the question is, what now can be done?

This estrangement is not too unlike the relationship between Alma the senior and Alma the younger. Alma the younger became very sinful and rebellious and took an active part in secretly seeking to destroy the church of God. Yet his own father was the head of the church.

"Now the sons of Mosiah were numbered among the unbelievers; and also one of the sons of Alma was numbered among them, he being called Alma, after his father; nevertheless, he became a very wicked and an idolatrous man. And he was a man of many words, and did speak much flattery to the people; therefore he led many of the people to do after the manner of his iniquities.

"And he became a great hinderment to the prosperity of the church of God; stealing away the hearts of the people; causing much dissension among the people; giving a chance for the enemy of God to exercise his power over them.

"And now it came to pass that . . . he was going about to destroy the church of God, for he did go about secretly with the sons of Mosiah seeking to destroy the church, and to lead astray the people of the Lord, contrary to the commandments of God, or even the king." (Mosiah 27:8-10.)

Yet, with all of this, Alma, the father, continued to love his son and to pray for him in faith, believing that the

Lord would somehow get through to his son. I imagine he had every reason in the world to give up hope and his prayers, but he also had every reason in the world to keep at them. Eventually, in the Lord's time, his prayers were answered. An angel of the Lord appeared to Alma the younger and the four sons of Mosiah.

"Nevertheless he cried again, saying: Alma, arise and stand forth, for why persecutest thou the church of God? For the Lord hath said: This is my church, and I will establish it; and nothing shall overthrow it, save it is the transgression of my people.

"And again, the angel said: Behold, the Lord hath heard the prayers of his people, and also the prayers of his servant, Alma, who is thy father; for he has prayed with much faith concerning thee that thou mightest be brought to the knowledge of the truth; therefore for this purpose have I come to convince thee of the power and authority of God, *that the prayers of his servants might be answered according to their faith.*" (Mosiah 27:13-14. Italics added.)

What is the main point to all of this? Basically it is to suggest that the highest form of influence is God himself; and if a faithful father or mother continues in faithfulness, never giving up on the wayward son or daughter but doing everything in their own power to reach them, then continues in offering the prayer of faith, the Lord may take a hand in the situation in his way and in his time. This doesn't mean he will force anybody, for this would violate his own principle of free agency. The appearance of an angel to Laman and Lemuel did not convert them to righteous living, but it gave them a supreme opportunity to know what was right and what was true. Alma the younger didn't have to obey the counsel of this angel, but he did.

"For, said he, I have repented of my sins, and have been redeemed of the Lord; behold I am born of the Spirit.

"Nevertheless, after wandering through much tribulation, repenting nigh unto death, the Lord in mercy hath seen fit to snatch me out of an everlasting burning, and I am born of God.

"My soul hath been redeemed from the gall of bitterness and bonds of iniquity. I was in the darkest abyss; but now I behold the marvelous light of God. My soul was racked with eternal torment; but I am snatched, and my soul is pained no more." (Mosiah 27:24, 28-29.)

There are many other illustrations in the scriptures of the power of the prayer of faith. If you are interested in modern examples, I suggest you pick up the Doctrine and Covenants and, using the index, study the various references listed under prayer and faith. You might begin with Doctrine and Covenants, Section 10, verses 46-52; 37; 39; 41:3; 42:14; 43:12; 44:2; 103:36; 104:80.

I don't really know how the prayer of faith works, but I believe in the following principles concerning it: First, in order to exercise the prayer of faith, a person must be living very faithfully so that he feels inside that his life is acceptable to God. As James put it, "The effectual fervent prayer of a righteous man availeth much." (James 5:16.)

Second, the prayer of faith consists largely of a kind of testimony of the Lord's goodness and power and wisdom, a total commitment that his will be done, an expressed willingness to obey that will and to be used in any way the Lord desires, and then the believing attitude that if it be right, the Lord will grant the blessing requested. To a degree a person may be very active in the Church yet lose faith in the unseen realities and the power of God in working his miracles of conversion. A positive, believing attitude will never come out of individuals who inwardly have been defeated, who have the person or the situation labeled, and who really believe "it can't be done." Many people, unconsciously perhaps, negatively meditate on people or situations they long to have changed. All of that negative meditation is a form of defeat. There can be no exercise of faith—nothing constructive, nothing creative in it.

Meditate and think deeply on this promise of the Savior, which he gave to the Nephites and which has been repeated in various forms in all dispensations, including this one.

"Behold, verily, verily, I say unto you, ye must watch and pray always lest ye enter into temptation; for Satan desireth to have you, that he may sift you as wheat.

"Therefore ye must always pray unto the Father in my name;
"And whatsoever ye shall ask the Father in my name, which is right, believing that ye shall receive, behold it shall be given unto you." (3 Nephi 18:18-20.)

To me it is encouraging to know that I must never give up hope; that I must never give up faith; that the Lord loves all his children, including my own, and doesn't want one of them lost. He wants to reach them, just as I do. He has the power to do it, and he usually works through trusted servants who exercise faith in him. He will never violate true principles. I, as a parent, can be such a trusted servant, and if I continue to exercise faith, the Lord may in his way and in his time take a hand in the matter.

Principle No. 8: Practices Consistent With Principles

Practices should follow principles and always be consistent with them. This is also a principle. Otherwise we are guilty of living a double standard, professing or teaching one thing and practicing another. Some of the Lord's most scathing denunciations focused on such hypocrisy.

Let us consider various practices, with the suggestions that parents should prayerfully develop their own. We can teach true principles, but you cannot tell people what specific practices they should follow to handle this or that situation any more than you can prescribe glasses for eyes you have not diagnosed.

First, the practice of having traditions: Family traditions serve as a kind of emotional grounding for individuals as they go through life. These may be such traditions as those surrounding birthdays and such holidays as Thanksgiving and Christmas, traditions in saying hello and bidding farewell, traditions of all the boys planning and preparing for missions, of family prayer, of temple marriage, of the family hour, of Sunday dinner, of Saturday afternoon activities. These are security points in young people's lives, something they can depend upon, something they associate with joy and happiness, pleasure and love, and

221

will always be able to identify with throughout their lives.

I have found it useful to also establish special traditions with each child—to have a special experience with a child and then to have a particular object or word represent that experience so that whenever that object or word is used, a flood of pleasant memories returns.

Second, the practice of private visits: While in the mission field my children wondered why the missionaries had the privilege of visiting privately with their father without any interruption, while they didn't. I would sometimes do things with them privately and play with them, but we seldom, one to one, sat down and talked about their concerns and problems and feelings. So they began to ask for these "interviews."

Today it is a regular practice, and whenever they feel need to talk things over, they ask for an "interview." The basic ground rule in this "interview" visit is that Daddy only listens and tries to understand. It is not a time for moralizing, preaching, teaching, or disciplining—there are other times for those important responsibilities of parents; this is a time to merely listen and understand and empathize with. I am honestly amazed at the freeness and the fullness of expression in those visits and also of the nature of the concerns, problems, and feelings. Sometimes I want terribly to move in and advise, teach, judge, or sympathize, but I have inwardly determined that during these special kinds of visits I will only attempt to understand and sustain, and to affirm and help them see clearly their own feelings and thinking and alternatives.

I have also found that as they share their problems, they become open to my problems; and many times I share some problems with them and find that by involving them in family problems they begin to take more responsibility in solving them.

Third, the practice of "dating" each member of the family: I believe in the one-to-one relationship in various activities, in doing things as well as in talking and visiting together. I have found that if "dates" are established far enough ahead and the child largely plans the content of the date, that the very anticipation is, in itself, almost as pleasurable as the date. To take the time to plan a date, to involve the other, and then to carry it out is an affirming and worth-producing experience for children to have with their parents and for wives to have with their husbands.

Fourth, the practice of morning and evening family prayer: Prayer is a privilege, not just a duty, and everything should be done in the home to inculcate a privileged feeling around family prayer as well as private prayer. The attitude of the parents regarding this special prayer or family devotional is the most crucial factor. It should take a little time and special effort. Perhaps it might involve a special place to go. Perhaps it will mean kneeling at the breakfast or dinner table. An effort should be made to gather each person, with no one left out; then the family gains a sense that in the eternal circle no one should be left out. If anyone is left out, he is missed. If there are ill feelings present and insufficient time to achieve reconciliation, perhaps those with ill feelings would not participate in this family prayer. It shouldn't come at the end of the rush of various tasks, but rather more at the beginning, when there is more of a sense of timelessness and when people don't feel pressured.

Fifth, family home evening: I have been very interested in the kinds of problems people face and complaints they have with the family home evening program. First of all, I sympathize with them, because I know it's not easy to suddenly have the parents set up a new program in an already crowded and sometimes fossilized family schedule. It is not a matter of just doing a few minor things. It often involves a fundamental reorientation of the family to have successful family home evenings. I know that some older youth resent being talked down to and sometimes call some of the things "Mickey Mouse." I know that some parents feel they can't take the time and really don't know how to effectively present and teach the lessons, let alone prepare them. Sometimes the communication patterns in the family are so firmly set that it is down-right frightening to try to open up new ones and to look those you live with in the eye and teach gospel principles.

Many parents feel they already have such a good and healthy relationship and/or that they are already so heavily involved in church activity that they don't need such an "artificial contrivance" as a specially set-apart evening for these lessons. Others feel that the lessons don't meet their particular needs and don't give sufficient opportunity for initiative and creativity, and even the newer, shortened lessons are criticized by some as being too long and complicated.

Many of the younger children just don't like sitting that long and only want the activity part.

I don't want to moralize on these feelings, because I know they are real, and I think they explain in a measure why more families do not hold family home evenings than do.

Again I repeat the magnificent statement of Henry David Thoreau: "For every thousand hacking of the leaves of evil there is one striking of the root." I believe that all of these feelings and problems do represent the leaves, and as long as we think at that level and give answers to these problems and feelings at that level, we will never strike at the root.

The root is spiritual. It involves a vision and a commitment to that vision plus the discipline to carry it out.

First of all, a successful family home evening program, one that is truly effective, can be one of the most powerful forces in a family to unite the family and keep it on the right track. But it also takes a major commitment and a good portion of time in the preparation. I suggest we accept the Prophet's counsel on this matter and the promises of all of our Church leaders, in faith alone, if necessary at first. By following this program, we will have the blessings of God come to our home and families. Let's not intellectualize or rationalize it away. The time may come in some places when the gospel can only be safely taught in the home.

Once parents make a commitment and have the will, then the next important step is deciding how to make home evenings most effective. Unpleasant and ineffective home evenings can undo their purpose and certainly serve to undermine the resolve and desire to hold them consistently.

In support of the helpful suggestions made in the family home evening manuals, I emphasize the following techniques:

First, involve the children in the preparation and presentation of home evening lessons and programs. Also, involve them in some of the problems, and receive their ideas and suggestions. You will be amazed at what will happen to the commitment and cooperative attitude of the older youth, particularly, when they are meaningfully involved and not manipulated.

The father is to preside at all home evenings, but as in any church meeting, others might conduct and participate—some to lead the singing, others to offer prayers, and so forth. Different individuals may take turns teaching the lessons or part of the lessons, conducting activities, and preparing refreshments. Again, meaningful involvement is the key. What do I mean by meaningful? Essentially, that suggestions and opinions are respected and carefully considered before final decisions are made.

The family home evening manual is an excellent tool, a resource. The primary resource is the inspiration of the Spirit of God, which the father as patriarch of the home, using his own priesthood, can receive in directing the content and activities of the home evening.

Second, use visual aids. It takes a little extra time, but they are worth it, particularly if you can get some tapes or films or filmstrips, a blackboard, and charts. Variety and visualization are keys to maintaining interest.

Third, the spirit doesn't have to be tight, rigid, and formal. Successful home evenings can emerge very naturally right out of an evening meal's discussion, a family council meeting, or some other family activity. But there does need to come a time in these evenings when the parents look their children in the eye, do some explicit teaching of the gospel of Jesus Christ, and bear testimony. These meetings are not just for good social family gatherings and interchanges, which are most worthy purposes in themselves, and may have to suffice for a time in some family situations. But, in the long run, the lifting power is in the vision of the gospel, in the spirit of the Holy Ghost, in the power of bearing testimony in love, and in discussing gospel principles in connection with real family problems, needs, and concerns.

There must also be a fun and enjoyable spirit around home evenings. Some fun is spontaneous and arises naturally, but there is also great fun in anticipating a carefully planned family activity that is to follow a home evening lesson. There must be plenty of time for interaction, for personal visits, for family games or activities, and sometimes a special activity out of the home—something that the youth can look forward to, can help choose and help make successful.

There are many other useful practices families have to encourage righteous living. One is the establishment of a mission fund for all the young men and sometimes the young women of the family. When young children earn much of the money they put into these mission funds, the quality of their motivation in preparing and planning on a mission will be far more spiritual than it is social.

I can testify what a difference that motivation makes in those first few months in the mission. While the others thrash about trying to find themselves, filled with their own needs and problems, those who have a deep spiritual motivation, born of years of personal financial sacrifice, planning, and preparing, are dealing with the problems and needs, the eternal needs, of other people.

Summary

The most important point or principle of this entire

subject is the first one—that of the transcendent importance of the responsibility of parenthood in the character development of their children. (The problem of how to effectively discipline children, which is certainly central and fundamental in this discussion of parenthood and character development, is presented in the next chapter.)

Some may feel that I have overstressed the responsibility of parents and underplayed the responsibility of youth. If I were writing this chapter primarily to the youth, I would discuss their responsibility, their need to obey, to honor, to appreciate, to live true. But since this chapter is not primarily written for the youth, I focus almost exclusively on our responsibilities as parents.

22

To Parents:
Principles of Effective Discipline

How to effectively discipline children and youth is a universal concern. The study of discipline from the standpoint of the gospel plan of life and salvation is extremely interesting and enlightening.

Chapter 42 of Alma is the most illuminating scripture on the subject of discipline I have ever found, and I suggest a careful study and analysis of the wise counsel Alma gave to his rebellious son Coriantum. He is attempting to explain the principles of justice and mercy, which are central to discipline. Let us look at some of the elements: first, the importance of law; second, if an individual violates the law, this is called sin; third, punishment logically and naturally follows sin.

"Now, how could a man repent except he should sin? How could he sin if there was no law? How could there be a law save there was a punishment? (Alma 42:17.)

This is justice. What about mercy? Can mercy rob justice? No.

"What, do ye suppose that mercy can rob justice? I say unto you, Nay; not one whit. If so, God would cease to be God." (Verse 25.)

Then where does mercy come in? On the conditions of repentance. In other words, through the power of the

Lord's atonement and vicarious sacrifice for our sins, this plan of mercy can meet the demands of justice to those who repent and exercise faith in the Savior and his atoning sacrifice.

"For behold, justice exerciseth all his demands, and also mercy claimeth all which is her own; and thus, none but the truly penitent are saved.

"Therefore, O my son, whosoever will come may come and partake of the waters of life freely; and whosoever will not come the same is not compelled to come; but in the last day it shall be restored unto him according to his deeds.

"O my son, I desire that ye should deny the justice of God no more. Do not endeavor to excuse yourself in the least point because of your sins, by denying the justice of God; but do you let the justice of God, and his mercy, and his long-suffering have full sway in your heart; and let it bring you down to the dust in humility.

"And now, O my son, ye are called of God to preach the word unto this people. And now, my son, go thy way, declare the word with truth and soberness, that thou mayest bring souls unto repentance, that the great plan of mercy may have claim upon them. And may God grant unto you even according to my words. Amen." (Verses 24, 27, 30-31.)

This may appear to be abstract theology, but it has tremendous significance on the subject of disciplining children. Let us again examine the elements.

First, the importance of law. Many times parents do not clearly establish what the rules are in the home, or if they do establish them, they change them on the mood of the moment, so that often their children never have any secure sense of exactly what the limits are and what is to be expected. Constantly shifting limits and arbitrary rule making destroy the whole concept of justice; and if this concept is distorted, then all that follows—sin, punishment, mercy, repentance, etc.—will be distorted.

"And if there was no law given, if men sinned what could justice do, or mercy either, for they would have no claim upon the creature?" (Verse 21.)

But if there is a law given and a clearly understood punishment affixed, and if repentance opportunity is granted, then children will have a sense of both justice and mercy.

"But there is a law given, and a punishment affixed, and a repentance granted; which repentance mercy claimeth the creature and executeth the law, and the law inflicteth the punishment; if not so, the works of justice would be destroyed, and God would cease to be God." (Verse 22.)

Second: Now that a law or a rule has been clearly given, is it accurately communicated so that the children understand it, or is it merely understood by the parents? Is the punishment to be given also clearly understood and is it fair; that is, is the penalty equal to the offense? Children can be trained in this concept of fairness, but I believe they have an innate sense of it. If time is taken to clearly discuss, when the atmosphere is not surcharged with emotions, what the rules are, the reasons for the rules, and the nature of the punishment, good training is effected.

Third, follow-through by parents. Are they consistent? When they consistently follow through, the children sense they "get what is coming" to them, and this reinforces their sense of justice, out of which much of their personal security comes. If the parents are not consistent, but become arbitrary, giving in and indulging one moment and then being strict the next, disciplining on the mood of the moment, the children never know what is to be expected. With no sense of justice, their personal security is undermined. They will then learn how to escape the natural consequences of their actions. They will learn to find shortcuts, to pretend, to deceive, to get by on appearance and a clever tongue. They will strive to manipulate their parents, to get one parent at variance with the other, and to work on the most lenient one to mediate their battles and wants. This often causes feuding and disunity between the parents, which plays back on the whole emotional tone of the home so that the disciplining chore becomes often bitter and angry and much worse than the original misbehavior or problem requiring the discipline.

I have found in my own family, for instance, that I have a tendency to be more lenient, indulgent, and permissive, and my wife, in order to compensate, leans over backward in the other direction. The children sense this and sometimes try to test "which way the wind blows" and then wrangle to get their own way.

To illustrate how children "test the wind": I returned home late one night and was doing a little work in the study when, as if from nowhere, my four-year-old son appeared and just stood there staring at me, expressionless. Things had gone well with me that day and I was feeling good, and I was ever so happy to see my boy, so I blurted out, "Hi, Michael Sean! How are you?" to which he said nothing but immediately whipped around, ran to the top of the stairs, and yelled "Hey, Stephen, he's nice!"

Can't you just imagine the conversation between my two boys on hearing me come into the house? particularly after their mother had been "at them" to get back in bed for a couple of hours?

If my wife and I take the time to sit down and carefully plan a unified, harmonious approach to discipline, commit ourselves deeply to consistent follow-through, and if we then will take the time to carefully sit down and discuss rules and the consequences of honoring or breaking them, and if we are then consistent in following through, it is amazing what this does to everybody's sense of justice and happiness and learning.

All of this points up again the supreme importance of parents communicating with each other and planning and then communicating with the children.

Does this mean that these rules are inflexible, that there are no exceptions? Some rules might be inflexible, such as damage to personal property, but with other rules —such as family schedules and work assignments at home —there would certainly be a place for flexibility. When consideration is given to individual differences and individual situations in these kinds of rules, children begin to feel involved and respected, and then they grow in a sense of fairness and being responsible. They also learn the plan of mercy, that sincere repentance (including restitution when possible) for a particular misbehavior may meet to some extent the demands of justice.

Purpose of Discipline

In a discussion of discipline, the practical question often focuses around forms of discipline that many equate with punishment.

Let us first ask, What is the purpose of discipline? Would we not all agree that the purpose of disciplining is to teach, and to teach in such a way that the children learn a correct principle?

Let us further ask, What is the purpose of teaching a correct principle? Wouldn't we agree that the purpose is that the children, or individuals involved, learn to apply that principle in their own lives? Isn't that really what learning means?

If this reasoning is sound, we must conclude that the purpose of parental discipline is to build *internal* discipline.

Now we have a more clear standard or criterion by which to judge different methods of discipline, which is: Does this practice or form of discipline encourage my child or the individual involved to exercise self or internal discipline in obeying true principles?

When you think about it, isn't this the whole object of the gospel plan? Isn't this the central test of life?

The purpose of the Law of Moses was to serve as a schoolmaster or a form of external discipline to bring the people to Jesus Christ, who taught internal discipline. Much of our school system today is geared to this idea of providing a system of external requirements, or what we would call external discipline, on the theory that gradually students grow and mature to a position where they are capable of using their freedom in increasingly responsible ways. Grade school generally is very structured. High school is also, but not quite as much as grade school. More freedom and alternatives are available in college, but it is still basically an external discipline system at most universities. Graduate school, however, is largely a movement toward internal discipline—to create opportunities for the graduate student to apply the skills, tools, and knowledge he has acquired and to pursue a course of study in his own interest.

The Aaronic Priesthood is largely a system of external discipline; that is, certain basic service and social requirements are clearly defined and outlined. The Melchizedek Priesthood, however, involves a specific oath and covenant that each man makes with the Lord, which includes commitment to follow the Lord's direction given both through his servants and through the still, small voice, in magnifying this priesthood (doing more than outlined).

The ward teaching program, in practice, was largely a system of external discipline—a specific message to be given by the ward teachers to families on a monthly basis. Home teaching, however, has moved considerable distance toward a program of internal discipline. No specific message is given, no number of visits are prescribed—only an objective has been assigned. That objective is to discern the needs, temporal and spiritual, and to act accordingly. Many home teachers would almost prefer to go back to the old ward teaching program, where the demands were not quite so heavy, so they wouldn't have to exercise internal discipline. They would prefer to give a specific message; then they wouldn't have to discern, under the influence of God's Spirit, what the problems and needs are. They could handle it mechanically and then complete their duty. But in home teaching, much more responsibility and freedom is given, and a great deal more internal discipline is required.

It is precisely because most people lack internal—or self—discipline that we see the rise of many institutions in society. Take installment financing, for example. This is a system of external discipline simply because people do not have sufficient internal discipline to save before they spend. With this system they first spend and then are forced (externally disciplined) to save in order to meet the periodic payments. It not only costs them more money for service and interest charges and the loss of the cash discount, but it also costs them in character growth. They are not learning thriftiness, frugality, and industry, careful budgeting and planning. These great virtues are being programmed for them by outside institutions.

Multi-billion dollar industries have been built around people's lack of internal discipline in the areas of exercise and dieting. With enough will power and internal discipline, a person could learn to keep his body in good shape and form by following the principles of regularity and moderation in exercise, diet, and rest. But because most persons lack this internal discipline, they buy external discipline exercise schemes and go on one diet after another, forever looking for a simple shortcut to health and figure.

Consider adult education. A high percentage of the population, as soon as they finish their formal schooling, make no systematic attempt to continue on with schooling of a formal or informal variety. This would take internal disciplining. Why read when television can think for you, entertain you, mesmerize you?

Methods of Effective External Discipline

We see, therefore, that many forms of external discipline condition people to increased dependency on external disciplines, which is the opposite of the real purpose of discipline (that of building internal discipline or self-control, as discussed above).

What forms of external discipline build internal discipline?

First, I suggest that by far the most important form of external discipline is example. Albert Schweitzer once put it this way: "There are three basic principles in raising children: First, example. Second, example. Third, example." I don't personally agree that example is everything, but I do believe that it is most of everything and certainly the foundation on which all other principles can work.

Therefore, before I make up my mind to be firm with my children, I must first make up my mind to be firm with myself and to exercise self-restraint and wisdom, that my discipline may be geared to one purpose—building internal discipline in my children so they learn to choose on their own to obey true principles.

Second, it is important to have a fairly firm family schedule, with regular hours of rising and retiring, particularly on school days.

I found in the mission field how tremendously powerful a daily schedule is. It is a form of external discipline, but gradually this becomes a habit, and once it is a habit it tends to become internalized. When missionaries learn to work and study according to this very rigorous schedule until it becomes part of them, they find themselves capable of applying that kind of self-control to many other fields of endeavor both on their mission and after it. This is not to say that there is to be no flexibility, but if you set up a firm schedule and decide to follow it, most of the "would be" exceptions go by the board, the entire family becomes healthier and happier, and much more is accomplished.

Third, coupling privileges with responsibilities. For instance, I have found great value in spending time in a family home evening, planning carefully the entire week, particularly fun family activities, where the anticipation of togetherness and of certain privileges is in itself quite an effective form of positive discipline. Children then know what is to take place, what responsibilities are theirs, and they gear themselves accordingly. When people accomplish significant things by their own planning and follow-through work, they have a great sense of self-mastery, achievement, and satisfaction, and this positive spirit diffuses itself into the whole atmosphere of the home.

Fourth, another powerful form of external discipline is an intelligent system of chores or duties around the home. There is value in involving children and older youth in helping to choose some of these chores and perhaps in rotating and in assigning others that were not volunteered for. I believe in the value of assigning the result to be accomplished more than in assigning the method to accomplish the result by. This gives the children freedom and an opportunity to develop internal discipline, initiative, resourcefulness, and creativity.

All members of the family need to understand there are certain things that must be done to keep a household running smoothly. Use a large chart or a blackboard to help visualize some of these things; then put your own responsibilities as parents on it so that the children understand your role and your part.

If a child does not perform his chores, the parents should spend time with him trying to find out why and perhaps providing a little training, but they should not take back the duty by doing the chore themselves. They should realize that the character development of the children is more important than what other people might think if the lawn is temporarily left uncut or a room unkempt. Perhaps the chore was too much. Perhaps the child is really lazy and trying to get by. Perhaps the child didn't clearly understand. In other words, the parent must focus on the real problem, which may lie with the child rather than with the particular task to be done.

An effort should be made to have some of the tasks or chores pleasurable or naturally satisfying, and if possible to arrange some chores as near to nature as possible, such as gardening, taking care of animals, or preparing food. These kinds of tasks provide natural rewards. Children can actually see what they have produced, which is satisfying.

Fifth, punishment is another form of external discipline. What do you do when the rules have been clearly spelled out and understood and then violated? What is the punishment to be? Generally speaking, I believe in the philosophy of what has been called "natural and logical consequences"—allowing that which naturally or logically would take place through the violation of a rule to be its own punishment.

For instance, if a child dawdles around in the early morning with the full understanding of the family rule to be at the breakfast table at a certain time and to leave for school at a certain time, then the natural consequences might be no breakfast and/or being late for school. If the parents are setting a good example themselves and giving encouragement and emotional support, then *allowing* these natural consequences to take place will gradually teach the child to accept the responsibility for living by these rules.

A friend once told me that he had overheard his children talking to each other in the morning, and one said: "If Mommy doesn't get us up soon, we are going to be late for school." This statement forcibly brought to the attention of the parents how they had gradually, even though unknowingly, taken the responsibility from the children to get themselves up on time.

Two divine principles seem to be threading themselves through how the Lord handles his children. First is the principle that he never does for them what they can and should do for themselves. If he were to do so, he would rob them of growth. The second principle is that he seems to work on the basis of natural consequences. If man abuses his freedom, he loses it. If he disobeys the commandments, he gradually destroys himself. This is not to say that the Lord does not intervene or does not maintain a constant personal interest. He created the universe; he governs it by natural eternal law, and his interventions are entirely consistent with this natural eternal law.

One of the real problems in connection with this natural and logical consequence form of discipline or punishment is that we, as parents, sometimes are not really willing to let this process operate, but rather desire to intervene or interrupt it in a way that robs the child or individual of the lesson to be learned and that often teaches that the only real harm is in getting caught. Sheltering people from natural consequences teaches irresponsibility. Perhaps our love is too possessive and lacks faith in the process of growth and development. If so, it may be that we have never learned these natural laws for ourselves. Perhaps we ourselves never had to deal with the natural and logical consequences of our own actions, and have become increasingly oriented to unnatural and social forms of punishment and discipline.

What are logical consequences as distinguished from unusual consequences? I can see my child's missing a meal because of not being responsible, but I can't allow the natural consequence of my child's running out into the street, or associating with youth of low standards and morals, or reading pornographic material. In some way I should decide on and clearly communicate what logical consequences follow what acts of obedience or disobedience. What might be some of these logical consequences?

If the child isn't willing to stay in the yard and insists on running into the street, then the privilege of playing with others, until he feels he can do so responsibly, quarrels and fights with others, then the privilege of playing with others until he feels he can do so responsibly should be withdrawn. If the rules regarding television and other entertainment opportunities are violated, then perhaps the privilege of these opportunities should be withdrawn for a time.

In a sense I am protecting or shielding or sheltering my children from some of the natural consequences, but I believe this is consistent with the way the Lord has worked with his children from the beginning. He is very concerned with the environment that surrounds his children. The program of the church itself is an attempt to structure the environment so as to make the living of gospel principles "the thing to do." Gradually the purpose of all of this kind of structuring and shielding is to build internal restraints and disciplines within the individual so that he might be able to effectively deal with the external temptations and compulsions he will inevitably face throughout his life. It isn't an all-or-nothing matter. It depends largely on the level of growth and responsibleness of the person as well as on environment factors.

Whenever the question of how to effectively discipline in such and such a situation is raised, it can generally be successfully handled if the parents involved would ask themselves, "What are the natural (or logical) consequences of such an action?" and then discipline accordingly.

A mother once wrote me, as mission president, regarding her missionary son and asked that I allocate her monthly check on a weekly basis to her son because he had never learned to handle finances responsibly. Inwardly, I said to myself, Well, is this missionary ready for a mission, if he can't even handle finances? How has this mother trained her son? I was upset by the request and I complied very begrudgingly. However, I was unrealistic. You have to hit from where your fist is, and you have to begin where the reality is. This missionary came into the mission field undisciplined and irresponsible. I couldn't change this fact. I could wish it otherwise, but this wouldn't make it so. I would only learn it myself the hard way later, which would then stir up other problems. I had to accept the situation as it was; and once I became aware of how really irresponsible the elder was with finances, I was more than happy to comply with the mother's request. We began there at step one and gradually moved to step two (more freedom, more responsibility), then step three, and so on, until the missionary, by the end of his mission, became very responsible, filled assignments of substantial trust, and developed considerable internal discipline.

While we should forever work to do the right things for the right reasons, we must never stop doing the right things for less mature reasons. The direction of development rather than level of development is the crucial factor.

Summary

I don't believe that the crucial factor is the method or form of discipline or punishment (spanking to some parents is a natural consequence) so much as it is three things: (1) the quality of the relationship between the individuals; (2) whether there is a clear mutual understanding of exactly what the rules are and what the consequences are if there is disobedience or obedience; (3) and consistent follow-through with that which has been agreed upon.

And, most important, underlying these three factors is the depth of the harmony and unity between the parents on these matters and the quality of their own example (internal discipline).

23

To Parents:
Communicating With Our Youth

About six months ago a young man came into my office. He was a member of the Aaronic Priesthood, about eighteen years old, with a great potential, with plans for a mission in his future. But I was somewhat alarmed by the report that he was planning to run away and get married, so I asked him if he would come in. He told me how he felt, that his parents were living hundreds of miles away, that they were recently separated, that they had been psychologically separated for years, that he had never felt within himself that they truly loved and cared for him, and that no one really cared for him except a girl who lived in another state. Every chance he had, he went to visit with her over the weekends. He said, "She understands me, and she accepts me, and she loves me."

I tried to reason with him: "You realize, brother, that this girl is not a member of our faith. You must realize the implications of that in your life. They are eternal. This will mean you will marry out of the temple and marry out of the faith. Think of the significance of that throughout all of the years you are going to live together. Think of the impact of that upon your children."

"Yes, I know, but I don't know what to do. I believe I can convert her and that she will be baptized and then someday we can get married in the temple."

Again I reasoned, "Brother, don't you realize that of all of those who plan to get married in the temple but who initially marry outside of the temple, a high percentage never do? These couples are not those who get married out of the temple initially and wonder whether they want to be married in the temple or not. These couples fully intended to get married in the temple. These are they who say as they enter into this temporal marriage, 'No question about it. I am going to get married in the temple. It is a matter of a year or two. A few things in our lives to get ready, to get worthy, and then we will go to the temple.' Of this group a good percentage never get married in the temple. You know this girl. Her father has been a spokesman of another faith and has had a very strong, dominant influence upon her. She has had this deeply ingrained within her since her youth. It seems to me that the chances are very, very slim that you will ever get married in the temple."

Then he turned and tears welled up in his eyes and he said, "But bishop, I love her."

Then he fell back somewhat in despair and did not know what to do. He said, "I could resolve now not to run away and get married, but I want to discuss it with her first."

I said, "Do you think you can carry that resolve out when you visit with her, when all of the emotional circumstances are conducive to running away and getting married?"

"I don't know. I just don't know."

Now here is a good example of a leader, his leader in the Church, giving what I consider to be good advice. I think it is logical and reasonable. Logic—that was my language. What was his language? What was it that concerned him primarily? His feeling, his emotion, his sentiment! What happens when you talk the language of logic to an individual who understands the language of sentiment? How can you communicate?

This to me is an enormous problem that we have with

our youth in the Church—the logic of eternity versus the sentiment of the moment—and I would like to give my analysis of this problem in terms of what I call filling the gap. I want to outline three gaps I believe must be filled before we can successfully solve this widespread problem.

The first gap is this: People in their youth, during their teenage period, are at the crossroads of life's decisions—that is, the decisions they are making at that time are more crucial and more strategic in their impact upon their life than perhaps at any other time in their life. By far, also, it is the most impressionable period. They are most vulnerable to the feelings of other people, particularly to what is called their peer groups—their friends, their gangs. This presents us with a dilemma: the nature of the activity and the decision—long-range; the nature of the emotional perspective—short-range. Should I go on a mission? Should I go on to college? What career should I go into? Should I get married? Whom should I marry? Should it be a temple marriage? Every one of these questions is an eternally significant question because essentially they amount to a man's life in this probationary period and are tremendously far reaching. Yet we realize that people are motivated through their emotions, how they *feel* about things. If they feel strongly about eternal things, they tend to act on that eternal, long-range perspective. But when they are immature, when they are susceptible to the policing of other people's opinions—particularly the gang, the group—then something happens to that emotional perspective. It reduces in size and becomes short.

A good story is told of a college president who was very concerned about the excessive smoking among the coeds on the campus. He tried two approaches. One was to bring in a very eminent physician who laid down a very persuasive and eloquent case about the direct and immediate relationship between smoking and lung cancer, that smoking unquestionably causes lung cancer. A very powerful message. A study was taken. Something like 3 per cent of those who smoked quit, and within six months, only a few of those had quit permanently.

He attempted another approach. He brought in a woman who had done a great deal of sociological research. This woman gave an excellent speech on the direct relationship between kissability and smoking. You are less desirable as a kissing partner if you smoke. Again a very powerful message. She gave researched statistical evidence that those who smoke are not kissed as often and are not as desirable to be kissed. Follow-up studies showed this approach influenced almost ten times as many people as were influenced with the other approach. Yet we see an inverse relationship between the "wisdom" of the message of the first and the "wisdom" of the message of the second. However, that is our wisdom in our thinking as adults; but the wisdom of the sentiment of the youth, that is another kind of wisdom. How do I talk to that "wisdom"? It is powerful and immediate!

There is a girl who was sold on getting married to a fellow in my ward. He had promised her that he would quit smoking and drinking. I interviewed them. He really had no interest in the Church, but he promised her that he would develop one if she would marry him. It became readily apparent to me that he would probably never really become devoted to the Church. His whole orientation, his value systems had been focused around physical, material, and social values. He admitted that he had never really prayed. But he had quit smoking and drinking for one full week! This was convincing evidence to her of his love, and convincing evidence to me that love can be blind. I saw them sitting there on the couch. She tearfully looked at him and said, "We love each other. I love him. I have faith in him. Bishop, are you asking me not to have faith in him, not to trust him? Is that not a teaching of the gospel? I have faith in him. I love him and he loves me."

Three weeks after they were married, she called me and was again tearful. He had come home drunk and had started involving himself with other girls. Short-range perspective; emotional perspective.

Our youth may intellectually understand this dilemma, this gap, but it is the emotion out of which people act, how they feel about things, not what they think about them, and this is particularly so the less mature they are.

Now let us look at the second gap. This compounds the first problem, for it is built upon it.

Inasmuch as the decisions have long-range consequences, and the perspective is short, who is to bridge the gap? Well, obviously the authority people in their life, people who have had more extensive experience, who possess wisdom, for they have gone through similar problems and they know what is happening—teachers, leaders, and above all, and most importantly, parents.

But here is the real gap. There exists with many teenagers a huge gap so that they tend not to listen to the wisdom of their parents or to trust authority figures. They tend to discount their parents, to write them off as not being "with it," as not really understanding them, as not really caring, as just preaching, moralizing, evaluating, judging, lecturing. All of these kinds of emotional attitudes they see in the parents.

A sociological survey was taken among teenagers, who were asked: Do you feel close to your parents so that you would go to them if you had personal problems? A high percentage said they do not feel close to their parents. They said they would not go to them, and they would not go to their teachers in their schools or in the church because they only get one major response—judgment, a lecture, a moral teaching. "They don't understand me. They don't really care. They are just preaching to me again. I don't want to go to my father; I know what he will tell me. I can predict it."

You see, the assumption is often made by parents, teachers, and leaders that merely an intellectual understanding of right and wrong is adequate to motivate people to do that which is right. And yet we know that many of them know exactly what they should do, although they don't do it. So again the question becomes one of knowing how to eliminate or reduce the gap between their intellectual perspective and their short-range emotions out of which their actions more frequently flow.

If parents and teachers do not fill the void, who will? The group—the group they go along with. What are the central values of most youth groups? Social, material, and physical values—"the clothing I wear, my looks, the way I behave, feel, talk, think, look, the friends I have, the status symbols I can accumulate in my life. These are the things that give me belonging and acceptance in this group."

But whom is the group made up of? "It is composed of people just like me who have short-range emotional perspective, who are concerned almost entirely with short-range things—material, social, and physical—and unless I comply and conform, I fear rejection and ostracism. I need to belong, to be accepted. Therefore, I have to comply. I am almost forced to, *unless* the gap is filled by someone else."

Who is to fill that gap? It has to be the parents, the leaders, and the teachers. But how, when there is such an enormous communication barrier or gap?

I suggest to all of us who are concerned with this problem of youth—and all of us, I am sure, are—that there is another gap that must be bridged before you can really bridge the communication and the motivation-perspective gaps. This is the gap in our own lives between our beliefs and our actual behavior—including our emotional, attitudinal behavior. That is the crucial void.

To summarize, *if parents, leaders, and teachers obey the laws of love, they encourage obedience to the laws of life.* If, on the other hand, they disobey the laws of love, they encourage disobedience to the laws of life. Let me give some definitions so this will take on some meaning. What do we mean by the laws of love? These evolve essentially around this idea: I affirm you and your right to be. I acknowledge you with great reverence and respect your existence, that you are a person of worth, that you have a divine Father, that you in your very humanity are worth loving. This is apart from your performance or your behavior. I may not like your behavior. I am upset with it, but I affirm you, I respect you. I honor you as a person, I listen to you, I try to understand.

Again, if I as a parent can live the law of love by that affirmation, I encourage obedience to the laws of life. What are these laws of life? Stay faithful in the Church and to all of the teachings of the gospel—the laws of repentance, the laws regarding education, the laws that have to do with the growth and development of a personality toward the eventual position of exaltation in the celestial kingdom, a celestialized personality.

A man whom I respect greatly, a stake president, had a son who did not desire to go upon a mission. He strongly wanted and had raised his son to go on a mission. He knew of the great benefits that it would reap to him and to all of those that he would touch in the mission field. He said, "Son, I want you to know that I want you to go on a mission, but I also want you to know that that decision is yours, and that if you should decide to go on a mission, your mother and I will be very delighted. We will honor you in your decision. If you should not decide to go upon a mission, your mother and I will also honor and respect you in that decision."

The son, with that kind of freedom, with that kind of affirmation given to him, went through quite a period of time in which he decided, "I don't want to go on my mission. The sacrifice is too great."

And with that superstructure of feeling behind him, he later responded to spiritual values and said, "Yes, I want to go on a mission."

He made an internal commitment himself, and I believe that internal commitment will reap its benefits the rest of his missionary life.

Another man I know said to me, "My parents want me to go on this mission."

"Do *you* want to go?"

"I don't know. Maybe. Sometimes I don't think so, but they want me to go, and it is very important to them. What I fear most is that I don't know how they would feel toward me if I didn't go."

What kind of commitment is he making? Well, he went on a mission, and within a short time he returned home without filling it. Were those parents living the laws of love? They did not affirm his right to be, to exist, to decide. They manipulated, they pressured, they coerced, and I believe that encourages (not determines) disobedience to the laws of life.

Once I talked about this in one of my classes at which a faculty member was present. He had been somewhat cynical about some of the teachings but was interested because of a very poor relationship and communication with his son. After visiting my class once, he said, "Wait a minute. I have lived my life, and I know exactly what kinds of problems my son is having, and therefore I understand him. I can see the dangers and the pitfalls in the future if he does not take my advice."

I said to him, "Let me suggest to you that you try making the assumption that you do not understand your son and that you start from the beginning by listening to him and what he says, without any moral evaluation after his expression."

"I don't believe it," he said, "but I will try it."

At eight o'clock in the evening his son stated, "Dad, I just don't think you understand me at all." Later this man told me, "Inside myself I said, 'I know I do. Do I have to go through all this?'" But he had promised himself he would listen. He said, "All right, son. I'll assume that I don't. Now tell me about yourself."

He was planning to end the conference at nine because of another commitment, but they went on until 11:30—three and a half hours. He later told me with new gratitude that he never realized he did not know his son at all, that he had never really allowed his son to express himself, or to be. The son always had to be what the father wanted him to be. If he did not quite fit the mold, an attempt was made to impress the mold upon him. The man said, "My son and I have refound each other. We are friends again."

If he can maintain that kind of relationship, can you see how that gap, that first communication gap, will be filled, so he can talk to his son and give the emotional support necessary for his son to act on the long-range perspective? But the key was in seeking to understand.

One day a mother who was beside herself with anxiety called me. "My daughter is becoming interested in a person who has no interest in the Church. She is really becoming involved."

The more she talked, the more I was convinced that the problem was not so much with the daughter—it was with the mother. At every opportunity she took that daughter and lectured her and preached to her and used her boyfriend, who later became her fiancé, as a weapon against her by saying, "Look at the kind of a boy he is. Do you want to marry a boy like that?"

"I love him."

I advised the mother, "Be careful you don't drive her into his arms. The more you deny her rights to be and to exist and to live, the more she'll feel to fight by behaving opposite to your expectations."

She could not understand this. Intellectually she could, but she was so subjectively involved that she could not risk another approach. She had never known another. Well, they were married, and from all I hear neither of them is very happy. The girl realizes what she has done now. There is even a bigger gap because the parents tend to use it as a weapon against her to say, "We told you so."

What is it, then, that can fill this most important gap in our own lives as parents, teachers, and leaders—

the gap between what I say with my mouth (and intellectualize with my mind) and how I behave (how I feel
down here in my heart)? I think that void must be filled,
because I feel the pressure and you feel the pressure to
meet the expectations of society. We ourselves are also immersed in all of these value systems—social, material,
physical, intellectual value systems. We are anxious to have
children who obey and conform. And when we see non-
conformity, we tend to take it personally. We become
subjectively involved and value our own acceptance more
than the essential intrinsic worth of our children. And so
we tend to disobey the laws of love—we try to manipulate,
force, push, cajole, and use logic or any other means
necessary to get people to do the right thing.

From my illustrations you can see two forms of disobedience—open rebellion and doing the right things for
the wrong reasons. The second is where people conform,
but they do not really care about it. They have to do it to
buy their parent's love, to buy their leader's approval, to
buy their teacher's acceptance. It is like the Duty to God
awardees who were caught involved in gang thievery. Hundred percenters—gang thievery. What had happened? All
those meetings—and the gospel had never really pene-
trated inside!

The answer in filling this gap between my feeling
about others and my verbal behavior and my intellectual
belief is in the depth of my conversion to the Lord Jesus
Christ, where I begin to feel in my heart that he loves me
with an infinite and a divine love and that therefore I can
love with great reserves, with great affirmation. Then I can
discipline, yes. Then I can give advice, yes. But this is
based upon a relationship of unconditional love and acceptance of the person. Often in our attempt to build a
relationship with the Savior we project our own human
experiences, which may be unforgiving, judging, and rejecting; we do not see the Savior literally as a elder
brother, as an intimate associate whom we can get to
know and feel deeply in our hearts, and therefore we often

will not allow the gap between us and him to be bridged. But I know it can be done. The scriptures tell us that if you will pray unto the Father with all of the energy of the heart, you will be filled with this love. Jacob 3:1-2 indicates if you will become pure in your heart, you can feast upon the love of Christ and then he will become "thy advocate in the heavens." Then righteous parents acting on the laws of love can actually influence the heavens to bless their children and can exercise enormous influence.

To the youth I would like to direct a word. Try to understand this problem—this gap in your lives—that you do tend to act upon short-range emotional perspective. Seek out the wisdom of your elders. Seek out a relationship with them—the kind of a relationship I have been speaking about. But try to understand why that relationship is difficult to achieve. In other words, try to understand your parents; try to affirm them in *their* right to make mistakes and to be imperfect and to grow through the mistake-making process. All of us are mistake-makers. If you will do that, then you can lean on the wisdom of the gospel and make decisions that have long-range perspective in them.

If you have faith in the divine potentiality of people, you can give them some freedom. When you give freedom, you affirm them. When you affirm them, you give them the emotional support to fill that void, to bridge that perspective-motivation gap.

Think about this short sonnet from Shakespeare, who tells about the powerful impact of a special relationship:

When, in disgrace with fortune and men's eyes,
I all alone beweep my outcast state,
And trouble deaf heaven with my bootless cries,
And look upon myself, and curse my fate,
Wishing me like to one more rich in hope,
Featured like him, like him with friends possess'd,
Desiring this man's art and that man's scope,
With what I most enjoy contented least;
Yet in these thoughts myself almost despising,
Haply I think on thee, and then my state,

Like to the lark at break of day arising
From sullen earth, sings hymns at heaven's gate;
  For thy sweet love remember'd such wealth brings
  That then I scorn to change my state with kings.
                                          (—Sonnet XXIX)

If you can love—deeply, richly—in affirming another person, you will help him to change, to develop, to grow. It is almost ironic, because some people think that if you do that, you make the other person become complacent and stultified. I believe that the very opposite results.

The highest principle in the gospel is love of God and people, not love of the principles. If you love people, the principles will become fused with strength and purpose. If you love principles as ends in themselves, others will sense your using those principles as weapons, and they will often rebel. Otherwise your love of them will draw them to obey true principles.

24

To Teachers:
The Power and Methods
of Involvement Teaching

A. Learning Is Changed Behavior—Your Divine Objective

Teachers! Leaders! Parents! Let this thought permeate your whole soul: the purpose of teaching is learning; learning is changed behavior. Your objective then is to inspire and help the learners to develop Christ-like character through more Christ-like living every day. (See 3 Nephi 27:27.)

Simple? Obvious, you say? Perhaps. However, carefully reflect on the strong tendencies in preparing and giving lessons to serve other objectives: "to cover material," "to get through the points," "to get the facts across," or even "to stimulate intellectually," "to involve," "to impress."

Divine knowledge or learning, the Savior taught, is a function of living or doing "the doctrine." (See John 7:16-17.) Peter beautifully taught this same vital principle by emphasizing that a *knowledge* of Jesus Christ was the fruit of *living* or obeying divine principles, beginning with faith and ending with charity or divine love. (See 2 Peter 1:3-8.) Knowledge is more than information—it is conversion.

Saturate your heart and your thinking with this lofty eternal aim and you'll discover it will constantly shape your preparations and teaching methods and dynamically influence your teaching relationships. *The most important single ingredient in teaching is your motive, your real objective.*

B. Why Involvement Teaching?

Unless the learner is involved and dynamically participates in the learning process, very little, if any, learning (changed behavior) will result. This growth principle underlies our entire church philosophy and tellingly distinguishes us from the professional "one man" approach to religion.

The more the whole person (mind, heart, soul, and senses) is involved, the more real, deep, and permanent the learning or change.

1. *Involving the learner helps to bridge the gap between the abstract (theory, principle, theology. "what should be") and the concrete (actual living, "what is").* Why? Because when the learner participates, you bring reality (feeling, real problems, actual behavior) to ideality (principles, theory). Unless this gap is bridged, application of the principle or lesson to life is unlikely, even though there is a momentary inspiration and resolve to "do the thing." But later, in the midst of the pressing and buffeting realities of life, old habits and attitudes reassert themselves. Something must be done in the learning process itself to inculcate new *attitudes* and to develop new *skills,* in addition to acquiring more informational *knowledge,* upon which new habits of life will be formed.

For instance, to convince others of the importance of a loving, creative, spirtual home atmosphere is most worthy. "But *how,*" she asks herself, "when my husband won't cooperate?" How helpful, practical, and motivating it would be to this sister and perhaps other sisters to develop a step-by-step program, starting with "what is" and moving to "what should be." Of even greater help is to give *training* in developing the priceless skill of communicating (empathy) with husbands and children, through demonstration and actual *practice* opportunity in the class itself.

2. *Involvement teaching facilitates two-way communication.*

Communication is mutual understanding, and therefore, it must of necessity be two-way to be effective. This means listening in order to understand. Such listening requires patience and courage, faith in and respect for others. The enemy of honest, unguarded communication is the tendency to judge, label, reject, manipulate.

Unless the learner feels understood, feels that his "unique" circumstances and problems are considered and that he himself is important, liked, and respected, then nothing that is taught "quite applies." Teachers, if you want to maximize your influence, particularly among those you haven't yet reached, start listening and stop judging or criticizing within yourself. Build a relationship—try to feel the pulse and adapt your lesson accordingly.

C. How to Effectively Involve the Learner

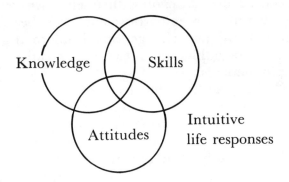

As illustrated, you note the interdependency and relationship between knowledge, skills, and attitudes. Influencing or changing one will to some degree affect or change the other two. Involvement teaching methods generally aim at all three simultaneously, thus maximizing the influence. People remember most of what they do, little of what they hear.

Reading a lesson manual aloud, lecturing, and conducting an abstract intellectual discussion, while useful methods in efficiently covering material, are generally ineffective teaching (learning) methods. They are often used out of fear or inadequate preparation or out of simply not knowing what else to do.

Effective involving methods include:

1. *Case discussions* of real-life problem situations, embodying certain principles in the lesson and calling for decisions and plans of action.

2. *Role plays* (spontaneous or arranged beforehand), in which learners live out the plan of action in a simulated reality or learn how to communicate or practice other human skills.

3. *Buzz groups*, formed by breaking the larger group into smaller, less restraining groups to achieve any number of purposes, such as discussing the application of the lesson to life, considering practical problems, analyzing one part of the topic, making decisions, and determining a specific plan of action.

When people can express themselves without fear of ridicule, censure, or embarrassment, they become more open to influence and change. Small, informal groupings tend to encourage this and to release the creative capacities of more individuals.

4. Other excellent involvement techniques include *panel discussions, symposiums, tableaus, individuals giving special reports, sharing experiences, testimonies, giving part of the lesson.*

Try new methods. Don't be discouraged or judge first attempts too harshly. Be patient with yourself. Involvement teaching skills don't develop overnight. As with any skill, proficiency only comes with preparation and *practice.*

D. Intellectual-Emotional-Spiritual Involvement

Involvement occurs if the learner's mind and heart are "in gear," even though he may not express himself verbally.

1. *Testimony—spiritual appeals:* We have all experienced soul-stirring involvement in listening to a powerful, inspiring message of a great leader or teacher. Our minds have been enlightened by the comprehensive eternal plan and view, our hearts softened and perhaps convicted by a spiritual message of repentance, our souls thrilled by a

testimony of the Living Christ and his marvelous work and wonder.

Teachers, never underestimate the power of sincere testimony. Bear yours fervently, naturally, frequently. Preaching the word of God has "more powerful effect upon the minds of people than the sword, or anything else." (Alma 31:5.) The Holy Ghost will confirm your testimony in the hearts and souls of the hearers. This is the most effective involvement, for it pierces to the very core and works on the roots of life.

2. *Use a physical or natural illustration to teach a spiritual principle.*

Jesus Christ was a master in this with his use of parables. He would vividly describe real situations from the peoples' own experiences and draw out divine lessons. Then each time the experience recurred or the scene reappeared, his divine lesson would be retaught.

You can do the same thing. Cultivate your powers of observation, imagination, and description. Teach inductively—infer from the specific to the general. Often it's more powerful than *deductive* teaching—inferring from the general to the specific.

Constantly draw spiritual lessons from the "seen" natural and physical processes in life. Let me illustrate:

1. In teaching the divine principles of love, faith, patience, and supportive understanding in relationships, illustrate the *seen* process of slow, natural physical growth in children. What about the *unseen* emotional, social, spiritual growth processes?

2. In teaching justice or the law of the harvest (you reap what you sow), ask an untrained person to play the piano or to sing a solo. Apply the obvious learning to the development of any skill (cooking, tennis, or communicating). Observe the farming process from planting in the spring to harvesting in the fall. There is no shortcut in farming, in school, in raising a family, in teaching Relief Society or priesthood lessons, in building relationship, in achieving any *real* success.

3. In teaching that the things of God, including a testimony, are given by the Spirit of God (1 Corinthians 2:9-14), pretend blindness and ask others to describe what it means to see. Technical information, analysis, and intellectualizing about sight won't help at all. To know God, one must experience his spirit, which comes from searching, prayer, study, worthiness—not from human reasoning.

4. In teaching that faith is born of obedience (desire, experimentation, diligence, patience—Alma 32:26-43), blindfold someone. Then ask three voices (one true, the others false) to direct him to his billfold hidden somewhere in the room. When he finds it, ask him how he discovered which voice was true and which false. Then try organizing the group into buzz groups to discuss the many additional insights and principles involved.

Teachers, you are only limited by your imagination in drawing the spiritual out of the physical.

The Roots

Effective involvement teaching isn't easy. It is highly demanding and spiritually exacting. Fundamentally, you teach the quality of your spirit. Therefore, your most vital preparation is spiritual. Learn to first master yourself; then get into the lesson content. You teach what you are, no more and no less, in the long run.

Gethsemane was a private battlefield—Calvary a public one. Private victories precede public ones. Shallow spiritual preparation, mechanical prayer, and heavy reliance on lesson content and teaching techniques will not deeply influence others to change, though they may be impressed.

The important problems you face as a teacher, or in your life generally, are rooted spiritually (though the branches appear practical or technical), and the key to their solution also lies within yourself.

"Out of the heart flow the real issues of life." (Proverbs 4:23.) Learn to examine your heart. Root out double-mindedness, the father of instability. Repent and covenant. Eliminate hypocrisy. Pray from your heart, privately, earnestly. Study the word of the Lord every day to feel and know the Author and his ways. "Let the solemnities of eternity rest upon your minds." (D&C 43:34.)

"I am the vine, ye are the branches: He that abideth in me, and I in him, the same bringeth forth much fruit: for without me ye can do nothing." (John 15:5.)

25

To Leaders:
The Character Foundation
of Leadership

It has truly been said that an institution is merely the lengthened shadow of its leader. His own character and attitude, example and practice diffuse themselves down through the entire organization and leave an indelible impression upon every person, every practice, every process.

It is of vital and fundamental importance that every church leader and teacher understand the tremendous far-reaching influence of his own personality and effort. More than any other one single factor, he will determine the success or failure of his group or project. This is a humbling, staggering thought—almost terrifying, particularly in church work, where we are dealing with the souls of men. But the Lord has taught us that if we will but come to him, he will make us equal to the demands of our calling. ". . . for if they humble themselves before me, and have faith in me, then will I make weak things become strong unto them." (Ether 12:27.)

Study carefully the illustration that follows, to see various ways in which a leader can respond to his calling. First of all, notice the wide gap between the demands of his calling and his own native abilities. You will observe that in church work the highest demands of one's calling are spiritual. Without the assistance of the Spirit of the Lord, it is impossible for a leader to succeed. His human

To Illustrate the Acceptance or Rejection
of Leadership Responsibility

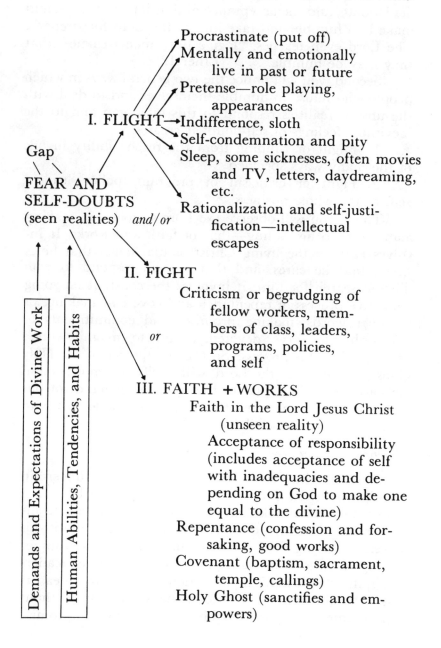

Procrastinate (put off)
Mentally and emotionally
live in past or future
Pretense—role playing,
appearances

I. FLIGHT→Indifference, sloth
Self-condemnation and pity
Sleep, some sicknesses, often movies
and TV, letters, daydreaming,
etc.
Rationalization and self-justification—intellectual
escapes

Gap

FEAR AND
SELF-DOUBTS
(seen realities) *and/or*

II. FIGHT
Criticism or begrudging of
fellow workers, mem-
bers of class, leaders,
programs, policies,
and self

or

III. FAITH + WORKS
Faith in the Lord Jesus Christ
(unseen reality)
Acceptance of responsibility
(includes acceptance of self
with inadequacies and de-
pending on God to make one
equal to the divine)
Repentance (confession and forsaking, good works)
Covenant (baptism, sacrament,
temple, callings)
Holy Ghost (sanctifies and em-
powers)

Demands and Expectations of Divine Work

Human Abilities, Tendencies, and Habits

skills, social knowledge, and good mind are simply not sufficient. Not only does he usually feel inadequate—he is inadequate, and the acceptance of that inadequacy should make him humble and take him to the Lord for strength. The Lord even teaches, "I give unto men weakness that they may be humble. . . ." (Ether 12:27.)

Second, you will notice the two general ways in which people who refuse to humble themselves and to deal with the unseen realities respond to this huge gap and to the inevitable feelings of self-doubt it creates:

1. Flight or running from the responsibility in one of the many ways specified.

2. Fight or criticism of program, policy leaders, self, or the whole business.

Third, you will observe the Lord's process in making man equal to his calling—that of faith and works. It involves faith in the living Christ, actual belief that he is there, that he cares, and that he will respond to your diligent search for him. It involves the constant on-going educative process of repentance and covenant making, or in other words, making promises and commitments to live right, to serve devotedly, and to magnify one's calling. Why this process? So that the power of the Holy Ghost, the Spirit of the Lord, will purify our motives and empower us to be equal to the spiritual demands of our callings. With man, many things are impossible, but with God, nothing is impossible.

Character and Motive

Paul taught, "For if a trumpet give an uncertain sound, who shall prepare himself to the battle?" If a leader is eager to make impressions and has an eye to his own reputation, his doublemindedness will uproot his power. In giving forth an uncertain sound, his trumpet may spread the same contagious disease in other leaders and in the people in his organization or group. In his eagerness to be all things to all people, he will end up without respect from others or from himself. He may compromise the magnificent principles and programs of the organization's purpose, in the name of expediency. He may find himself exaggerating for effect, struggling for loyalties from others based on false principles, manipulating and masterminding others, becoming a hovering supervisor, finding fault with others, and criticizing. This process leads to a loss of faith in others and to discouragement and unhappiness.

Let a teacher or leader examine his motive and exert all his power to develop a single and pure one—to serve God by serving his children through the revealed program. He is an appointed agent of the Lord, called by prophecy and the laying on of hands. He does not seek praise, for he is an agent, nor is he discouraged by criticism.

Let there be no mistake about it—"A double-minded man is unstable in all his ways." (James 1:8.)

Purpose of the Church

The purpose of all Church programs is to help in the perfecting of the Saints. One of the most basic distinctions between revealed religion and the religions of men is in the nature of God's work and glory. "For behold, this is my work and my glory—to bring to pass the immortality and eternal life of man." (Moses 1:39.) Man's growth and development in becoming a "celestialized personality" come from heavy involvement, the give and take of activities, not professionalism or so-called successful "programs" without the extensive participation of others.

Each church leader must think very clearly about this matter, for it is central to everything else.

While many Latter-day Saints are active and strong in the faith, there is a great marginal group of people that are not, and how they're treated and involved may either "make them" or "break them." This group is composed of embittered people, of some rebellious youth, of some offended auxiliary workers, of some "plain Janes" plagued with fear and self-doubt and loneliness. Whoever is tender in the faith, who can be easily offended, who have shallow individual testimonies, these are they who are in this all-important marginal group. How they "feel inside" matters to them most and will direct their lives.

In planning and in organizing and in carrying out plans, the leader must constantly ask himself what effect these plans and decisions and actions have on those in this group. How will they feel? Liked? Needed? Wanted? How much can you expect of them without overly frightening them? What do they naturally like to do?

This is a matter of tremendous importance, because these people (and they sometimes form a majority of potential participants) are in the most "influenceable" period in their lives and literally on its crossroads. It's fairly easy to gear the program to the faithful, solid nucleus, but infinitely important to consider this impressionable group seriously in every phase of planning and activity.

Shepherd: Sheepherder or Sheep?

The good church leader is a *shepherd*, and his people are his sheep. The shepherd knows his sheep, and they know him. He knows their voice, for he knows their aspirations and fears, their worries and doubts. He knows their family and their problems. He knows them because he has genuinely listened to them. The shepherd cares for his sheep; he cares very sincerely. He genuinely appreciates them. He loves then so much that he would lay down his life for them if he had to. He shows his love in innumerable ways—little acts of kindness, patience, forbearance, understanding, compassion. He'll go the second mile for his sheep. When one of his sheep strays, he leaves the ninety-nine and lovingly brings it back into the fold. This spirit of valuing the one lost sheep is the same spirit that keeps the other ninety-nine in the fold.

His sheep also know him. They have heard his voice. He has not pretended to be someone he is not. He is no "tin god" who stands apart and is difficult to approach or talk with.

	Shepherd	Hired Sheepherder	Sheep
Motive	Love of sheep	Love of wage	Safety Belonging
Communication	Honest ("for they know his voice") Two-way ("and are known of mine")	Dishonest, disguished ("know not the voice of strangers")	Self-concerned, one-way
Leadership	Lead in front by example through love.	Drive from behind—carrot-and-stick approach.	Follow—no vision—just go along like a good guy.
Consequences	Safety—salvation, self-realization, eternal life.	Sheep deserted in stormy times (when wolf approaches) leaderless and scattered.	Course of least resistance.

The shepherd leads his sheep. He does not need to drive them, because they know his voice and will follow it, and therefore he can go before them. He leads them from the front.

The *sheepherder* has to drive his sheep. He has to push and cajole and beg and hover in order to get things done. He has to drive because he does not know his sheep, and they do not know him. He has never really listened to them. He doesn't really care for them, because he cares for his wage. He's a hired sheepherder, and he's working for "what's in it for me." His wage may be glory or honor, or the power and control a position bestows. He may even aspire to a higher position or one of greater social honor. Because of his double-mindedness, his voice rings hollow and is the voice of a stranger. This officer or teacher does not need to wonder why his attendance is low, why the activities lack "punch." If he's honest, he'll examine his own heart and study the roots of the instability.

Then when things don't go well, or when he's criticized (approaches of the wolf), this hired sheepherder leaves the sheep. He leaves by giving excuses, by asking for another job, or by indifference and complacency, or by becoming one of the sheep himself.

As a sheep, he merely "goes along," and as a sheep leader and teacher, he may do just that which he has to do in order to "get by"—no real drive or enthusiasm or fire anymore! Everything becomes dead-level mediocrity. Then, rather than acting upon this unhappy situation and striving to radiate a new spirit, this sheep rather absorbs the existing spirit. He's an imitator—not a creator. He's a victim—not a master. He's a sheep—not a shepherd. Officers and teachers—leaders! Think on this shepherd, sheepherder, and sheep analysis, and look at your own leadership role.

The most important factor is this: How much do you really care for your people? How much do you feel this deep inside, this sincere caring for each of the individuals in your MIA class, in the Scout troop, or whatever class or activity or group your assignment is with?

Leaders are often tossed and turned by every wind of "new leadership doctrine." Should they be more democratic or more autocratic in action? Firmer or more permissive? Tell more or ask more? What are the best techniques for getting things done through people?

These questions are important and must be considered, but they are secondary questions. The primary question is: How much do you really care? You answer that question correctly, and you can make some mistakes on the other questions and still be very successful. But if you answer it incorrectly, you may have all the right answers to the other questions, but you cannot succeed.

To become a shepherd, follow the true Shepherd. (Study John 10.)

Two Vital Dimensions to Every Group—Task and Relationship

Everyone is excited about the great dance coming up. It's going to be a smashing success. That's the first dimension—the task.

The dance committee get along well with each other, except for Tom and Richard, and they don't "get on" well at all. That's the second dimension—relationship.

The church leader must be constantly concerned with both sets of problems—getting the job done and the relationships between the members of the group doing the job.

To neglect either challenge or problem is to neglect both.

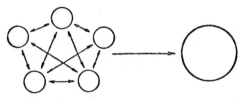

Relationships   Task   Objective— successful dance

It is easy for a task-oriented leader just to keep pushing things along and unintentionally to ignore the feelings that are aroused and the relationships that develop in the process. The leader must take time to look at this dimension—even if it seems that it is not related to the task. The leader must take time to see that people are properly informed on "what is coming off," on what is expected of them. He must also take the time to listen to them; their feelings and problems must be important to him.

A good leader must be humble enough to admit that he can't perform all these leadership functions, and that he needs others to help him to initiate ideas, to support ideas, to make decisions, and to carry out those decisions. These can be called task leadership functions. Group relationship leadership functions would include harmonizing, understanding, communicating, and everything that will enable each individual to find personal satisfaction from his contribution to the job.

If there is no personal satisfaction and no personal reward, then the individual simply will not contribute. People do not invest themselves if there is no hope of reward.

Rewards come in various forms. Friendship and warmth are real social rewards. Recognition and the opportunity of self-expression and participation in decisions that affect oneself are real and important psychological rewards. The leader must constantly see that there is opportunity for both social and psychological rewards, as well as for the spiritual and self-fulfillment rewards.

The leader must concern himself with an intangible called the "climate." This is the working atmosphere that reflects the morale of the group—the group spirit, the sense of co-operation and teamwork.

The leader must concern himself with people's feelings and with relationships, because he really cares—not just because he's supposed to. If he takes an interest merely because he should, he will be both wrong and unsuccessful. He will be wrong because regard for people should be seen as an end in itself. He will be unsuccessful because he will be "found out."

Leadership Must Be Flexible to Adjust with Reality

There are different patterns of leadership for different situations. Some will be effective in one situation but ineffective in others; for instance, a committee has planned a traditional spring party. Planning requires creativity, and creativity demands a free and spontaneous and permissive atmosphere under a more laissez-faire kind of leadership ("hands off").

However, this isn't the kind of leadership called for during the opening exercises of MIA. The leader will direct and control the meeting by following his prearranged plans. This is *authoritarian* leadership and serves its rightful purpose.

And there are times and situations that demand another style or pattern of leadership, which involves widespread participation and also some direction and control by the formal leader.

In determining the leadership pattern to follow, if we are to be good leaders, we should analyze the situation, the time pressures people are under, the nature of the problem or project being worked upon. Also, we must consider what our own leaders expect from us and what has gone on before. What about the members of our group? What are their abilities and aptitudes? What are their interests? What do they expect from us as leaders? What do they expect to contribute? What do they want to contribute?

What about the forces within ourselves? How much can we delegate to others and still feel comfortable? What about our strengths and weaknesses? What things can we do, and what things can't we do?

All of these questions are important, and answers to them will be good guides in determining our leadership pattern. We must be flexible. We can't play golf with a tennis racquet or tennis with a golf club. We can't build a house with a hammer alone. We need several tools—each one to serve its own purpose. "The eye cannot say to the hand, I have no need of thee." (See 1 Corinthians 12.)

Generally speaking, however, the more others are involved and the more widespread the participation is, the greater the individual growth. Therefore, the greater the purposes of the Church will be served.

Participation Versus Manipulation

Participation encourages involvement of others. It is based on faith in others and their creative potential. Manipulation, on the other hand, involves masterminding others or creating subtle pressures and forces on others, so as to "make them conform." This philosophy is based on an absence of faith in others. It places faith in one's own leadership techniques in getting things done through people; for instance, do we allow others to *participate in setting their own goals and objectives* in an area where the Church or your leaders haven't already set them? Or do we set them ourselves and then try to sell our objectives to others? They may passively go along, but where there is no internal commitment, don't be surprised when the objectives aren't achieved. A sense of personal responsibility flows naturally from honest participation.

What about evaluating the performance of people? Do we do it only through reports? Have we ever considered encouraging them to evaluate their own performance?

We will discover, if we allow people to help set their own objectives, perhaps with some consultation with us and others, and do it in such a way that they really mean it when they say, "These objectives are mine," that they will often set them higher and be far more rigorous in their evaluation of their own performance than we would ever dare to be.

Do we ever go to a meeting with our minds made up as to what we want done and then ask for an open discussion as to what should be done and use subtle directioning to bring the group around to our point of view?

This may work fine for a while, but eventually the "news will get out," and people will sense we aren't really interested in their feelings and opinions. Then we'll wonder why they don't participate as frequently and as spontaneously as they once did, and why they have little sense of personal responsibility. We must believe in people and be honest with them and genuinely listen to their contributions, and appreciate them and learn from them and change our minds sometimes, so that literally *our people do exercise a real influence in making the program successful.*

Man is not lazy or indifferent by nature. His natural and spiritual endowments give him boundless energy and enthusiasm. Every day we see these qualities manifest in activities in which he discovers personal meaning and significance—such as creating a business or a hobby, preparing for a vacation. Theoretically, church service should have more personal meaning and eternal significance to him than anything else, but often leaders rob others of this feeling of meaning and significance by turning them into robots, or by leaving little opportunity for creative expression. Healthy, maturing people resist being treated in immature and childish ways, and often their resistance takes the form of passivity, indifference, and even subtle forms of resistance and rebellion. When we see these signs, we must be careful we don't just look critically "outside" at them. We must study our own leadership process and see if we first don't have to change.

It has been proved again and again that where a real opportunity for creative participation exists, the release of energy and intelligence and resourcefulness and other human potentials is frequently unbelievable! Why? Because man is literally a child of God, his Father in heaven, and locked within his system is Godlike potentiality.

"Psychology" Is No Substitute for Basic Morality

If the auxiliary secretary prepares her reports poorly and she knows it, the principle of justice and honesty is violated if she is complimented for her fine performance in the name of "good psychology."

It is violated if the MIA superintendent expresses his "heartfelt appreciation" for the wonderful work and support of all of the officers and teachers, and then later that night he privately criticizes certain MIA officers and shows his basic dissatisfaction with the way things are going.

It is violated if a ward officer resents the "unwanted intrusion" of a stake board leader and expresses his unhappiness with the policies and recent directives of his own leaders, then a little later, in the name of "good human relations theory," gives an inspiring talk to his own officers and teachers on the need for greater unity and loyalty and to avoid faultfinding and backbiting and the questioning of those in authority.

J. McDonald taught: "To be trusted is a greater compliment than to be loved." Leadership is not so much a matter of techniques and practices as it is fundamental character and integrity, humility and morality. A great development in the field of leadership psychology and human relationships has taken place in the last decade, and this is all to the good, as long as the greatest emphasis stays with the development of the fundamental "common" virtues. "Though I speak with the tongues of men and of angels, and have not charity, I am become as sounding brass, or a tinkling cymbal." (1 Corinthians 13:1.)

Two Kinds of Results: Quantity and Quality

Statistics reflect quantity but not necessarily quality. Study carefully the quality factors behind the statistics— factors which are difficult to report, the kinds of results that many people never learn about. Therein is our greatest reward.

Learn to get both kinds of feedback to our fellow church workers. Teach them how reports are used and how they can be used as a great tool in planning and decision making. This report consciousness develops a sense of accountability, which in turn encourages the attitudes of humility and mutual respect. People then are constantly reminded that this is the Lord's kingdom, not theirs, and that their calling is divine, not human. The benefits of this constant feeling are self-evident.

The church leader must constantly realize that he is dealing with the souls of people, and that spiritual salvation is at stake. The more he can *build the program around the Living Christ, the principles of the gospel,* the more sure he will be that their foundations are secure, and that they will grow to become responsible adult parents and leaders in God's kingdom. If, on the other hand, he turns this encouragement and motivation into mere contests and gimmicks and cheerleading sessions, he'll gradually discover that even though these have a certain "punch" for a time, they gradually lose their punch; then one day, "when the chips are down," spiritual shallowness will be evidenced. The program, the teaching, the leadership must be Christ-centered.

Summary

Note again the teaching of Solomon: "Keep thy heart with all diligence; for out of it are the issues of life." (Proverbs 4:23.) A good leader in the church is one who looks frequently into his own heart for many of the answers to the problems and dilemmas in front of him. He knows that he needs to be a shepherd in helping to bring others to the true Shepherd. He knows that before he can lead, he must follow. He knows he must care for his sheep. He must learn to know his sheep and their voice and give them the opportunity to know him and his voice.

He knows that he teaches only what he is—no more and no less; that what he really is matters far more than what he says or even what he does. If he is firm with himself, he can effectively be firm with others. If he genuinely sustains his own leaders, he will teach that attitude to his followers, and they will sustain him. He knows that to live by the sword of criticism is to die by the same sword.

The good leader knows what real sincere prayer is— prayer from the heart—and that kind of knowledge is "caught" by his associates and members in his class. The leader knows that unless he really comes to his own meetings prepared, with plans well laid out, he will teach his group members the shortcut philosophy of just "getting by." He must be the supreme example of preparation and excellence in planning.

So on with every trait. As with the leader, so with the people. Over the long run, you teach exactly what you are.

The leader is humble enough to accept his own agency, and not to behave like a little tin god who throws his weight around in order to have a sense of domination and control. He is a good leader because he is the servant of all and is accountable to the one over him. This attitude of agency and accountability is tremendously powerful. "He that speaketh of himself seeketh his own glory: but he that seeketh his glory that sent him, the same is true, and no unrighteousness is in him." (John 7:18.)

The leader uses his intelligence. He thinks and reflects. He reads the feedback and strives for understanding. He learns to listen. He adapts to differing situations by using different patterns of leadership. If his problems are fluid and changing and dynamic, his tools are creative and multiple. If his problems involve church policy and procedure, then he gives clear instruction and unswerving directives in such a way as to inspire immediate obedience.

Throughout and in everything, the true leader is constantly reminded of the ultimate purpose of the Church and places the highest value on the work of the individual, testing his decisions and activities by this criterion: What does it do to the individual and to his possibility for divine growth, to his dignity? This singlemindedness builds strong lives, brings stability and a sense of purpose and direction in group effort, and inspires loyalty and confidence in relationships. Each individual then finds a real sense of personal satisfaction, purpose, and self-fulfillment—a divine kind of fulfillment—in his contribution to the "task." (Study D&C 121:34-46.)

26

To Leaders:

Four Great Keys in
Successful Church Leadership

Leaders—stand back. Take a long look at the problems you face. What fires are you trying to put out? Any conflict situations? A lot of last-minute scurrying about to do? Chasing down details? Someone let you down?

Most of your pressure, headaches, and frustration are but the leaves of a great tree. Too many communication breakdowns. Too little long-range planning. Too much "leadership by crisis."

Instead of working on the symptom level, what if you could work on the roots of the causal level? Would you like to apply preventive rather than remedial medicine? Your real problem exists and will be solved in the underlying processes of leadership and administration. These are not the seen problems but rather the unseen, like the great iceberg mass that lies under the surface of the water.

Look into your own heart and measure yourself against the following four great keys of stake and ward leadership and administration. Take fresh courage. And in humility turn these four keys in your own heart. You will discover over the weeks and months that you are truly hacking away at the roots of your problems.

Are you willing? It will take tough-mindedness. It will involve developing new leadership habits and attitudes, requiring concentration, patience, and dogged persistence in their practice.

It won't be easy. For a while, you may stand alone.

First Great Key—Planning

"Wars are won in the general's tent."

Planning must be of two kinds—long range and short range. Long-range planning must be done first and is of the greatest importance. If it is done correctly, short-range planning will flow naturally and easily.

First, plan your over-all calendar for the year. What are the major events? The minor events?

Second, plan what kinds of preparations must be started now (where? why? who? how?) so as to avoid big frustrating pushes to meet deadlines.

Short-range planning includes details and preparations for meetings. Carefully work out the meeting agenda. Send them to those who will attend the meetings several days prior to the meeting so each can come prepared to report and to discuss wisely. After meetings, send complete and accurate minutes (use carbons) with assignments to each participating member.

Unless you follow this agenda process, you will discover the hard truth of Parkinson's first law: "Work expands to fill the time available for its completion," and also another of his famous laws, "The time spent on a matter is in inverse relation to its importance."

Your meeting agenda should include:

1. *Review:* Last meeting's minutes read, assignments reported on, vital correspondence discussed.

2. *Short-range detailed planning* on the activities and problems of the week or month: Who to do what? when? where? and how?

3. *Long-range planning* by looking at the basic question: What are the root problems we face? How can we better train? Get more involvement? Increase unity? Spirituality?

Long-range planning is creative. It requires concentration and a real belief in its value. The natural tendency, often a habitual tendency, is to get bogged down in details and neglect this essential creative, mental activity.

"Things which matter most must never be at the mercy of things which matter least." (Goethe.)

Planning is a skill. Like any skill, you become good at it only through continual practice. Then practice planning —your results will literally amaze you.

Second Great Key: Communication

Remember first this principle: Unless communication is two-way, there is no communication. Communication is simply mutual understanding.

For stake and ward leaders, communication is the bread and water of your activity. You must cultivate the ability to understand and to be understood. Most human problems are communications problems or misunderstandings.

1. Important verbal communication, particularly of assignments, is to be followed up by clear, written communication with all involved receiving a copy. Then adopt a consistent reporting practice on these assignments. This system of assignment and reporting is divine and will instill a sense of divine stewardship and agency in your entire organization. It will breed unity, spirituality, sustaining support, and the attitudes of obedience, humility, and respect. (Keep accurate, current files of all written communication, assignment sheets, agendas, and reports for future reference.)

2. When changes and adaptations in a program are necessary, make certain special communication to all involved is sent out in sufficient time. Then everyone will feel fully informed and know what is expected. Otherwise some will feel neglected or slighted or lose faith in the integrity and consistency of the program and its leadership. Personal upsets and disappointments to those tender in the faith can turn them away altogether.

More important than the techniques of communication is the attitude of communication: the willingness and desire to listen for understanding. Avoid snap judgments. Use the third ear, which can hear the feelings of the heart.

Third Great Key: Follow Through
The Administrative Process

ANALYZE
(problems, reports)

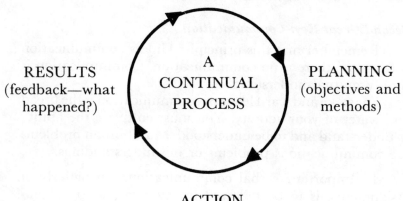

RESULTS
(feedback—what
happened?)

A
CONTINUAL
PROCESS

PLANNING
(objectives and
methods)

ACTION
(communicating and doing)

1. Your finest follow-through tool is a *checklist* that includes all the items that must be considered in fulfilling an assignment or project. It should be as detailed as possible. For instance, a monthly dance would include such assignments as publicity, physical arrangements, entertainment, refreshments, music, decorations. Each of these in turn can be broken down into greater detail.

2. The second follow-through tool: Fix responsibility on one person. "What is everybody's responsibility is nobody's responsibility." This person can hold other assigned people responsible to follow through, but you will be the only person who will follow through on him. Don't bypass unless you want the responsibility back. He will feel respected and trusted and sustained. Trust is the highest motivation.

Cultivate a follow-through philosophy—"there are no excuses." Develop the spirit that excuse making, buck passing, and complaining are worthless, negative activities.

In reporting meetings, develop the spirit that each person would either state, "I have accomplished the assignment" or "I have not accomplished the assignment, but will by (a certain date)" rather than "Well, this came up" or "Brother Jones let me down" or "I didn't know." Over a period of time, if this philosophy is consistently applied, it will develop a deep sense of responsibility and almost force long-range planning and effective two-way communication.

Sometimes we hear the complaint, "They let me down" or "They just aren't dependable." This is the very reason you are a leader—to train the undependable. If people were already dependable, they wouldn't need training. It is because they're often not dependable that they need your training, help, and leadership.

3. Third follow-through tool: Learn to use visual charts and graphs that give a clear picture of all progress as well as future plans. This will motivate and foster a sense of achievement. Why visual charts and graphs? You'd be amazed at how little understanding some people have of what is expected and of where you're going. Rather than "appearing stupid," they often sit silently back and then you assume they understand. People remember far more of what they see than of what they hear.

Planning, communication, and follow-through are interwoven with each other:

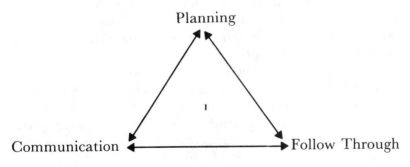

One cannot be successful without the other. To successfully do these three things, you must change habits—

thinking and doing habits, which are deeply ingrained. This is not easy. Understand why there may be resistance, fear, and self-doubt. Many people have simply never learned to plan even for their own future. Many have simply never learned to communicate with their own wife or family or even with themselves, let alone with an entire organization. Many have never carried responsibility and been held accountable. This new planning, communicating, and follow-through leadership can frighten and offend—or it can help tremendously! It all depends on the application of the following key—by far the most important.

Fourth Great Key: The Attitude of Faith, of Understanding, of Appreciation, of Involving

The natural reaction to situations where responsibilities exceed abilities is either fight or flight (escape). The gospel's answer: faith plus works.

In stakes and wards, your spiritual responsibilities are always greater than your natural ability, because you are dealing with spiritual forces and purpose. Faith often begins when it "can't be done."

As a stake and ward leader, understand why people criticize, offer excuses, or take various escapes. Do not yourself become critical or escape your responsibility to understand, train, educate, inspire, help. Understand that people can only act out of their own experiences. You must help give them spiritual experiences with divine attitudes. It is futile to criticize, find fault, or label someone as "incapable" or to judge someone as being "this kind" or "that kind" of a person.

You will exercise your faith in God if you believe in his children and their limitless potentiality. It is your duty to learn the processes of releasing that potentiality. These processes are spiritually demanding on you. They involve a real, continuous effort to understand. This takes time and patience and the attitude of humility.

You must learn to listen and to *empathize* (to see the world from another's point of view). This involves *accepting* people as they are, *appreciating* their every effort, *recognizing* work well done, and *affirming* their right to be an individual, to feel and think differently.

Learn to *involve people* in the decisions from the planning stage on. Only sincere participation in the endeavor will tap their greatest potentials and desires.

Accepting, understanding, appreciating, and involving comprise a divine experience that will lift and edify.

If you give another human only the experience of judging, criticizing, or rejecting, what have you done? Built barriers of defense, communication breakdowns, fighting and flighting, bad feelings.

Such attitudes of faith and respect are self-fulfilling prophecies. As Goethe put it, "Treat people as they are and they will remain as they are. Treat people as they can and should be and they will become as they can and should be."

Leaders, do you want a glorious experience? For one month, act on four assumptions and watch what happens. You'll be joyfully amazed.

1. *Assume good faith on the part of others.* Don't impugn their motives. Assume that they are right from their point of view. Assume they are trying to do their best as they see it, although this may not be as you see it. When communications break down and bad feelings develop, assume that others mean to do their best, and then go to them and talk it over. Clear the thing up. Don't believe rumors. Go to the source yourself and talk it over. People stop fighting when they are accepted as they are. Defense drops when they sense your sincere interest and desire to understand and help rather than to judge and reject.

2. *Assume that every negative situation or trouble can be turned to the Lord's advantage.* When you encounter a complaint, obstacle, or problem, ask, "How can we turn this to the Lord's advantage?" Then seriously discuss it.

You'll find yourself thinking and speaking positively about a so-called "negative" situation. The accomplishing power of a positive mind is unbelievably great. It is like the mind of the Lord, the great Creator. The evil one inspires negative thinking and defeatism. Just as faith without works is dead, so also is works without faith.

3. *All problems ultimately are spiritual,* not technical, financial, or practical (2 Nephi 3:7). Since the ultimate problem is spiritual, one of desire and faith, the ultimate solution must also be spiritual—more conversion to the gospel, the stake and ward program. This involves teaching, patience, testimony bearing, and expressing love and appreciation. Expecting too much and judging too harshly discourage people to try, to get involved, to strike out, because these efforts involve the mistake-making process of growth and possible criticism. They then feel that "to do nothing is safer." Remember that the greatest of all things is the human soul; the Church, the gospel and its principles, and the stake and ward programs are all developed solely to assist the human soul in its divine growth. Never confuse means and ends or become more focused on programs than upon people.

4. *Your problems begin first in your own heart.* "Keep thy heart with all diligence; for out of it are the issues of life." (Proverbs 4:23.) Have the courage to look into your own heart first. Earnestly seek the Lord. Ask him to reveal to you your weaknesses. (See Ether 12:27.) This takes deep, sincere, private prayer from the heart.

More than all else, your sincere humility and great courage to look into your own heart and turn the key found therein will inspire others to look inwardly and turn the key in their hearts.

Summary

These four great keys or activities will probably take no more than 20 percent of your time, and yet they will dynamically influence 80 percent or more of the success of your stake and ward program. Make your mind up to use them. Make it a habit.

Sink your spiritual roots deep by drinking deeply from the divine fountain of daily sincere prayer and scripture study and by "starving" yourself from the worldly fountains of life. Then when the times of stress or storm come, you will not be uprooted or blown away. With deep spirituality will flow a power from within to love your people, to have faith in them, to involve them, to appreciate and understand them. From this you will develop the powerful leadership skills to plan, to communicate, and to follow through. Thus, you will work on the roots of success rather than on brush fires, deadlines, crisis, frustrating details.

You will rediscover the central spiritual truth: *You teach what you are.*

27

To Missionaries:
Ten Basic Principles of
Effective Missionary Work

I. Teacher or Salesman?

Are you a teacher or a salesman of the gospel? There is a difference. A vital difference. Let us explore it.

To the salesman, his product is apart from his person. To the teacher, it is not. His product *is* his person. He effectively teaches only what he *is*. It is "caught," it is felt, it is sensed, it communicates, it edifies. Christ said, "I am the way, the life, the truth." In the very person of Christ was embodied the fullness of every teaching he uttered. There was no separation. To attain a knowledge of his utterance and his divinity meant that we too must become like him. Knowledge is a state of being. True conversion, true testimony is only found in what you *are* —not in what others think you are or even what you hope you are or hope that they will think you are.

1. The Motive

The salesman is motivated for some kind of gain, whether it is a sense of achievement or a form of recognition.

The gospel teacher is motivated by genuine regard and a sincere valuing of the other. This is what the Greeks termed *agape* love, or selfless love. This is what the Savior meant in his repeated question, "Lovest thou me?"

It isn't the fact that Peter loved Jesus Christ that mattered so much, but rather that Peter would feed His sheep or His lamb (and thus demonstrated the quality and depth of his love of Christ).

2. The Product

To the gospel salesman, the product is baptism. In his self-justifying manner he may label his baptism as a convert baptism or as a conversion; nevertheless, he has essentially sold when he baptizes. This brings him the recognition of the sale, which thereby satisfies his motive. He loses interest immediately afterwards in the fellowshiping process, because this does not feed his motive. His morality is a statistical morality. People become numbers.

To the gospel teacher imbued with a sense of sacred responsibility and a true understanding of conversion, the product is a changed life. The product is a soul committed to the higher level of living, committed from within to keep the commandments of God and to follow in the footsteps of the Christ. He knows that such a commitment *must* come from within. He also knows that this eternal commitment can be nourished and cultivated from without by his own love, his testimony, his patience, his understanding, his faith in the man, and his "inside" eternal power to commit and to come into the Lord's kingdom. He would never manipulate ("work them about") into commitments, for that would mean that he made the commitments for them and that shortly thereafter when he leaves them, they will leave the Church. When the first storm comes, they, being built upon sand, will be washed into the sea.

The gospel teacher is constantly aware of not only the quality of the convert but even more importantly of the quality of the conversion. This is particularly so with youth who can more easily be "talked into" the Church. With them the gospel teacher makes doubly certain, takes extra pains to see that they are properly taught, that they learn how to pray, and that they *do* pray. He knows that young persons' mentalities and environments are such that it wouldn't take much for a storm to wash them out to sea even after baptism, and he therefore guards their castles with strong walls of protection, support, and fellowshiping, so that the foundations of the castle will become granite-like through continued commitments, activity, attendance, and service.

The nature of the product that the gospel teacher has is interwoven with what the investigator literally becomes. The greatest part of the conversion will come after baptism under the influence of the Holy Ghost, through the years of study, prayer, and service; but to the gospel teacher there must be an internal commitment that a man has freely made. To choose the way of life and salvation is the free responsibility and privilege of each.

Baptism becomes a prize, something of greatest worth to become worthy of, not something to be "talked into." The teacher strives to help the contact to become worthy of this "pearl of great price."

3. Technique

The gospel salesman earnestly strives to develop his skills, to increase his knowledge in using those skills, so that he might effectively "sell his product." As he confronts realities of every day, he learns the principle of expediency; that is, do what you must do to get your product sold. Therefore, the end, selling the product, would justify almost any means, including subterfuge, deception, various forms of subtle pressuring, creation of different kinds of social obligations, misuse of scripture, misquoting, or almost any other "small thing."

The gospel teacher is honorable to his core and knows that the means and the end are inseparable. He knows that manipulation hurts the quality of the conversion. But it isn't because he knows this that he doesn't manipulate or use deception or pressure, but rather because anything dishonorable is so foreign and alien to his own honorable nature that it simply would not flow out of him. It is repugnant to his sense of decency and virtue. Being whole-souled, he can use his knowledge and skills only as a literal part of himself and not as things he "puts on himself," like a coat or an affectation so as to leave "the right impression" upon another. Because of what he is, he simply can't use a gimmick approach. He couldn't use subterfuge at the door. He wouldn't attempt to "psych" contacts up to a fever pitch so they would "buy."

The teacher's underlying fundamental attitude of love and regard of a human soul makes his knowledge and his skills really effective. As he testifies, people sense his whole-souled integrity and the Holy Ghost burns within them. He is teaching what he *is*. It even matters little how polished his techniques or how finished his conversation or how eloquent his speech or how impressive his knowledge is. What does make the difference is that he teaches what he *is*.

4. *What He Is*

The gospel salesman believes that he is an important part of an important process in selling his product. It really matters little how he lives or what he does to sell it. All that matters is that he sells it and wins the praise. It almost reminds one of an early salesman of long ago who tried to sell a product (salvation) and desired that all of the "glory be mine."

The gospel teacher has the assurance of his own divine ordination, that he is called "by prophecy and the laying on of hands," and that through honor and truth alone will he successfully prepare the souls he teaches for the conversion of the Spirit and by the Spirit. Regarding the honor and the glory, he feels to say with Christ, "Father, thy will be done, and the glory be thine forever," or with Paul, "I have planted, Apollos watered: but God gave the increase. So then neither is he that planteth anything, neither he that watereth; but God that gave the increase."

Are you gospel salesmen or gospel teachers? It is a matter of degree, but it is also a matter of principle.

May the Lord bless us to climb continually upward toward the noblest calling of all: gospel teaching.

II. You Teach What You Are

One of the strongest convictions coming out of my own observations and experience is this: You teach no more or no less than what you are; that is, what you are as a person becomes the most powerful essence of your message.

For instance, if you are unable to make promises and to keep them, in all likelihood you will discover that your contacts do not make and keep commitments.

If your contacts "pack you in," you might ask yourself, "What part of the mission program have I packed in?" Do I lack faith? Vision? Am I immediately obedient to mission directives? Do I live the schedule?

When we teach people the Word of Wisdom, to honor the Sabbath Day, and to pay an honest tithing, we are essentially teaching them a discipline. This becomes a self-discipline, in which people learn to make moral choices between alternatives. They have the freedom to fail or the freedom to succeed. This freedom is basic to responsibility, and this responsibility is basic to all human growth.

We teach what we are. We can teach people the discipline spoken of above only if we ourselves are disciplined. If we are unable to discipline our lives into an effective program of work, study, and prayer, regardless of how we might teach otherwise from the lips, what we are really teaching is the lack of personal discipline. In a sense, this teaching is "caught" and not taught.

Even though we might express love to our contacts, if we do not feel and express it toward our companion, we tend to teach a lack of love and a lack of faith.

If we ourselves are doubleminded, we teach doublemindedness. If we are concerned with worldly concerns, we communicate these same concerns. In other words, we teach them to try to "have their cake and eat it too."

The key to your families is in your heart. From the Proverbs of Solomon we read: "Keep thy heart with all diligence; for out of it are the issues of life."

How true! How precious an insight!

For an answer to the questions you have regarding the families you are finding, teaching, and desire to bring into the Church through the waters of baptism, examine your own heart. What do you find there? Regardless of the words you use and technical perfectness of your discussions, the most powerful and compelling message of all is exactly what you are.

Are your families slow to hearken to your teachings? Are you slow to obey the directives and programs of the mission? Look into your heart.

Do your contacts hesitate to pray with all their hearts? Look into your heart. Do you pray with all your heart? Sincerely? Specifically? With *all* your heart? Privately as well as with your companion? Look into your heart.

Do your contacts do their homework? Do they study the tracts carefully? The Book of Mormon? Do you do your homework? Do you honestly prepare every morning for that day's labor, a good two and a half hours of companion and private study and planning? Look into your heart.

Are your contacts socially aspiring, and do they see Mormonism as a faulty rung in that social ladder? Are you aspiring? Are you genuinely happy with the successes and recogntions of others? Do you fear the opinions of men and "worship" at the altar of praise and public opinion? What is the supreme object of your devotion? Is it the true and living God or self improvement? Do you love him first?

Let each of us look into our own hearts at least once a day in a private, personal prayer to our Father in heaven and therein discover the answers to the problems of our families.

Have your contacts faced their moment of truth— that is, the moment of truth about themselves? Have they looked at their rationalizations and pretenses, fears and sins, and acknowledged them to be such? Have they come face to face with the truth that they desperately need the gospel, that it is indeed their Father's divine plan for their happiness and eternal growth, and that they need help from you and from the branch and from God, and that they want it with all their heart?

Have you faced *your* moment of truth, in which you have honestly acknowledged to God and to others, if offended or lied to, your weaknesses, your procrastinating spirit, slothfulness, disloyalty, impurity of heart and mind, aspiration for the honors of men? Have you taken these matters to the Lord and with all your heart asked him for forgiveness, relying upon the atonement of the Savior in faith and granting forgiveness to all who have offended you, that you also might earn that forgiveness? Have you then forgotten the past and gone forth with a renewed vigor and determination and courage to make it a new day for yourself, relying upon God's help?

The Prodigal Son faced his moment of truth. After he had spent his inheritance, he "came to himself," realized he had offended both heaven and home, and remorsefully returned.

One young missionary recently realized he had fooled and pretended his way through the first several months of his mission. He had spent his inheritance. Then he "came to himself" and to a desire to return, and with God's help he will return and he will succeed.

May the Lord help each of us to be true shepherds, who care terribly much for the sheep, and not to be sheepherders, who work for wages and who care little for the sheep and leave the sheep when the wolf approaches, and neither let us be sheep who "merely go along." We are here to teach and not to be taught. The shepherd leads because he cares. The sheepherder cannot lead. He does not know, neither does he care; therefore he must drive. No man can be driven back to the Father. This is what Satan wanted to do, and his wage was his own glory. This is why he was cast out. (See John 10.)

Our Lord *was* what he taught. He embodied perfection. He didn't say, "This is the way." He said, "I am the way."

III. We Must Become Christ-like

Proposition 1: We only trust our own experience.

Trust and faith are almost synonymous here. Each of us acts in terms of our own experiences. So also do our contacts.

We believe in Joseph Smith's experiences because we have had, in a sense, an experience with Joseph Smith. We have seen his work and fruits, read his testimony, and received in our own hearts the Spirit's confirmation of its truthfulness. Therefore, we trust Joseph Smith's experience because we have had an experience with Joseph Smith and found him trustworthy, and have had an experience with God's Spirit and found it good.

The only experience of many people with Mormonism has come from anti-Mormons or social disapproval. It's easy to understand their first reactions. They merely trust their own experiences. Can they do anything else until they have a new and different experience?

What is the reason, then, for a lack of faith in revelation or a revealing God in the world today? Answer: simply because of few, if any, divine experiences with God. Why? No revelation, no vision, no priesthood, false creeds: "The earth also is defiled under the inhabitants thereof; because they have transgressed the laws, changed the ordinance, and broken the everlasting covenant." (Isaiah 24.)

Proposition 2: Our highest responsibility is to introduce people to divine experience.

If people will actually experience the things of God and the Spirit of God, then they will trust this experience. At first they may mistrust it or suspect it, because their past experiences have taught them to do this. How can we introduce them to divine experiences?

First, by being an example of diety ourselves. By being a true servant of God and of them. Alma taught his wicked son, "Behold, O my son, how great iniquity ye brought upon the Zoramites; for when they saw your conduct they would not believe in my words." (Alma 39:11.)

Second, by showing intrinsic love to them. We do this in the way we treat each other as companions first, and then in the way we treat them and their children. As we would like to be treated, so we treat others. You can see the futility of criticism. Fruit comes by "abiding in the vine" (a divine relationship or experience).

Third, we give them the vision of the restored gospel. We share with them our testimony in the spirit of meekness and in the solemnity of our heart, and as we do so, the Holy Ghost will witness to them of its truthfulness. This is a divine experience.

People to a degree must first be converted to the messenger before they will become converted to his message. They must believe the messenger is true. The only scripture many of your contacts ever read is your own life.

Paul wrote to some Saints he had just left and said essentially, "Forget what my reputation was. What was your experience with me?"

Christ taught his Nephite disciples: "What manner of men ought ye to be? Verily I say unto you, even as I am."

Proposition 3: A person will know the truth to the degree he is true to the truth.

A person's experience in obeying God's commandments gradually makes him over, and he becomes a "partaker of the divine nature." (John 7:16-17; 2 Peter 1:3-11.) The divinity within him is released. His own nature testifies to him of God, and he feels God's love and feels that he is a child of God.

What is true to you is truth to you. If your contacts do not yet know the Church is true, it is because they are not yet true enough to the Church. Perhaps you must first be more true to them so that they will have sufficient trust in you as a messenger to believe and obey your message.

Proposition 4: You will encourage obedience to the laws of life if you will live the laws of love.

"By this shall all men know that ye are my disciples, if ye have love one for another." Truth begets truth.

Pride becomes the natural defense people develop against the possible hurt of new experiences. They resist change. They count costs and consequences of change. They feel that if they jump off the treadmill they are on, the new ground will upturn them.

Your responsibility is to give them a new experience with this ground to show it is secure and firm and that they enter into a new, glorious friendship and fellowship with the Saints and the Spirit of God.

It also follows that if you disobey the laws of love, regardless of what message or testimony you give, you will encourage disobedience to the laws of life. Why? Simply because people will only trust their experiences, and if they have an experience with lovelessness, force, manipulation, sarcasm, light-mindedness, impatience, or unkindness, they will trust that experience and reject your testimony.

Proposition 5: You are "as God" to your contacts.

The true and living God, who is the Father of our spirits, is a stranger to most people. You must introduce him to his children by first showing what he is like in your own life.

If you listen to them with real respect, empathy, and caring, they will come to believe God will also listen. They will pray with faith. If you refuse to listen with understanding (lack of empathy), they will likely pray mechanically without faith, for their human experience will teach them about the divine experience.

If a parent is unkind to his child or shows prejudice and favoritism, or if he is moody and selfish and constantly changing, then this becomes the concept of God the child will grow up with. He will live in fear of an arbitrary, changing, mean, selfish, non-caring God. He will pray only out of duty, never out of desire. If he sins, he is never quite sure he is forgiven, even after sincere repentance. He carries regret, fear, and guilt all his life, and this stifles his personal growth and creativity, freedom and capacity to love and enjoy others in the world. He becomes grasping and selfish, eager to accumulate the facades and symbols of success in order to better cover up his deep self-fears and self-doubts.

If we cannot be trusted, and we are to show God to them, "How can I trust God?" they may reason.

If we can be trusted, our contacts will be encouraged to begin to live the commitments. Faith is born of obedience and contact with the Spirit (unseen reality). Then they will begin to have a divine experience that can be trusted and that will motivate a higher and higher order of obedience, eventually leading them back into the presence of God their Father.

Proposition 6: "The child is always father of the man."

This means that the first few years of childhood become the dominant influence on the entire life. It is a true statement, but it is an incomplete statement, for it does not consider the possibility of the second birth.

A person can undergo the second birth with Christ as the new Father, and this childhood will become the dominant influence of an entire new life. You are the midwives in this second birth process. You are shepherds to lead people to the true Shepherd. But at the present you are the only shepherd they know, and you must be a true shepherd, for they will not follow strange voices, nor will they follow the double-minded sheepherder who tends sheep for what's in it for him. Nor will they follow a sheep, for the sheep follow them.

Proposition 7: Every person you meet is as Christ.

"As you have done it unto the least of these my brethren, ye have done it unto me."

As you treat every person in terms of his unseen,

divine potential and divinity within him, it will to that degree spark a release of that divinity.

"Let your light so shine before men that they will see your good works and glorify your Father which is in heaven." Your own divine attributes will reveal God to them, both in you and within themselves.

Proposition 8: You essentially bring three things: vision (testimony), love (empathy), example (divine experience).

Example must come first, for they need to have a little trust in the giver before they will believe in the gift (the vision of the restored gospel or your testimony).

Love must come second, for there must be a relationship of caring and sincerity before they allow a teaching experience. After this, message or testimony (vision) can be given. Then the three mingle continuously together, providing a great and divine experience that will bring people to a new well of trust and faith and knowledge, peace, joy, and happiness.

If they drink deeply of the waters from this well, they will never thirst again.

When you empathize, you receive a person to yourself. When you testify, you give a vision to that person. As you live uprightly, you provide an experience with divine attributes (divinity). Testimony gives truth. Love motivates. Example breeds trust.

The root cause of all real problems in man is estrangement from the Father, which began at the time of the fall and continues each time man transgresses the Father's laws.

The root solution to this problem is found in the atonement of Christ. He atoned for both the fall of man through Adam's transgression and for the fall of each individual through transgression, if a man will receive his gift through obedience to the principles and ordinances of the gospel.

IV. We Reap Only What We Sow

The Apostle Paul forcibly teaches an eternal and immutable law. Study it carefully and apply it personally:

"Be not deceived; God is not mocked; for whatsoever a man soweth, that shall he also reap. For he that soweth to his flesh shall of the flesh reap corruption; but he that soweth to the Spirit shall of the Spirit reap life everlasting. And let us not be weary in well doing; for in due season we shall reap, if we faint not." (Galatians 6:7-9.)

The lesson contained in this marvelous scripture is taught us again and again, just like a recurring theme throughout the scriptures.

We literally reap as we sow. This means if we sow a good morning's preparation, we will reap a good day of contacting and teaching. If we sow enthusiasm and positiveness in our heart, we will reap enthusiastic responses at the door and positive commitments in discussions.

If we pray sincerely and devoutly from the heart, we will begin to reap the works and the fruits of the Spirit; and if we think about physical and material and worldly cares, we will reap the works and fruits of the flesh. Misery and happiness are inevitably the output of what is put in.

Do you want to increase your teaching hours? To reap this result you must sow adequate preparation in terms of contacting and mastering discussions as well as living for the Spirit with its fruits of love and faith and courage and conviction and confidence. There is no mystery in this work. It is very simple. We merely reap what we sow.

Make Up Your Mind

There is only one thing to do, and that is to decide what you really want and be willing to pay the price to attain it. This is what we mean by making up your mind. Don't make up your mind only to succeed, but also make up your mind to pay the price of success. Don't make up your mind to be well prepared, but rather make up your mind to get up at 5:55, have your prayer, and have a well-organized period of study and concentration. Don't make up your mind to get twenty "golden contacts," but rather make up your mind to ask the golden questions so many times today or to knock on so many doors today, and there is no question about it, you will soon have your twenty "golden contacts." No missionary can escape or dodge the truth of this law. Let a missionary say, "No living the schedule for me. I set no high and strict aims ahead of me. I see an unrestrained and easier missionary life." Has he thus escaped the law? No—he has plunged head foremost into the most terific self-denial in missionary life! Henry Emerson Fosdick wisely taught:

> "If we will not deny ourselves for a Christian home, we shall deny ourselves a Christian home! What more appalling self-denunciation can there be? If we will not deny ourselves a loose and unchaste life, then we shall deny ourselves self-respect and a conscience fit to live with. If we will not deny ourselves bad temper and a wagging tongue, then we shall deny ourselves friendship—God pity us! If we will not deny ourselves those habits of thought and life that keep divine fellowship away from human hearts, then we shall deny ourselves God. In short, if we will not give up evil for good, we shall surely give up good for evil."

The law of growth and success is acceptance of personal responsibility to obey laws. Convert baptism blessings are predicated on obedience to the basic laws of missionary work. If you obey the laws, the convert baptisms will inevitably follow. Disobey and no conversions will take place. The Lord is bound by our diligence. If we do our part, he will always do his.

The laws of missionary work are all summarized and embodied in the following revelation: "See that ye serve him with all of your heart, might, mind, and strength."

	→ Convert Baptisms
HEART	Law of Christ (humility, prayer, faith, integrity, love)
MIND	Law of Preparation (study and planning)
MIGHT, STRENGTH	"Law of Moses" (schedule living: basic work)

From this it's obvious that missionary work is not a short-range social pressure system of gimmicks and cheerleading; it is a sober, mature, spiritual, and intelligent effort to do God's eternal and majestic work among his children. "I am the true vine, and my Father is the husbandman. Every branch in me that beareth not fruit he taketh away, and every branch that beareth fruit, he purgeth it, that it may bring forth more fruit." (John 15:1-2.)

We reap as we sow. This is the fact of all life.

Note the following diagram illustrating both the man-made "law of the shortcut" and the natural, God-made "law of the harvest" as applied to life and missionary work.

Can you now understand why the Lord told the boy prophet that the creeds of the world were an abomination in his sight, that they teach for doctrines the commandments of men? Worship that does not change and transform and dynamically lift the worshiper is vain worship. Man-made churches all teach shortcut philosophies to salvation, either through "confession" or through the sacraments of the church. Death-bed confession in most churches today supposedly saves. This heretical man-made doctrine makes a mockery out of God and deceives his children. It attempts to palm off a counterfeit in the name of God and salvation, only to teach the shortcut philosophy of "something for nothing."

"He that entereth not by the door into the sheepfold, but climbeth up some other way, the same is a thief and a robber." (John 10:1.)

Thief? Of one's own soul.

Fellow missionaries, you alone have the true and complete teachings and revelations of the Lord that will lead the faithful to salvation and exaltation. Faith plus works plus the saving and exaltive ordinances of the restored gospel are God's law of the harvest of souls.

Mormonism is the message of the Father given in this dispensation. Patience is the heart of faith. Faith is born of obedience and perfected by works. Faith in the unseen powers comes from contact and experience with these divine powers.

The Divine Law of the Harvest vs. Man-made Law of the Shortcut

The Farm—law of the harvest (a natural or God-given law)	Human institutions that *may* teach the law of the shortcut (a social or man-made law)	Missionary work involving the natural law or God-given law of the harvest (shortcut artists are always frustrated and never succeed in the long run)
1. Plowing ground	1. School—Learning to cram, memorize, regurgitate, and soon thereafter forget all.	1. Solid daily preparation.
2. Planting the seeds	2. Social popularity through good looks, fashionable clothes, learning to play the roles.	2. Constant efforts to maintain spiritual mindedness through prayer, fasting, and scripture study.
3. Cultivating and pruning	3. Economic prosperity through human manipulation, something-for-nothing gimmicks	3. Keeping minds and hearts clean, pure.
4. Watering	4. Family-rearing philosophy: spoiling children through giving things to them only for the asking instead of earning things, and of gearing family life to the immediate satisfaction of human desires.	4. Absolute obedience to the commandments of the Lord's mission directives, proselyting programs, and leaders.
5. Weeding		5. Search for the honest in heart with real intent.
6. Etc.		6. Teaching by example and precept. Teaching commitments.
		7. Helping through the process of faith and repentance
		8. Covenant making in the waters of baptism, leading to the gift of the Holy Ghost.
The Harvest	*The Harvest*	*The Harvest*
Bread on the table (There is no shortcut, no substitute, no leaving out of one of the ingredients.)	Short-range, shallow satisfactions. Appearances of success. The shadow, not the substance.	Active involvement in the kingdom of God under the influence of God's spirit— perfects and sanctifies the human soul.

V. Prayer

"What men usually ask for when they pray to God is that two and two may not make four."

How true this Russian proverb often is!

We tell our contacts about the four steps in prayer. Let us also teach them about the spirit side of a successful prayer, not only about its letter and form.

There are three simple points on the spirit of prayer that comes from a sincere heart:

1. *Prepare your prayers.* Before you kneel with your companion, discuss between the two of you what it is that you really want and how much you really want that blessing. What kind of a price in effort are you willing to pay to obtain it? In other words, think through your life, your contacts, your mistakes, and your greatest needs, hopes, worries, and fears. The Lord is a loving Father, and he cares greatly and understands deeply. He knows what things you have need of even before you ask him. The purpose of the preparation in thinking, discussing, or meditating over our needs is merely to help you come to a clear understanding of what you *really* want and need and what you are really willing to do in order to get what you want.

Phillips Brooks taught, "God looks not at the oratory of your prayers, how eloquent they may be; nor the geometry of your prayers, how long they may be; nor the arithmetic of your prayers, how many they may be; not at logic of your prayers, how methodical they may be; but the sincerity of them He looks at."

2. *Make your utterances sincerely specific.* Thank the Lord for specific blessings, the blessings you feel deeply grateful for right in your heart. Then pray for specific things, for specific contacts to meet specific commitments and to work toward specific baptism dates. Pray specifically for an improved relationship with your companion, for an improved ability to concentrate, study, memorize, and teach. Acknowledge specific weaknesses and seek forgiveness. Pray to be led to "one family this morning in tracting"

that you can teach and baptize into the Lord's Church. Pray with feeling and with earnestness, believing that you will receive the blessings once off your knees.

3. *Make specific pledges.* Tell the Lord exactly what you are willing to do and what you *will* do to achieve the blessings you seek. If you feel it will take three hours of good, hard, solid tracting in the spirit and full of enthusiasm to find that family, and you feel you can honor those pledges and go forth believing, you may be assured that as surely as the night follows the day, so will the answers to your prayers come, sometime, somewhere, somehow.

If you want an improved relationship with your companion, tell the Lord what specifically you will do to improve it. If you want the ability to master the six discussions, tell the Lord how you are planning to study and specifically what you will do that day. As Brigham Young said to the early Salt Lake settlers, "Pray as if all depended upon the Lord and work as if it all depended upon you." Two and two will never equal five. Neither will half-hearted prayers and half-hearted work bring full success and full achievement.

Teach your investigators the same three things about prayer. Teach them how to pray from their hearts sincerely and to learn the great law that we reap as we sow. Teach them to tell the Lord what they are willing to do in acquiring the knowledge of the truth that they specifically desire and request and what they will do in order to get the courage to stop their smoking or tea drinking or whatever obstacle they encounter. Teach them to prepare their prayers by way of thinking through what truth means to them and what they are really willing to pay for it.

Our great blessing and assurance, elders and sisters, is that we know that God does live and that this is his truth, and he loves his children and therefore he will direct them and answer their prayers. We don't have to manipulate people or talk them into anything. We have nothing to fear. There is no force or enemy that can successfully oppose our best efforts. If we are on the Lord's side, the Lord is always on our side. He never leaves us. We only leave him sometimes.

How blessed these assurances are. How terrible and unthinkable it would be to try to do this work without these assurances. With these assurances we can literally depend upon the Lord to bring the conversion to anyone who will put his life through the conversion process of desire, study, prayer, church attendance, and applying the principles of the gospel in his life.

VI. *"I Will Do It"*

You and two others are entering into a partnership to purchase a business. Each is to invest $5,000. One of the other two says, "I *hope* to pay $5,000," or "It is my *intention* to do the best I can," or "Somehow I'll *try* to get my $5,000."

Would you put your $5,000 down on that kind of a promise?

As an insurance executive, would you unconditionally promise to commit the resources of your insurance company to a man who could not unconditionally promise to pay his premium?

Think seriously about this. Its significance to you in the mission field is profound and far-reaching.

A contract is a covenant. It is another word for a promise to perform on an obligation.

This gospel is a gospel of covenants. We make lower covenants, and by obeying them our capacity increases to make and obey higher covenants, until eventually we become sanctified and perfected and enter back into the presence of the Lord.

When we make covenants in the waters of baptism or at the sacrament table or in any of the holy ordinances of the priesthood and of the temple, they are all based on the idea that "I *will* do it."

To say, "I will *try* my best," or "This is what I *hope* I

will do," or "What I am *trying* to do" is to make *no* covenant at all.

Saying deeply within you and meaning it, "I *will* do it," gathers together all of the powers within yourself and focuses your energy and your discipline on your objective. It also pulls down from God his divine power, for he is bound by his contract or covenant with you. (D&C 82:10.) And he will not let you down!

Think about it. One of the finest and highest ways we can demonstrate our faith in the Lord Jesus Christ is to make an unqualified pledge or covenant with him to do one thing or another that we know must be done, particularly when it is something that we know we cannot do by ourselves. Thereby, we demonstrate we have faith in his integrity to honor his promise to us and also in his power to enable us to do things far beyond our own capacities.

Unless you promise what you will do (in specific acts), you have no contract that will be valid. The Lord promises only when you promise. In other words, if you don't promise, you have no promise. When you do promise, then you have *all* his promises.

Do not promise something you will not do. But focus and organize the forces within you so that your mind is truly made up, and then enter into a contract or covenant with him—a covenant to make any sacrifice to be successful; then you can trust him entirely, for as you honor your covenant he will honor his, and "you will have power" such as you have never known before. You will "speak with authority." You will find that God will "disperse the powers of darkness from before you" and "cause the heavens to shake for your good and his name's glory." He will "shew forth his power unto the convincing of men" and "be with you at every time of trouble" and "support you against all the fiery darkness of the adversary." He will "send his angel before your face." He will "be on your left hand and on your right hand, and his spirit will be in your heart." The greatest blessings and promises of eternity are yours when you promise unconditionally with a mind made up by saying "I will" and then doing it. (Study slowly and carefully D&C 50:17-29.)

If you make and observe your covenants, you will teach covenant-making and obeying—or in other words, to be baptized. Remember, we teach what we are.

If *we* refuse to make and obey covenants, and since baptism is a covenant, what then are we teaching our investigators? We are teaching them to not make covenants, or put in plainer terms, "don't be baptized."

What is your honest opinion of an investigator who will say he will "try" to pray? Or he "hopes" to make it out to church, or he "hopes" to quit smoking, or he'd "like" to quit his tea?

What would you think of an individual who would say at the time of the marriage covenant, "I'll try" or "I hope to" or "I'll do my best," instead of "I will" or "I do."

We really don't have to look anywhere for answers as to why certain areas don't produce. We should look to our own hearts. The Lord's power will be with us only if we obey his laws. The Lord tells that we *may* partake of the waters of eternal life freely if we *will.* Many missionaries are discovering and are often amazed by this great covenant-making power. Others have not really taken it into their personal lives yet, but merely think about it.

This is the answer to bringing down the fullness of the Lord's blessings upon our heads: If we will make covenants and observe them by sacrifice, we will teach others to make covenants, and we will bring many truly converted souls to the waters of baptism.

"Yea, he that repenteth and exerciseth faith, and bringeth forth good works, and prayeth continually without ceasing—unto such it is given to know the mysteries of God; yea, unto such it shall be given to reveal things which never have been revealed; yea, and it shall be given unto such to bring thousands of souls to repentance, even as it has been given unto us to bring these our brethren to repentance." (Alma 26:22.)

"You Teach What You Are"

You covenant

They covenant
(are baptized)

I. To obey
   A. Law of Moses
      (schedule, tract-
      ing, teaching)
   B. Law of Preparation
      (prayer, planning, study)
   C. Law of Christ
      (faith, love, consecration,
      humility, integrity)
II. To sacrifice
   A. Worldly pleasures
   B. Taking the course of least resistance in testifying
      and teaching.
   C. Too much time in our room and in activity
      (busyness) without accomplishment.
   D. Pride, selfishness ("What's in it for me?")
   E. Mediocre effort
   F. Light-mindedness
   G. Criticisms and murmurings
   H. Unvirtuous thinking

Study the scriptures and your patriarchal blessing;
pray earnestly for the spirit of covenant-making, and make
only those covenants you know you will keep. By so doing
you will grow in faith, power, and integrity, and your
capacity to make greater covenants will increase.

VII. Five Keys to Make Your Devotion Effective
Effectiveness means convert baptisms. Effectiveness
means to teach good discussions to good people. Effective

activity brings accomplishment, results. Ineffective activity (busyness without results) brings frustration and can breed discouragement and an unbelieving or defeatist attitude. Effectiveness—accomplishment—success: one and the same thing.

Learn well this idea: 80% of your success comes from 20% (or less) of your activities. That 20% will give life and meaning to the other 80%.

ACTIVITY   SUCCESS

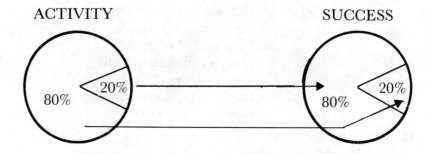

What are the five great keys of effectiveness or success? These five keys will take less than 20% of your time, but they will make all of your time effective. If you use this 20% right, the other 80% will also be right, and you will baptize converts.

First Key—Communicate

To communicate means to understand and to be understood. Keep your communications in order so that they are really honest and humble and sincere with three persons: (1) with God in earnest daily prayer—particularly the private prayer of faith, the believing prayer; (2) with yourself in meditation, in listening, and in making your own mind up; (3) with your companion. If these communications are in order, a sweet, secure, and powerful spirit will be in you when you tract, work through members, and teach. The best way to have your own heart understood is to truly strive to understand the heart of another, including the Lord's. Have empathy.

Second Key—Plan Ahead.

Plan your week; plan each day. Plan where you want to spend your time and with whom, doing what. Planning is faith. Planning is setting goals and a program to achieve them. Planning is thinking. Planning is serving "with your mind." Half an hour in daily, careful planning will double or triple the effectiveness of your ten hours of work. Planning requires mental discipline, patience, and a lot of practice. Do not become discouraged in your struggling initial effort to develop the planning skill. Stay with it in faith. Plan your study class carefully, and you will double its effectiveness. You will master more discussions, memorize more scriptures, keep on top of the Study Guide. Plan your work; work your plan. Use daily planning cards.

Third Key—Simplify.

Simplify means to eliminate non-essentials. "Things which matter most must never be at the mercy of things which matter least." Simplification means to continually bring your contacts back to the fundamental discussions. The best evidence of the Apostasy is the Restoration. The best evidence of the Restoration is the Book of Mormon. The best evidence of the Godhead is the first vision. The best evidences of Joseph Smith are the Book of Mormon and the fruits of Mormonism. The best source of testimony is obedience (John 7:16-17). Scriptural and doctrinal arguments are futile and evasive, for they evade the responsibility of a personal quest for truth in repentance, in earnest, humble prayer and obedience. That's simplification. Put first things first.

Fourth Key—Be Strong.

The main goal of the First Discussion is to set a good baptism date. That's being strong.

Faith is born of the spirit of the Lord, which comes initially in your fervent testimony. Repentance means to live commitments. Commitment teaching means teaching to repent (change of heart—conversion). Be strong in love on commitments. A spirit of love and empathy is the essence of teaching to convert.

To be strong with others, you must be strong with yourself, for you teach what you are. Command your own body; be up at 5:55, to bed at 10:30, out at 9:30 a.m. and 6:00 p.m. President N. Eldon Tanner has said, "Self-discipline is doing what you know you should do when you don't want to do it."

Being strong is making a covenant, and covenant makers baptize covenant makers.

Being strong means to mentally concentrate in your prayers. (Praying out loud may help discipline the mind and increase concentration.)

Being spiritually strong is to accept your role as an agent (eye single) of the Lord and to give to him, the principal, all of the glory and the honor. (This "plan—simplify—be strong" formula is the personal philosophy of one of the world's great missionaries, Elder Franklin D. Richards, Assistant to the Council of the Twelve, who presently helps in the supervision of several missions.)

Fifth Key—Multiply Yourself by Using Members.

One team feverishly works to loan ten copies of the Book of Mormon a day. Another team spends part of the day committing *members* to loan copies of the Book of Mormon. They end up loaning 50 and arranging several group meetings. Members loan these books to golden families with whom a relationship is already established. They are then committed to help fellowship them during the teaching process and after baptism. They help shepherd your contacts through their Gethsemane moments in conversion and help them live the Word of Wisdom. While you bring a family to Church, your committed member team workers bring a family also.

Learn to be effective by using these five great keys. It won't take more than 20% of your time, but the spirit of them will burn like fire through the other 80%. *Communicate, plan, simplify, be strong, multiply yourself.*

VIII. "Bring the Husband and the Wife Along Together"

"It's okay for my wife if she wants to join the Church, but not for me. I am really not interested or religiously inclined. She can do as she likes."

Is this attitude untypical, or maybe the opposite: "Well, if my husband wants to join, that's fine for him, but I have some real doubts myself."

Let's listen to these two individuals, in not too untypical fashion, six months later. Take the first couple. The wife has joined the Church. Listen to the husband: "You and your church! You're always putting that church ahead of me and the kids." And listen to her retort: "It's the only satisfaction in my life. If you'd only have the courage to give up the smokes and listen to the elders, you'd know what I mean." Nag, nag, nag.

Take the second couple. The husband belongs, the wife doesn't. Things went okay at first, but then the Church became a real competitive force in the family. The husband feels unsustained and lacks the courage to carry through and has become inactive. Kicking against the pricks within himself, he rationalizes his inactivity by expressing doctrinal doubts.

I offer four observations:

1. *Begin the teaching process with both parents there—* preferably the entire family. If you begin with the wife, and she responds positively and the husband responds at a slower rate, this becomes a source of embarrassment to her husband. It makes him feel inferior and inadequate, and rather than admitting such inadequacy, he may begin to criticize or fight and resist further teaching. If you do begin with the wife, make certain you take extra pains to bring the husband up to her level, without making him feel foolish or ignorant. Keep it simple and express commendation for every kind of progress. Express your faith in both.

2. *Look to the man as the head of the household.* Be respectful; pay deference to him. If possible, get him to

take charge of the meetings, to call on those he wants to pray. Build him up in the eyes of his wife and his children. He will see you as a source of sustaining help in his own household, and generally he will sustain you in your efforts.

3. *Learn to teach the husband and wife together and equally.* If you sense that the wife begins to move out ahead of the husband and catches on a little quicker, unless you take pains and patience to bring the husband up to her, you actually may be sowing the seeds of later discord and disunity. The husband can become very defensive when he senses his wife is moving ahead of him and can take out his bitter feelings against the Church and against her interest in it. The same thing can happen if the husband is ahead of his wife.

4. *Deal with each person in the family personally,* making each feel important, allowing each to participate, and listening with respect and patience to each. Gather the older children around and teach them to pray, each in his own turn. Teach the whole family to have a family prayer. Give them a few scriptures to read together. Conduct a family home evening for future ones. Teach them to honor and respect each other.

5. *Let them see by the way you treat your own companion* the kind of love and respect family members should have for one another. And how do you teach these things? You teach them in your own manner, in the way you honor and respect your companion. You teach them in the way you literally serve that family. Love them, get to know them, help them, pray with them and for them, and call on them frequently. Make sure there's a daily contact with someone in the Church. Go out of your way to bring back the stray one, to comfort and understand, and to give help. Literally love a family into the Church and you will experience a joy beyond anything you've ever known.

What should you do if they simply don't come along together? Never baptize a woman without the consent and sustaining influence of her husband. Try also to gain the consent and sustaining influence of a wife if the husband wants to be baptized and is worthy.

The basis for judgment is this: If you sincerely believe that by baptizing either the wife or the husband, assuming permission of the other is given, the Church will become a source of help and inspiration in making the baptized member a better wife or a better husband, one with more love and respect and acceptance of the other, and a better father or mother, then go ahead and baptize him or her. If, on the other hand, you see the Church becoming a new source of competition and of disunity in the home, it might be wise to struggle more with the family, to take more time in teaching them and trying to bring them together. There may be some impossible situations where baptism now of one of the family members is best, but if you have the above frame of mind and you work and pray earnestly to that end, I believe you will bring in more complete families than ever before.

IX. Don't Ever Let the Ninety-Five Teach You About the Five

Past experiences often act like chains on the present and the future. Early impressions become lasting impressions. Habits work themselves into ruts. A mental attitude that "nothing will happen here" or that "it can't be done here" becomes a self-fulfilling prophecy.

Never let the ninety-five teach you about the five.

It has always been the case that the gospel of Jesus Christ will appeal to a relatively few selected souls. In all likelihood these are souls who committed themselves in the preexistence to the acceptance of the everlasting gospel during their earth life. Those who are of the blood of Israel come from such a spiritual heritage; and when they hear the voice of the Lord as the missionary teaches and testifies, there is something eternal, some divine spark, that cries out "Abba Father."

Don't ever let those nine doors that reject you and your message teach you anything about that tenth door.

Go to each door with an alive, fresh, eager, positive, and spiritual approach, believing that the Lord is with you, that his spirit will go before you and soften the hearts of the hearers, and that at "this door" you will find one of those selected few who are sufficiently humble, open, and honest so as to hear the voice of the Lord calling to them. How they treat you, they may have treated the Savior.

Don't ever let the ninety-five people you meet in the street survey who pass you by indifferently teach you anything about the five who will respond to the survey and show interest.

Don't let your past experiences blind you to the promise of the present moment.

From what source, then, do we find our learning, if not from our own human experiences? That source is the Spirit of the Lord. Over and over again we learn that this is an essentially spiritual work, and to try to involve oneself with anything more or less than this misses the mark by a wide mile. (3 Nephi 11:40.)

"Again I say, hearken ye elders of my Church, whom I have appointed; Ye are not sent forth to be taught, but to teach the children of men the things which I have put into your hands by the power of my Spirit; and ye are to be taught from on high. Sanctify yourselves and ye shall be endowed with power, that ye may give even as I have spoken." (D&C 43:15-16.)

This is exactly the meaning of faith, or "the assurance of things hoped for, the substance of things not seen." You hope. You believe that somewhere among those thirty people you will contact this morning there will be one or two families who will positively respond. The unwise missionary will learn lessons from all those who reject him to the effect that he will believe that no one will accept, that the area is sour and no good, that it has been "tracted out" or that "the people (as if one could make broad sweeping generalization about all of the people) are simply "not interested."

There *are* people who are interested. Go about with the philosophy of searching, and believe that there are people the Lord would have in his Church and who will come into his Church if the gospel is properly and spiritually presented to them.

Faith, courage, and the worthiness to be taught from on high are the sources of your knowledge—not people, not the area, or not some disillusioning experience.

Never let the ninety-five teach you about the five. Let the Lord teach you about them. "Follow me and I will make you fishers of men."

X. Be Strong in the Hard Moments

There are certain crucial moments in any human endeavor which, if *excellently used*, become the determining moments. These moments will determine the course of future events. This is doubly valid in divine endeavors.

"For this reason came I into the world." The Savior's entire earthly ministry, the establishment of his church, the teaching of his gospel, in fact, his entire eternal role, was to be climaxed and culminated in the great atoning sacrifice that took place in Gethsemane and on Calvary. The entire plan of life and salvation fulcrums around the crowning act in which the Savior performed the vicarious sacrifice that not only guaranteed immortality and resurrection to all mankind, but also opened up the way to eternal life. Everything that the Savior ever did is and was hinged upon his atoning sacrifice. All of human history will revolve around this single transcendent event. Jesus rebuked Peter for smiting off the ear of the high priest's servant (in order to protect his Lord from arrest), and said: "Put up thy sword into the sheath: the cup which my Father hath given me, shall I not drink?"

Can you and I not ask ourselves the same question? When it comes to those crucial moments when the real work of our ministry is performed, "Shall I not drink?" These crucial moments, ironically, are also the hardest moments of our missions. That is, they are moments when we find a very strong conflict between that which we should do and that which is the easiest thing to do (the course of least resistance or what we might consider to be the more natural and human thing to do). We must also say with the Savior, "For this purpose came I into the mission." Or a strong companion (senior or junior) must say to his weaker companion, "The cup which my Father hath given me, shall I not drink it?"

I suggest there are *three crucial moments* that in a sense comprise the Gethsemane and the Calvary of your mission— three hard moments when the cup must be drunk if our missions are to succeed and if we are literally to find the kind of joy and fulfillment that is possible here.

These three moments are: (1) *getting up at 5:55*, (2) *the initial contacting*, and (3) *being strong with love in commitment*.

1.   5:55 symbolizes the schedule, the Law of "Moses" in missionary life. Why is it hard? Because of the pull of the flesh. It is the beginning. To miss getting up at 5:55 by only a few minutes is to fail in it, and sometimes that failure, that few minutes behind, will carry itself throughout the day from one activity to the next.

2.   Why is initial contacting so difficult? Because it's so much easier to just slide by and not tract but to do other "important" things. It's hard to contact a stranger— at first. (Then by practice it becomes easier.) At first it's easier, it's more natural, it's more human to take the course of least resistance in working almost exclusively around those we know or a youth program, and to just hope that adults and families will come to us. But for this reason came we into our missions. This is our "Gethsemane," and each of us must drink that cup. This is divine. Admittedly it is not human. It is divine.

3.   Why is being strong with our contacts in commitment teaching such a hard moment? Because each of us would like to be liked, to be popular, not to offend or to risk the possibility of embarrassment to ourselves or others. Always remember that where the risk is great, the opportunity for success is greater. The human, natural way is to merely engage in gospel conversations, to passively discuss the gospel, to intellectualize about it, to philosophize

about it, to speak of it as something "out there." The far more difficult and divine way is to talk about its personal implications in the life of the investigator. This is why teaching the discussions is the crucial teaching, not just engaging in gospel conversations, though they can serve a very useful softening-up purpose. But there comes a point where we must drive home the commitments to the people—literally—to pray, to study the Book of Mormon, to attend church, to repent. (Study Alma 38:10-12.)

The Latter Stages of Conversion

The latter stages of conversion begin mainly with the Word of Wisdom in the third discussion, when the people really begin to realize the impact the message is going to have on their personal lives. This is their Gethsemane moment, when they are essentially faced with the great personal question, "My will be done or Thy will be done?"

Don't back off from this moment or allow some obstacle to disturb you. Learn to be strong in this moment, for this is the very moment that you were sent to be strong in. It is this moment that you are to be a shepherd and to give the most support and love and pour the most faith in.

I am convinced that we "pack in" more people than "pack us in." By this I mean we give up too early when they begin to throw up objections or to balk a little or to seek some escape. We often say, "They packed us in." But I wonder if we simply didn't "pack in" our responsibility in this hard moment.

If you yourself are an example of the Gethsemane attitude and if you have successfully surmounted your hard moments, you will understand deeply their feelings in their hard moments, and you will be willing to "die with your people" as they go through these hard moments.

If you abide in the vine, and if the Lord's words abide in you, you will begin to bring forth a little fruit. Then the Lord will purge you and give you the power to bring forth more fruit, and you will successfully bring people through these hard Gethsemane moments, and they will prepare for their baptism. (See John 15.)

Conversion literally means "a change," and unless a behavior change has taken place, there is no conversion, and if there is a baptism without a change or conversion, then almost inevitably the new member becomes washed overboard by the first wave or wind that smashes into the boat. We inherit all of our own workings. We cannot avoid it, though we may like to do so. The Church will grow no faster than the quality of the conversion, and statistics cannot reflect quality—only quantity. Numbers do not reflect quality. Numbers can be very deceptive and may suggest something that is absolutely not so. Quality is eventually reflected in branch (or ward) growth, branch activity, branch attendance figures, and the quality of branch meetings.

I urge upon each of us a sense of personal responsibility, a sense of personal commitment, of urgency, of dedication. I urge the Gethsemane spirit. I urge partaking of the cup the Lord has given us to drink. Let us be strong in "the hard moments."

28

Advice to Returning and Returned Missionaries

In the mission field you experienced a quality of spiritual and service life likely unknown to you before. Many of you felt after leaving home that you had left the Garden of Eden and gone out into the "lone and dreary world." But gradually, as the months passed, and through the divine process of missionary work, study and prayer, your heart and your world changed from a physical, social, self-centered one to a spiritual one where all of your energies and enthusiasms and time became focused on one grand goal—that of bringing souls to the Lord and his restored Church and gospel.

This is why to a great degree you felt far more wrenched on leaving the mission field than you did on initially leaving home. Your heart had changed, and so had your world, and you felt you were truly leaving your Garden of Eden to go back into the "lone and dreary world."

And now a major question looms on your personal horizon: How can I maintain the sweetness, the purity, the simplicity and beauty of spiritual life and work when I leave the mission field and return "into the world"?

Many other major and subsidiary questions follow in the wake of this dominant righteous desire. How much church work should I do when I go home? What about education? What should I go into? Where's the money going to come from? What about courtship and marriage? What about the girl I left behind, or who left me behind? How will I know when I'm in love? How will I know who's the right one to marry? When should I get married?

How is my family going to accept me? Will they recognize and appreciate my mission experience? Will they allow me to be changed? How can I build close relationships with them? How can I keep my testimony alive and active? Will I have a difficult adjustment? What should I say at my homecoming?

Many anxieties and emotional feelings rise to the surface. Fears and self-doubt, confusion and uncertainty are among these feelings. Sometimes a desire to stay in the mission field is prompted by the urge to escape responsibilities of family life, education, earning a livelihood, facing the "cold, cruel outside world." In the "secure world" of the mission field you don't need to earn a living by the sweat of your brow; many of your personal needs are continually met by others; a great brotherhood and friendship is fostered; the work is deeply satisfying and joyful; love and appreciation are given and received in sincere, simple manners; you are able to labor single-mindedly, receiving the admiration and the support and love from those abroad and at home.

From "listening" to both modern and ancient church leaders, I see threading through their counsel five points, or five great principles, which, if honored and obeyed, guarantee to you that you will maintain the spirit of the Lord, that your faith and testimony will be alive and active, that Christ will continue to be the light and life of your life, that you will have the internal stamina and spiritual strength to resist worldly encroachments of the physical, social, and intellectual temptations of reality, and which, from a long-term perspective, will guarantee temple marriage, a long life of faithfulness and service, love and happiness, joy in your posterity and eternal life with the Father of your spirit.

POINT NUMBER ONE:
The habit of daily, private, and sincere prayer from your heart.

See for the Lord earnestly to understand his will, and make your mind up to obey it—every morning and every night. Take time to meditate and think about your blessings, the greatness and goodness of God, and express your gratitude with all your heart.

In your mind's eye think through the pressures and temptations of the day, and internally commit yourself in that private mental battle to the principles of righteousness. Fervently ask for God's spirit in the believing attitude to assist you in resisting temptations and in giving you the power and the peace within you to grow, learn, obey, and contribute, to serve, love, and remain humble and spiritual minded.

If you will spend a half hour in the "presence" of the Savior of this world every day, you will spend eternity in his presence. He will become your friend and your Master. You will have a natural association, for he will be no foreigner and stranger to you. He will provide the motive power behind your life. You will walk in his light. On leaving this life, you will find it natural to want to spend eternity in his presence, and you will do so because you spent much of your earthly life in his presence and found it natural. How can this be? Simply because you obeyed his laws and feasted upon his love and drank deeply from his fountain rather than from the worldly fountains of this earth, and you discovered for yourself the priceless truth he told the Samaritan woman: "If thou wilt drink of the water which I give unto you, you will never thirst again."

To pray sincerely in public and in private is often a great test. You will often feel tempted not to do so, and you will often feel no great need to do so. Your circumstances may be such that, if you are really honest with yourself, you don't feel a need for God. You aren't forced to be humble—you will have to be humbled because of the word—the word of God. (See Alma 32: 13-15.) This is why you must stay very close to the scriptures and let the words of the Lord flow continually over your mind.

You learn in the mission field the difference between prayer from your heart and prayer from your lips.

You learn that prayer thus involves the following principles for maximum efficacy:

1. You must prepare yourself for your prayer through meditation and scripture reading. Make a reconciliation with those offended; strive to clear up internal confusion and double-mindedness. Think through the temple ceremonies and other glorious spiritual experiences, or whatever activity or thinking process subdues your spirit and sobers you and prepares you to enter into the presence of the Lord.

2. Ask the Lord for specific blessings and express gratitude for specific blessings so that you avoid vain repetitions and meaningless generalizations. Let the things you ask him for and thank him for be things you deeply feel and mean in your heart.

3. Pledge to him the specific laws that you promise to obey, upon which the blessings you request are predicated. If you take this idea seriously, you will find you will be very hesitant to ask for certain blessings because of your own inward hesitancy to obey the laws upon which those blessings are predicated. This will force self-honesty and objectivity, and you will gradually discover that such self-understanding and self-honesty will give you a true basis for growth and a basis to know all other things outside yourself as well.

4. Learn to listen in your prayer. Don't just talk all the time. Empathize with the Lord, with his thinking, with his feelings, with his ways of doing things. Meditate, ponder, consider, value, appreciate, love, worship. Let the affections of your heart be placed upon him. Be open, sensitive, and receptive to his inspiration and heavenly impression. Keep your mind open and believing.

5. Pray in the believing attitude and realize the power of the prayer of faith, that truly the Lord has promised that whatsoever you ask of him in righteousness, believing that you will receive, if you ask it in the name of the Savior and if it is right, you will receive it.

In a sense you are defining your belief in God. You are bearing your testimony to God of his goodness and power and greatness, of your inner assurance that he can and will grant the blessings you desire if they are right for you. Then when you rise off your knees, you will need to act as if those blessings were granted to show forth your believing, faithful attitude, nothing doubting. As you pray in the name of the Savior, do it in the full realization of his divine role as Advocate and Mediator, and as the Holy One of Israel who atoned for your sins, who suffered and bled and died for you that you might find life and freedom.

6. Don't rush out of his presence when you conclude your prayer. Stay there, and think and ponder and appreciate. Rise up off your knees committed, inwardly resolved. Your mind is made up. You are fully aware of the forces and realities that will surround you that day, or that did surround you that day, and you have won your private battle. It is now merely a matter of living out those decisions and victory in public. The private making up of one's mind in the presence of the Lord is a great and necessary act that will guarantee public success. Private failure is merely the prelude to public failure, but a true private success guarantees public success.

You will have to work at your prayers. You have to yearn in them. You have to yearn for them. You have to bring self-discipline into your prayers to make certain that you pray regularly and that you mentally concentrate. It may help to vocalize your feelings in your prayers, for to speak out loud forces the kind of mental concentration that often is necessary when your mind has a tendency to jump around or when it is preoccupied with earthly forces, pressures, and fears.

To pray alone is vital in developing sincerity and in growing in personal faith. The first thing the Savior taught about prayer is that it should be alone, in one's own closet with the doors closed—that you should pray to your Father in secret, and he will see and hear in secret and reward you openly.

POINT NUMBER TWO:
Study the scriptures every day.

Study them from the point of view of personal edification and insight to understand the will of the Lord for your own life. Don't study them only from the point of view of intellectual understanding.

In a sense your soul can become confused by diverse pressure and aspirations of life. You need an instrument to interpret the real needs of your soul. Just as the Urim and Thummim served the Prophet Joseph Smith as a divine instrument in translating the reformed Egyptian language, so the holy scriptures can become your Urim and Thummim to translate the will of the Lord and the needs of your own soul, to reveal your pride and double-mindedness, to motivate repentance and learning, to foster clarity and spiritual sureness and internal commitment to the principles of righteousness. By thinking daily on the word of the Lord, you will seek your honor from him rather than from men.

You will realize that the Law of the Harvest is an immutable law, that you will reap as you sow, and that it is impossible to do otherwise. You will realize that your spiritual life and happiness are not subject to human judgment, appreciation, or recognition, but that the Lord knows and cares, and all you need to worry about is that you live your life according to true principles and trust in him for the outcome.

Get into the habit of studying the scriptures for a few minutes before retiring and for a few minutes every morning, so that your mind is spiritual before your sleep and spiritual on your awakening. This will become as food to you, as food to your soul, and just as sleep unravels the jangled-up nerves and tired tissues of your body, so will prayerful and earnest meditation on the scriptures unravel a tempted soul or the internal weariness that comes from earthly desires and double-minded living.

"Search diligently, pray always, and be believing, and all things shall work together for your good, if ye walk uprightly and remember the covenant wherewith ye have covenanted one with another." (D&C 90:24.)

In order to study and pray sincerely, you must live sincerely. An understanding of the scriptures will be revealed to you to the degree that your life is of the quality as to receive the spirit of the Lord. Otherwise the scriptures or the word of the Lord will have no natural appeal to you. You will prefer to read other things more naturally interesting and stimulating. The scriptures will be boring to you, and the Lord will gradually become a stranger to you, just as anyone with whom you do not communicate sincerely over a long period of time becomes a stranger. You both begin to live in different worlds, to feel different feelings, to think different thoughts, and you have very little in common anymore. If you are not continuously careful, such can happen between you and the Lord.

Remember that duty can bring you to desire. If you find yourself slipping, if you find the scriptures are starting to lose their natural, spontaneous appeal, then "gird up" the loins of your mind, and out of duty (to begin with) get back into the regular habit of daily scripture study. Stay right with it. Go back to them on a habitual daily basis and drink deeply from them, and you will gradually discover the natural loveliness and sweetness of God's word and prefer it infinitely to man's word and man's ways and thoughts.

The scriptures will become to you a check list on your spirituality. They will become a divine interview. If you earnestly seek to discover your weaknesses through the scriptures, as suggested in Ether 12:27, you will come closer to the Lord. Your weaknesses will be revealed, and if you "stay in there fighting" in faith and faithfulness, your weaknesses will become your strengths.

POINT NUMBER THREE:
Honor the Sabbath day as a day of worship and service.

The one great opportunity to bring back the sense of single-minded spiritual service of your mission days is the Sabbath—one full day out of seven set apart for nothing but worship and devotion and renewing your covenants.

Organize your affairs so that the "pig doesn't get into the mire" on the Sabbath and that you don't need to do any studying at all for your school work. If necessary in order to meet some special Monday morning deadlines or to prepare for a Monday test, miss that date on Friday or Saturday night, but do not violate the sanctity of the Sabbath day. You will do far better in school and have much more balance and joy in your life by following this counsel than you will if you try to cram and study on Sunday. You will enjoy neither your study nor the Sabbath.

Retire to your bed at least by midnight Saturday night so that you can get a good night's rest and go to priesthood meeting refreshed and grateful. Rather than napping all afternoon or joy riding, serve in your Church office in some way, or study the scriptures, or in some other way have uplifting relationships that edify and strengthen yourself and others. Bear brief testimony frequently in fast and testimony meeting.

Avoid "social" dating on Sunday. If you take a date to Church or a fireside following sacrament meeting, do so with a single-minded intent to worship and to learn and to continue to honor the Sabbath.

If you partake of the sacrament righteously, your soul will be filled and will not hunger for the world's things and ways, and your perspective in life and your purpose will be regained.

The Sabbath is truly the key day in maintaining a

depth of consistent spirtuality, and each of the other six days will be richer and more productive because of honoring the Lord's day. If you have any question about what can and cannot or should and should not be done on the Sabbath, ask one question and sincerely answer it: Is it worshipful?

POINT NUMBER FOUR:
Keep yourself morally clean in thought and in action.

The natural biological temptations are there. Today's worldly atmosphere is saturated with sensual suggestiveness, and this requires you to exercise great self-control toward those situations or temptations that come in such rich doses. Read clean literature. Avoid trash. Go only to uplifting, entertaining movies. Avoid the sick ones, which appeal to man's baser motives and lower nature. Most movies will be avoided.

Avoid sitting alone in cars late at night. Promise yourself and your God that you simply will not do any necking, and that you will regard a kiss of affection as sacred, not to be participated in frequently and promiscuously. A kiss of passion or desire and a kiss of affection are completely different, and each person knows the difference within.

If you can control your thinking in your heart and maintain purity, your actions will be also pure. If you do not, you will be led to necking and then to petting, and perhaps to a complete loss of virtue. This will destroy, unless later sincerely repented of, the spiritual strength and divine power acquired in your missionary labors.

Often the best way to resist temptation is to remove it. "Lead us not into temptation." Double date; go in groups; get in fairly early; have private prayer, and when appropriate, prayer with your date. Watch out for the beginnings, and you will never have to worry about the endings.

Keep in your mind a vision of purity and cleanliness and a temple marriage. Never let anything mar that vision. Go to the temple at least once a month to regain that vision, to set your path straight, to recommit yourself, and to perform a great vicarious labor of love.

If you get pinned or become engaged, have an agreement and understanding on absolute purity. Develop a deep relationship of respect and sincere friendship.

Virtue is lost a little at a time, by degrees, just as righteousness is acquired here a little, there a little, line upon line, precept upon precept. Beware of rationalization, thinking all is right "in the name of love," or thinking nothing is really wrong unless you "go too far." Be honest with yourself and honest with your God in your private prayer. Your inner heart knows. Down deep where you live, be clean and pure. Resist and overcome temptation, and you will absorb into your character the strength and fury of those temptations and be made that much stronger each time. This will pay dividends to you and yours the rest of your life and throughout eternity.

POINT NUMBER FIVE:
Magnify a Church calling and your priesthood.

Magnify means to do more than what is minimally required, more than is asked of you. It means to go the second mile. It means to serve anonymously. Service for social rewards and recognitions is fine to begin with but will not sink your spiritual roots deep into God's soil, and when the day of stress and storm comes, you will find that you can be uprooted. On the other hand, works of righteousness done in secret and kept in secret and all other forms of anonymous service, beyond the blessings they confer upon others, build a deep reservoir of spiritual strength within you. When the stresses, strains and storms of life come, you will be able to draw upon this reservoir and receive internal succor. "Out of your own belly shall flow the water of eternal life." "And without compulsory means it shall flow unto thee forever and ever."

Go to all the meetings asked of you, including leadership meetings. Give excellent preparation in your assignments. Sustain your leaders, regardless of their weaknesses and inadequacies, and give them your loyal, dedicated, humble support.

Of course, you will keep the Word of Wisdom absolutely and pay a full and honest tithing. If there is a portion of your money over which you do not exercise control, then pay tithing on that portion of your money over which you do have control. Pay it regularly. Pay it willingly and gladly, and great blessings will come upon your head and heart. Everyone can at least pay tithing on their spending money, even when supported by others in school.

Remember again—rationalizations are no good; there are no excuses.

Fast two meals on fast day in the true spirit of fasting and prayer. Pay your fast offerings and bear your testimony.

Go to the temple frequently, at least once a month. Go with others who feel as you do (fellow returned missionaries—a regular group perhaps) so that you can have spiritual conversations before and after the sacred vicarious work. Renew your dedication and your understanding of the great laws and covenants. Look beneath the symbol level to the eternal meaning level, and then strive to translate those eternal principles and truths into real practices of everyday life. Go spiritually prepared, hungry and thirsty, having the faith that you will be filled. And you will be.

Simply be that kind of person of whom the bishop will say out of your presence: "This is someone who is truly consecrated to the Church, on whom I can depend absolutely. He is faithful and pure and powerful in his righteous use of the priesthood."

These Five Points Are Interrelated

If you violate one of them, you will find that you will violate to some degree all of them. You will need to honor them all in order to honor fully any one of them. Sincere spiritual life is a fruit and the roots of that tree must be deep in God's soil. This is why it is so important that you avoid evil companions; that you associate yourself, particularly in social activities, with those of very high standards and spiritual thoughts; those who will lift you and edify you; those whose conversation is free from coarseness, vulgarity, slang, swearing, taking the name of the Lord in vain, light-mindedness, impure practices, cutting sarcasm, cutting speech, social falseness. Cultivate authentic friendships in which you understand one another and are striving to maintain and deepen your commitments to the principles of eternal life.

Watch out for the gradual erosion of your testimony through pride, vanity, and intellectualization. Watch out for sophistication, which is worldly wisdom. Worldly wisdom is foolishness to God.

Remember that faith in any system but Christ's is pride. True faith in Christ will bring humility. Humility is the opposite of pride. Pride is the mother of all vices, and humility the mother of all virtues.

Build your foundation upon Christ and his true principles, and no storm can tear you apart or expose rotten 2 x 4's behind a shiny facade.

Remember the three temptations of Christ—to the body, to pride and vanity, to worldly aspirations. Remember the divine instruments given to you to overcome them—your body itself, your companions and family members, and your opportunities to serve others anonymously. Remember the great covenants you have made, the temple laws you agreed to obey. Each is built upon the other, and only through obedience to the lower law is the capacity to obey the higher law obtained.

Unless you are your own master, you cannot become a consecrated servant of the Lord. You first must master your body and mind. You need to develop a reservoir of power, strength, and inner peace so that you are not policed by the opinions of others and your own fear of disapproval and hunger for human approval.

Look carefully over the five points. Talk with friends or others who have similar interests and desires. Visit with your bishop and other spiritual advisers. Counsel with them and receive admonition from them. Avoid the spiritual decay of intellectualization, of double-mindedness, of materialism, of sensuality.

What About Education?

In today's complex, specialized world, it is most important that you get as much education as possible. If you have strong enough desires, you will find that the means will be provided, and marriage or finances need not stand in your way.

Do not shortcut your long-range career by refusing to sacrifice and build an investment within yourself. The main value of education is not financial or occupational, but it is personal and spiritual and character-building. You can become a better husband and father, wife and mother, citizen, church worker. You learn to think analytically and creatively. You learn to write and communicate clearly and persuasively. You learn how to read with discrimination. You develop a way of thinking about life and problems. Your basic knowledge is deepened and expanded, your horizons lifted. Your ability to sympathize and appreciate is increased. In every way you can become a fuller and more integrated, more capable, more wise human being.

But you will need to work very hard at school, and self-discipline must be your motto so that you follow a regular study schedule consistently and avoid the Law of the Shortcut. Remember, you reap as you sow, and cramming sessions deceive no one—certainly not yourself. People can get a degree if they are skilled in certain intellectual and social techniques and memorizing capacities, but they do not get an education unless they have consistently obeyed the Law of the Harvest and applied themselves day in and day out to their studies.

I wouldn't let anyone force or pressure you into selecting your major or a career before you honestly feel within yourself that you are ready. The first year or two of college can be used to satisfy general education requirements and to get a broad, liberal background. Expose yourself to different fields of human endeavor to get to know yourself. It is an advantage to be open and uncommitted at this stage, to ecplore various fields, even those which seem not to have a natural interest, rather than to merely go into those fields where you are already strong, for this can often make your strengths your weaknesses through a loss of balance and wisdom.

Seek to understand different fields and yourself in them rather than to judge prematurely. Once you understand, you will have a basis for wise judgment. And if you are prayerful, the Lord will guide you, for the career you choose will be one of the most important decisions you will ever make in this world. You will give the best hours and the best thinking and the best enthusiasm of every-day life, six days a week, for the next forty years of your life. You would certainly want this great gift of your life to be given to that which is right and uplifting and noble and which would be self-fulfilling.

If you like doing something, if you are good at it, and if it is the kind of thing that the world really needs— then you have found a good career. It must bring you happiness and a sense of personal meaning and contribution, or your job will gradually become a means to an end rather than having the qualities of an end in itself.

Remember in your studies that most of science is merely the knowledge acquired by man without faith in Jesus Christ, so beware of placing your entire faith upon any science or any philosophy of man. Use the scriptures and the modern oracles as the standards by which you judge life and other learnings, rather than the other way about. Beware of rationalization, which is often prompted by intellectual pride and personal trangression and a gradual inversion of values within you.

Be open to further growth and development. You can learn all that life can give to you, and it will serve you well as long as you are true and faithful to the eternal principles, to that learning which comes from God alone. Wisdom comes from humility and obedience, while learning may come from schooling. "To be learned is good if you hearken to the counsels of God."

Don't belittle yourself or take the course of least resistance. Don't settle for mediocrity. Don't lose your vision of your great divine potential and what you can contribute. You need a good solid education. Your ability to contribute in life will be largely influenced by it, and those who do not have it often feel inferior and somewhat defensive inside, even though they may hide it well. It isn't the most important thing, but it is a *very* important thing, in my opinion, that you get as much education as is possible, hopefully a college degree, regardless of the circumstances or financial difficulties in which you find yourself. A way will be opened up and means provided if your desire and determination are strong enough.

I would hope that your wife recognizes education's value and encourages you and is willing to make the sacrifices necessary. To receive dividends in life, you must be willing to make the investment.

Family Relationships

Remember, because of your experiences on your mission, you carry the responsibility to a great degree to inspire and unify your family. You are not to respond to the moods of others, but to radiate divine attitudes. Regardless of the difficulty, express your love and appreciation and warmth to your family. If you ever feel rejected, use self-knowledge and understanding of others; do not reject back. Watch out for self-pity. Draw from your spiritual reservoir, from your mission experiences the capacity to adapt and to turn every situation to the Lord's advantage. Expression of warmth requires practice, and practice makes perfect. Surely you will make some mistakes, but that is to be expected. So does the pianist before he becomes proficient.

Remember the H_2O analogy. H_2O can stand for liquid, gas, or solid, depending on the outside temperature and pressure. Almost every situation you are in or person you meet is like H_2O. They are in a constant state of radiation and absorption. If you will draw from inside your spiritual reservoir spiritual attitudes, you will radiate those and others will absorb them, and you will lift and edify. Otherwise your spiritual life will be shallow and you will absorb the radiation of lesser spirits. Rather than being the master of circumstances, you will become the victim. Rather than acting, you will be acted upon. There will be no true joy in this kind of life.

Your family carries with it a lot of emotional feelings developed over the years. You can become very subjectively involved in your own feelings, and this often compounds the problems. It is for this reason that you must seek out and use self-understanding and sincere prayer more than ever before so that you serve and bless your family, that your brothers and sisters are inspired to serve missions and be married in the temple, to live righteously.

Do not wear your religion on your sleeve and preach to your family, relatives, friends, or other people. Do not find fault with or judge your parents or others whose lives are not what you expected or hoped; be humble and live quietly the principles you believe in. Simply believe in the power of example. It is infinitely greater than precept, particularly with your own family. There will also be opportunities to do some teaching. Remember that example must come first, then sincere relationships of love and acceptance, and only then can you be successful in giving the vision of the restored gospel of our Lord.

What About Dating, Courtship, and Marriage?

For a while following your mission, do not trust your emotions too much. You will be going through an adjustment process and learning to define yourself in a completely new world and environment. You may find that your moods will range from moments of great elation to feelings of self-pity and depression. It would be a sad thing indeed to make eternal long-range decisions on either of these extreme moods. Wait until you get to know yourself a little and your moods level out a little before you make too many judgments and decisions, particularly when they have long-range consequences, such as engagement or marriage.

If you seek him earnestly and live righteously, the Lord will guide you in these matters and will give you a feeling of rightness within your being. Of all moments in your life that are important, this one is, and the Lord will not leave you alone. But you have to agree to live his law and to avoid playing cat-and-mouse dating games where people become skilled in manipulating each other's emotions.

To trust in the Lord means to follow true principles and to leave the outcome in his hands. To trust in the arm of flesh is an attempt to manipulate the forces of life so as to get the outcome you desire, whether that is the Lord's desire or not. You do not always know what is best for you. God does. Trust in him. Have a believing attitude, regardless of what others might think or say. God is a God of truth and integrity; his promises apply to you through your faith and faithfulness, and he will never let you down.

In your dating get to know each other under many different kinds of situations and circumstances. Don't just go to be entertained or to watch a movie, but engage in various activities and have rich, sincere conversations. Until you are certain of the "one and only," go with several and get to know them well.

Often when you return home you feel a little insecure and may have the tendency to grasp for any source of security or certainty. Many become pinned or engaged before they really should, because of this search for security, or they become victims of certain social pressures and obligations. They will inwardly resent this, and this resentment will come out in various ways. This is why it is so important to be very honest with yourself and others and to obey true principles, trusting in the Lord and leaving the outcome in his hands.

When you have found the one for you and you are certain, through sincere prayer and righteous living, that she or he is the one, then get married and begin your family and fulfill your divine obligations.

If you have the will, you can raise your family as you go to school. I don't believe the question of whether to have children or not is one of financial or practical difficulty nearly as much as it is one of desire and faith and spiritual determination.

Watch out for quick judgments when you return home, in one way or another, either for a particular girl or against a particular girl (or boy). Get settled and get to know yourself until you can trust yourself in this new environment, until you can trust your feelings.

I do not believe any time limit can or should be given to returning missionaries as to when they should get married. It depends too much on the people involved and their degree of maturity and responsibleness. It also depends somewhat on their circumstances of life. However, I would subordinate the latter to the former. Trust in God and act on true principles. Be patient. Don't expect perfection overnight. Be honest and have sincere dating and courtship relationships. Make your courtship a spiritual one. Pray with each other. Before marriage go to the temple several times, if this is possible.

Make certain that the temple marriage is your greatest goal and value, and that it is not eclipsed by all the temporal "do's" and preparations for marriage. Often in a Mormon community, temple marriage may be felt only the necessary social "thing to do" and can become second to the trousseau, to the tea, to the wedding dress, to the parties, and to all of the other preparations. Be careful. Keep the temple central so that your enthusiasms and interests and loyalties are focused primarily upon it. If they are not focused upon it, I would adapt whatever is necessary in order to maintain that focus.

Other Important Points

1. *Your homecoming talk.* Tell people about your mission area, about its people, spirit, and ways. Tell them

about the mission, about the responsibilities missionaries need to carry, about the growth and development of branches and Saints, about missionary and proselyting programs and strategies. Relate personal experiences on your mission that have given to you an internal conviction of the principles of the gospel. This is the most powerful way to bear testimony and to teach. And teaching is infinitely preferred to preaching, particularly at your homecoming. Give the experiences in detail and point out exactly how you learned various principles of the gospel, and he who has ears to hear will hear.

2. *What about the armed forces?* It is important to recognize an important obligation to serve one's country. Generally I would suggest trying to serve the country as an officer and with as much education behind you as possible.

3. *How soon after a mission should you go to school?* Individual circumstances vary, but I believe the sooner you get into school the better you will be able to retain the excellent work and study habits developed in the mission field, and you will become so busy in meaningful activity as to minimize adjustment difficulties.

4. Other than going on another mission, *how can you serve the mission field?* First, by exercising righteous influence on other young men to go on missions. Many young men are very susceptible to influence, and the right kind of relationship and counsel and assistance and interest at the right time can often help a worthy young man who might feel lonely or have some doubts or have a tendency toward waywardness or who might have a very poor relationship with his family or with ward leaders to go on a mission. Take every advantage to influence young men in this way. A kind word or act is often a key. Be interested in young men. Go out of your way to serve them and help them and inspire them and assure them a beautiful example.

When you get married, establish early the tradition

335

with your children to go on missions. Start savings accounts for missions.

You can always help missionary work by making contributions to missionaries and perhaps combining with others to send missionaries into the field.

5. *How can I help bring my non-Mormon family members into the Church?* First and foremost, by an example of sincerity, love and appreciation. Don't preach or judge or reject. Second, build honest, affirming, accepting relationships with them. Third, you might be able to do some actual teaching. At least you can share your feelings about your experiences, and these will generally be appreciated. Be patient and remember the tremendous power of example.

Summary

Your mission has been the greatest spiritual experience of your life. In it you learned the eternal lessons of life. You learned that happiness is a by-product of selfless service. You learned that you found your life to the degree you lost it in the lives of others.

Remember, *your life is a mission, not a career.* You were not placed here on earth to serve your own selfish desires and ambitions. Look upon your entire life, your education, your marriage, your family life, your career as a mission, and they will become a mission to you. Everything, if done with the right motive and an eye single to the glory of God, can be a spiritual activity. It is only when we lose this point of view that temporal labors and school work become selfish and self-serving and spiritually unsatisfying. "To the pure all things are pure." Then you won't need to hearken back to your missionary days. You won't need to live on the sweet memories or on a resurrected testimony for the source of your spiritual life.

When you were released from your mission, it was merely a transfer to another district to serve God in a different way, but still through the service of his children. Remember to keep your scriptures at your bedside.

Study them frequently, for the word of the Lord is the rod of iron that will keep you along the unmarked straight and narrow path, which will be obscured from time to time in your life by the mists of darkness or the temptations of Satan. Holding firmly to the rod of iron will carry you successfully through those mists, and you will partake of the tree of eternal life.

Develop your own personal study guide and follow it, using a check list. Let self-discipline in every phrase of your life bring you to Christ-like motives and works of wisdom, humility, love, and service in each of these phases of life.

Believe in the Savior. "But seek ye first the kingdom of God, and his righteousness; and all these things shall be added unto you." (Matthew 6:33.)

VI

A BEGINNING:
Spiritual Aerobics

29

A Beginning:
Spiritual Aerobics

My he looked good! Pleasant—tall—determined! His chest had somewhat "gone to pot" over the intervening years since his outstanding athletic achievements in college, but he'd been active in sports and he still looked good.

"Two lengths, Ed—as hard as you can go. Come on now," I challenged.

In he dived. He gracefully thrashed through the first length, turned about, and went as hard as he could on the second. Halfway back he suddenly gave out, paddled over to the side, rested, and then slowly crawled up on the bank. He just lay there—no motion, just breathing very deeply.

"What's wrong, Ed?" I asked, running up.

"I don't know. I feel dizzy and kind of sick all over."

He was nauseous all that day. He learned something about himself. You can't run faster than you have strength. You had better not overdo. You can't kid yourself—you've got to build up gradually.

Jogging has almost become a national craze. Why? What's behind all this active exercising, this jogging, running, walking, bicycling, swimming?

"Aerobics" stands for an active exercise program based on the idea of incrementally building up the reserve power in the body (heart and lungs) to supply the necessary oxygen through a healthy, developed, open circulatory system.

Take someone (probably, though not necessarily, older) who has been leading a sedentary life (very easy to do in our modern, mechanical, automated, gadgetized society today) and put him under physical strain.

Running for a bus, shoveling snow, hunting in deep snow in the mountains—the body cries out for oxygen. But the oxygen can't get through: the vessels and capillaries are undeveloped, clogged or closed.

Oxygen deficiency may bring on clotting, which may result in heart attacks, coronaries, or strokes (blood and oxygen deficiency in the head). The same kind of thing happens when we put too much "juice" on a limited electrical circuit. We blow a fuse.

Evidence shows that those who build up and *regularly* jog or swim or whatever will not only feel and look fitter but will also sleep better and can work longer and more efficiently than they otherwise would.

Such exercise as jogging takes no special equipment, costs nothing, and takes only a few minutes a day. The only requirement: self-discipline. A very rare requirement.

Spiritual Aerobics

There is also an emotional or spiritual aerobics. It is a daily exercise of emotional and spiritual fiber and muscle which, if regularly followed, will result in building reserve capacities of "spiritual oxygen" to be called upon in times of stress.

Most of us, under emotional strain, tend to "blow a fuse."

We're tired. It's been a hard day. The children are noisy. They're pressing their own needs. They're beginning to "bug us." We find ourselves irritated, angered. We lose patience and then watch out! Our intemperate spirit explodes! We fly into a rage! We say things we don't mean—things that wound and hurt and strain.

We've just had a spiritual coronary!

The healing, repairing process will take time, patience, and humility.

Or take this instance: You and your wife (or husband) just don't see eye to eye on the matter of family finances (or child discipline, or handling touchy in-law situations, or whatever emotionally charged issue brings out differences in upbringing or temperament). A situation comes up that demands a decision. In discussing the matter, you find yourselves unable to really listen to each other, to give and take. You're right—she's (he's) wrong. Now to prove it! Feelings become strained. Eventually one or both either loses his or her temper or withdraws. No communication— no understanding.

A spiritual stroke!

Again, healing is difficult. Sometimes it's not even attempted. The wound then congeals and lies deep inside, buried by new defenses of cynicism, sarcasm, and bitterness. It may fester and then under another provoking situation "break out" and provide new ammunition for the next round. Good marriages thus often deteriorate, little by little, fed by pride (fault-finding and self-justification) from one of deep meaningful communication to one of accommodation, then toleration, and finally hostility (either open or subtle).

What is this daily exercise, this spiritual aerobics? I suggest it is largely found in a daily effort to do two things: first, *to gain perspective* and second, *to make some decisions* in light of that perspective.

Of all God's creations, man, his child, alone has the capacity to transcend himself, to rise above himself and his own immediate situation—in short, to gain perspective on what's happening (present reality) and what should be happening (purposes, ideals, values).

We need to take time daily to reflect, to think, to meditate, to plan, to study God's word, and to hear with our heart the preachments of our conscience.

Then we need to make some decisions regarding what we are going to do in light of this understanding. Private prayer is the perfect time to recommit ourselves to an eternal perspective and to some specific practices for that day, such as patience, integrity, diligence, purity.

President McKay taught:

"We have today greater responsibility than ever before, as men of the priesthood, as women of the Church, to make our homes such as will radiate to our neighbors harmony, love, community duties, loyalty. Let our neighbors see it and hear it. Never must there be expressed in a Latter-day Saint home an oath, a condemnatory term, an expression of anger or jealousy or hatred. Control it! Do not express it! You do what you can. to produce peace and harmony no matter what you may suffer," (*The Improvement Era,* June, 1963.)

This daily exercise of meditation, scripture study, planning, and prayer may generally take 30 minutes. That half-hour will increase the quality of the other 23½ hours, including the depth and restfulness of sleep.

As with physical exercise, those of us who say we haven't the time for "spiritual aerobics" are excuse making and will find ourselves, whenever the situation calls for strength beyond our reserve, incapacitated by self-doubt, envy, jealousy, pride, fear, anger, bad tempers, all indicating a lack of spiritual oxygen.

We must never become too busy sawing to take time to sharpen the saw.

INDEX

A

Aaronic Priesthood, system of internal discipline, 233

Abraham, made convenant with Lord, 167

Acceptance, necessary to understanding relationships, 192; of others, 250, 281; of others, in rebuilding relationships, 130; of returned missionary, 318

Act, not react, 215

Activity, physical and mental, importance of, 75

Administrative process, 278

Adult education, 234

Advice, to returning and returned missionaries, 317-37

Aerobics, definition of, 341; spiritual, 341-44

Agenda, meeting, 276

Alienation, from God, causes insecurity, 44; of individual, 76-77

Alma's counsel of discipline, 228-29; estrangement from father, 218

Animals, give security to children, ͻ6

Anxiety, of returned missionaries, 318

Apathy, overcoming, 77-78; results of, 77

Apollo 11, and overcoming gravity, 168; what we learned from, 91

Appearance vs. reality, 22

Appetite, being slave to, 169; conquering and controlling, 29

Appreciation, as leadership tool, 281

Archbishop of Canterbury, 70

Armed forces, and returned missionary, 335

Aspiration vs. consecration, 25

Atonement, heart of gospel plan, 96; influence on relationships, 47; how to receive gift of, 47; meaning of, 47; relationship of, to marriage, 48-49

Attitude, and learning, 254-55; as key to successful Church leadership, 280

Auto mechanic, story of involvement of, 143

B

Baptism, follows obedience, 297; is covenant with God, 97; of wife without husband's consent, 310; product of missionary work, 285; second birth, 53

Behavior, and learning, 253; based on need, 113; influenced by laws of love, 199; understanding, 112-13

Behavioral approach to study of gospel, 2-4

Believing, necessary in prayer, 173

Birthday party, example of emotional level of child, 8

Blessings, predicated on law, 171; thanking Lord for, 157

Body, importance of in spirit world, 35

Bolyn, Anne, 68

Borrowing strength to build weakness, 11-13

Branch president, and communication problem, 183-86

Bread, meaning of, in sacrament, 95

Brother of Jared, 174

C

Calling, becoming equal to, 262

Callings, magnifying, 326

Calvary, definition of, 66

Caring, importance of, 267

Celestial personality, man may become, 4

Celestialized personality, 263

Changing others, how to, 133-37

Character, and motive, 262; formed by decisions, 115

Chastity, breaking law of, 162

Charts—activity and success, 306; follow-through, 278; how to involve the learner, 255; leadership responsibility, 261; planning communication, follow-through, 279; sheepherder, shepherd, sheep, 265; "you teach what you are," 305

Cheating in school, example of, 181

Checklist, as follow-through tool, 278

"Child is father of the man," 294

Children, communication with, 158; example of gaining cooperation of, 213-15; needs of, 210; one-to-one relationship with, 213; to obey and honor parents, 210; training and teaching of, 213. See also Communication.

Chores in home, involving children in, 235

Christ, Jesus. See Jesus Christ.

Christ-centered, leadership must be, 273

Christ-like, missionary must be, 291

Church, and self-esteem, 87; callings, magnifying, 326; programs, purpose of, 263

Cleanliness, moral, for returned missionaries, 325

Climate, of approval, necessity of, 118; working atmosphere of group, 268

Commitment, essential in motivation, 147; example of boy learning trust, 145; examples of, 165-66; follows hearing still, small voice, 165; internal, in conversion, 286; is covenant or oath, 166; must come from within, 285; necessary for conversion, 315; necessity of, 68; to family, 205; to family home evening, 224; to God, importance in overcoming habits, 93; to responsibility of parenthood, 206; with the Lord, 196

Communication, and conditioning, 117; attitude of, 277; between husband and wife, 8, 39, 106, 179, 212, 343; between parents and children, 8, 9, 85, 103, 106, 142, 176-88, 180-83, 213, 222, 231, 245; between teacher and student, 195-97; breakdowns in, 176, 218; causes of breakdowns in, 109; compared to iceberg, 104; creative, 89; definition of, 306; example of, between father and son, 248-49; example of, in mission field, 183-86; gaps in or barriers to, 199, 246; helps build self-esteem, 89; is mutual understanding, 152, 255; key to successful church leadership, 277; key to successful missionary work, 306; lies more in feelings than words, 105; spiritual roots of, 176-88; sunshine philosophy of, 179; two-way, helped by involvement teaching, 254; two-way process, 151; verbal, 277; with God, 39, 68, 72, 151-75; with logic and feeling, 189-201; with missionary, 216; with self, 194; within family, 110; written, 277

Comparisons, between children, 80; of children in school, 81; of children's growth, danger of, 14

Concept of threat, 115

Conditioning, barrier to communication, 117; past, 168

Conflict, in missionary work, 313

Conformity, to buy love, 250; enemy to man, 74

Conscience, and Huckleberry Finn, 160; counseling with, 59; is light of Christ, 45; still, small voice of, 59

Consciousness of victory over self, 32

Consecrated life, Savior was model of, 26

Consequences, logical vs. unusual, 238

Contacts, finding missionary, 312; in missionary work, 314

Contract, is covenant, 302-304

Conversation, example of children's, 158

Conversion, concern with quality of, 285; depth of, fills void between behavior and belief, 250; latter stages of, 315; meaning of, 54, 316; miracle of, 51-61; reasons for, 177; results of, 53. See also Missionary.

Convert baptisms, how achieved, 297

Converts, what in Church impressed, 41

Cooperation, of children, example of, 213-15

Coronary, spiritual, 342

Courtship, of returned missionary, 332-34

Covenant, at baptism, 97,; definition of, 167; how to, 98; is contract, 302-304; making, importance of, 168

Covenant children, 167

Covenants, in gospel, 302-304; obedience to, 186; of returned missionary, 327; renewal of, in sacrament, 97; results of, 98; with the Lord, 169

Cowdery, Oliver, 69-71

Criticism, of program, 262

D

Dancing standards, example of, 189-93

Dating, each member of family, 222; for returned missionaries, 325, 332-34

Days of creation, likened to levels of spiritual growth, 5-17